[Cipe Pineles: a Life of Design]

Cipe was witty, serious, sly, courageous, generous, fun-loving. She would stand up for her staff, her photographers, artists and her work. She rarely compromised but always seemed to gather the respect and support of those she needed. She was big and influential at a time when there were few women like her. Cipe was very important to me in ways that are hard to describe. It's like having a third parent. . . Cipe was always imprinted in me.

(Roger Schoening letter)

Cipe Pineles:

a Life of Design

Martha Scotford

 W. W. Norton & Company / New York • London

A NORTON PROFESSIONAL BOOK

Copyright ©1999 by Martha Scotford

The text of this book is composed in Bauer Bodoni and Helvetica Condensed Light with display in Helvetica Condensed Bold. Manufacturing by KHL Printing Co., Singapore
Book design by Martha Scotford

Library of Congress
Cataloging-in-Publication Data

Scotford, Martha.
Cipe Pineles: a life of design / by Martha Scotford.
p.   cm.
"A Norton professional book."
Includes bibliographical references and index.
ISBN 0-393-73027-1
1. Golden, Cipe Pineles. 2. Graphic arts-- United States--Biography. I. Golden, Cipe Pineles. II. Title.
NC975.5.G59S38 1998/1999
741.6'092--dc21
[b]
98-18053
CIP

ISBN 0-393-73027-1

W. W. Norton & Company, Inc.,
500 Fifth Avenue, New York, N.Y. 10110
http://www.wwnorton.com
W. W. Norton & Company Ltd.,
10 Coptic Street, London WC1A 1PU

0 9 8 7 6 5 4 3 2 1

facing title page: Portrait of Cipe Pineles in early 1940s (photograph by Richard Pousette-Dart).

title page: detail of Parsons poster, designed by Pineles, with illustrations by Janet Amendola.

Photo Credits:

Unless otherwise credited, all illustrations are used with permission of the Cipe Pineles Collection, Archives and Special Collections, Wallace Library, Rochester Institute of Technology, with thanks and appreciation to Carol Burtin Fripp and Thomas Golden.

Reproduction of published materials from *Vogue*, *Vanity Fair*, *Glamour*, *Charm*, and *Mademoiselle* by permission of The Condé Nast Publications, Inc.

Published materials from *Seventeen* are reproduced by permission of the artists and photographers; the author apologizes to any who could not be found.

Raphael Soyer painting is reproduced courtesy of Forum Gallery, New York and The Estate of Raphael Soyer.

Give Me a Bath; or Such is Life in a Big City is reproduced by permission of Rose Warren. Photography by Tracy Simon.

Painting of Agha's Office by Cipe Pineles is reproduced courtesy of the Joyce Knoedler Morrow Collection, Wallace Library, Rochester Institute of Technology.

Courtesy of Thomas Golden: photographs on pages 25, 30, 38, 56, 74, 83, 99, 100, 102, 129, 146.

Courtesy of Alice and George Forster: photographs on pages 18, 20, 22, 24, 26, 44, 50, 75, 83.

Courtesy of Mies Hora: photograph on page 157.

Courtesy of Joe and Evelyn Kaufman: photograph on page 76.

Courtesy of Estelle Ellis: photograph on page 113.

Other photographers are credited where known.

Some material has been previously published in *Eye* magazine, number 18, fall 1995.

The research for this book has been supported by an Individual Grant from the National Endowment for the Arts.

[D]edicated, with love and thanks,

to my first design mentors, my parents,

Anne Hahn Scotford and John Ryland Scotford,

and with love to my children,

Alexandra Proctor Lange and Jeremy Marcus Lange

[Contents]

[Designing a magazine is] a rationalist's dream —in which the elements of architecture, sculpture and film come into play. . . . A magazine is not simply a mise en page of type. It is a mise en page of meanings— expressed in type, photographs, illustrations or all together.

(Leo Lionni at 1985 magazine symposium)

[Preface]

Though I can no longer remember exactly how and when I first saw the work of Cipe Pineles, the value of her story and its potential as exemplar occurred to me at an important confluence. Several years' search for women in graphic design history had revealed some problems: Much of women's participation had been ignored; the variety of women's roles within the field was not acknowledged because definitions of roles were based on masculine models; male-female collaborations had gone unrecognized; judgments of historical significance depended on traditional connections to power, money, and institutions; little consideration was given to alternative kinds of mentors, the "unpowerful," such as family and friends; work for audiences other than male and mainstream was not valued; and the act of combining professional work with the demands of private life and family was not a factor worth mentioning in any assessment of a designer.[1] These skewed points of view painted a picture of graphic design history that to my eye was less than complete. Fortunately, through the generosity of her children, Cipe Pineles's archives had become part of the Graphic Design Archives at Rochester Institute of Technology, and the National Endowment for the Arts was well funded and still bestowing individual grants. Initially, the story of Cipe Pineles seemed rich in possibilities. In retrospect, I can say she has more than fulfilled them.

A range of ideas coming from feminist history, feminist art history, and current feminist critiques of design history has informed this discussion of Cipe Pineles and her work. Traditional history and art history have been criticized for focusing on the individual agent, and in most cases the male agent. Many now agree that the traditional perspective of history through the lens of male hero and male creative genius has created a skewed view of events, circumstances, experiences, values, and products. This view has also been distorted by biases surrounding class, race, and national and religious origin.

Though the subject presented here is female, I chose a traditional format that focuses on the individual agent. A monograph has been committed, when such forms are suspect. Historians speak of getting beyond the "bricks" of history and looking at the larger and more significant walls and buildings. They focus on this larger picture in an attempt to understand how the bricks fit together, how they got there, who built the edifice, and why it was built. However, we will not fully understand the structure of American graphic design history until we have more female "bricks." This book is a start.

My approach was to create a case study that would allow me to delve into the work and life of a historically important individual who was both a woman in design and a designer *for* women and *with* women. I wanted Cipe Pineles's case to serve as a model for studying women designers and to help advance graphic design history. Her experiences were varied, and I realized that she could be studied in several contexts: as a young woman breaking into professional design; as a seasoned designer guiding several women's magazines through years of important social change; as an established professional breaking down barriers in professional organizations; as a dedicated teacher during years when women's attendance in design schools was increasing; and as a professional woman involved in family life with two husbands who were prominent designers as well. I saw Pineles as the first independent woman designer to mix and balance the professional and personal. She had, by fine example, promoted the existence and acceptance of women in graphic design in the early years of the profession's development.

I began by studying all of Pineles's notes, sketches, dummies, letters, portfolios, notebooks, files, photographs, and ephemera. I then looked at the concentric circles the people in her life formed around her. To discover how she was perceived in her many different roles, I interviewed her family members; close friends; former neighbors; colleagues and collaborators, who were editors, artists, designers, photographers, and teachers; former students and assistants; and members of the wide design community who had come into contact with her through various committees, projects, juries, conferences, and other events.

The image of Pineles's life that emerged from these interviews was not a simple, straightforward one. This is hardly surprising, as Pineles was a successful professional women during decades when this was unusual. Nor is "success" easily defined or achieved, however effortless the practitioner may make it seem. In addition to "successful professional," the story of Cipe Pineles is many stories: child in wartime, immigrant, Jewish daughter, plucky career girl, wartime wife, struggling professional, editorial team member, working mother, widow, design partner, teacher, lover, friend, and colleague. This work has sought to enlarge the perspective around the subject, bringing in the many individuals who influenced Pineles's work and life, and to provide a wider social and historical context for her professional work.

My approach to Pineles was greatly influenced by *Composing a Life*, in which Mary Catherine Bateson writes that women's lives, unlike those of men, are rarely planned or linear. Instead, they are composed of a variety of activities, roles, and critical decisions often performed or made out of necessity. I have also taken into account the claim Carolyn Heilbrun makes in *Writing a Woman's Life* that the so-called natural plot posited for women's lives is one they seldom fit. Questioning the assumptions commonly brought to women's biographies (and even to autobiographies), Heilbrun explains that significant events in women's lives often occur at times other than those predicted by theories based on masculine examples. She encourages historians of women to break from convention, examine the important relationships in the subject's life, and notice what has been ignored or hidden from public record.

The inclusion of women in graphic design history has been a spotty endeavor. Histories available before 1983, when Philip Meggs's *A History of Graphic Design* was published, mentioned very few women, as did the first edition of Meggs's major work. Less than a handful of "anthologies" of women's design work exist; even fewer cover graphic design. Textual information has frequently been too basic, purely factual, and lacking in analysis, interpretation, and context. *Hybrid Imagery* until now has been the only book about an individual woman graphic designer; it was written by April Greiman, who followed the lead of many male designers and wrote of her own life in graphic design, thereby creating her own public record. Articles about women graphic designers in professional magazines and journals have become more common since the 1960s, as have the different venues for such articles. Still, public and professional notice has in no way kept up with the increasing numbers of women entering and succeeding in the graphic design profession.[2]

Reproduction in catalogs and books creates a public record of work that is often inherently ephemeral. Both of the major graphic design history exhibitions, *Graphic Design in America* (at the Walker Center in Minneapolis in 1989) and *Mixing Messages* (at the Cooper-Hewitt Museum, the National Design Museum of the Smithsonian Institution in 1996), were curated by women and included work by women designers. The catalogs for these exhibits to some extent help to correct the spottiness of the picture of graphic design history. They better show the involvement of women in American graphic design and the variety of roles available to them. One-fifth of the designers profiled in the Walker catalog are women, and Pineles is among them. The Cooper-Hewitt catalog includes approximately 300 different works of graphic design, one-third of which are credited to women. Pineles is mentioned with other designers of the 1940s and 1950s as one who mixed European modernism with healthy doses of wit and the colloquialisms of commercial vocabularies.

Conferences have been prominent venues for graphic design history for the past ten years, but only within the last five years has there been an explicit attempt to add women designers to the program discussions. In 1992 at the School of Visual Arts in New York City, critic Karrie Jacobs presented "Lost Women Designers," a lecture partly inspired by an experience Jacobs had with Cipe Pineles. Beginning a book project on Will Burtin, Jacobs went to talk with Pineles. Before Jacobs had even explained the project, Pineles (correctly) assumed the book was not about her. Jacobs was taken aback and considered this so unfair that she dropped the project and at the conference spoke against "myth-making" and "monographs."

Likewise, the publishing history on Cipe Pineles has been sparse. She was featured in *Print* in 1955 and again in 1985 as the cover story. *U&lc* ran a profile interview in 1978; a critical essay on her work appeared in *Eye* in 1995; and a summary essay was published by the American Institute of Graphic Arts (AIGA) in 1998. As the "pioneer" I believe she was and for her other important qualities, Pineles could have been included as the tenth pioneer and only woman in the important anthology *Nine Pioneers of American Graphic Design*; the case for her inclusion was argued in the *Eye* magazine essay.[3]

The decisions Pineles made and the paths she took during her life have inspired me when inspiration was needed. Carolyn Heilbrun recently commented on this phenomenon in *The Last Gift of Time*. Although Heilbrun is referring to writers, her words pertain to many kinds of women: "Women, I believe, search for fellow beings who have faced similar struggles, conveyed them in ways a reader can transform into her own life, confirmed desires the reader had hardly acknowledged—desires that now seem possible. Women catch courage from the women whose lives and writings they read, and women call the bearer of that courage friend."

Though I never met her, I now call Cipe Pineles friend; may you as well.

[Acknowledgments]

This book exists because Cipe Pineles was a collector with a large house and because her family had the generosity and foresight to give her materials, as well as those of William Golden and Will Burtin, to the Graphic Design Archives at the Wallace Library of Rochester Institute of Technology; because Roger Remington and Barbara Hodik developed such good relations with Pineles herself that she was involved in the plan; and because the developing archives have become an important and necessary haven for the materials of American graphic design practice.

During my work on the project I have been encouraged and helped by several colleagues at RIT. I sincerely thank: Roger Remington for early conversations (when I found out about the treasure that waited) and the loan of materials; Barbara Polowy, curator of the collection, for allowing me complete and flexible access; Jim Bodenstedt, Susan Williams, Kari Horowicz, and Ian Weber for practical and photographic help; and not least, Deborah Beardsley and Tim Engstrom for friendship and hospitality in Rochester.

While I developed this project and presented some preliminary ideas about women in design I was helped by the supportive words and actions of colleagues in design history and publishing: Steven Heller, Phil Meggs, Rick Poynor, Sharon Poggenpohl, Ellen Lupton, Maud Lavin, and Victor Margolin.

There have been many individuals to whom I had to appeal and I thank them for their help: Margo Karp at Pratt Institute; Robert Rindler from The Cooper Union School of Art; X. Theodore Barber at Parsons School of Design; A. Benno Schmidt for research in the Library of Congress; Lorraine Mead at Condé Nast; Judith Johnson at Lincoln Center for the Performing Arts, Inc.; Rick Barandes for old magazines; Ellen Mazur Thomson for remembering an anecdote; and the many artists and photographers whose work is reproduced.

North Carolina State University has been the site of my academic career; many people who make up this institution have helped me develop into a teacher and have allowed me the freedom to find my way as a scholar. I appreciate the small grants over the years that permitted me to explore several areas of interest. The graduate history seminar taught by Anthony LaVopa contributed to the methodology of this project.

The School of Design has been an environment for growth. From my own department of Graphic Design, I am grateful for the friendship, grant proposal help, and general career mentoring of Meredith Davis and the editorial work of Andrew Blauvelt on earlier writings. I have also been sustained by the enthusiasm of my students at North Carolina State University for this project; they have seen and heard bits over the years and kept asking for more. Graduate students Susan Curtis and Sunny Kwok provided research assistance and photography. My thanks to my colleagues on the school research committee for research grants to help with the smaller hurdles. Most recently, Dean Marvin Malecha has been very understanding of conflicting demands on my time.

The National Endowment for the Arts has twice provided funding for my work on women in design and I am continually thankful that I began my work before the current and undeserved decline of its fortunes.

It has been interesting to play several roles in the production of this book. After many years as a designer of books working with editors, to be on the "other side" as author was humbling. I have learned new appreciation for the objectivity and patience of editors. While it is literally true there would be no book without them, I want to thank Nancy Green and Casey Ruble for their labor to make it a much better book. The improvements are at their urging; the remaining faults are mine.

The usual suspects among family and friends have hung in there with me, through exciting days of discovery to dreary days of rewriting. I appreciate every smidgen of their interest and every minute of their listening to my complaints. Several members of this group also took the role of early "nondesign" readers to help me write for a broader audience; I am solely responsible for any lapses here. In addition, I want to thank those friends in design and publishing for their advice and help with technical obstacles.

There are two sets of parents responsible for the base upon which I have worked, and I am eternally indebted to them. John and Anne Hahn Scotford, themselves designers, provided a home where design and art defined the environment and our experiences. My sisters and I were imprinted by design; we lived with Eames furniture, learned architectural styles from the car windows, and could identify typefaces by age ten. My late in-laws, Kurt and Helen Lange, provided my most direct experience with European and Jewish culture. Knowing them encouraged my interests and, I believe, allowed me to understand Pineles in ways not otherwise possible.

This book exists because of the family, friends, and colleagues of Cipe Pineles who loved and regarded her so highly that they have continually aided, encouraged, and energized me throughout the project. Unique, irreplaceable, and utterly indispensable, they were willing to share their memories, letters, notes, and "pieces of Cipe" with me. It is my hope they will find in these pages the Cipe Pineles they knew. I will always be grateful for the generosity of:

Janet Amendola
Ruth Ansel
Lillian Bassman
Ivan Chermayeff
Seymour Chwast
Mildred Constantine
Tom Courtos
Rudolph de Harak
Lou and Anne Dorfsman
Kim Elam
Estelle Ellis
Helen Federico
Carl Fischer
James and Cleo Fitch
George and Alice Forster
Carol Burtin Fripp
Ken Garland
Sara Giovanitti
Thomas Golden
Albert Greenberg
Marcel Guillaume
William Helburn
Steven Heller
Barbara Valentine Hertz
Mies Hora
Isabel Johnson
Valentine Hertz Kass
Joe and Evelyn Kaufman
Dodie Kazanjian
David Levy
Janet Levy
Joel Levy
Leo Lionni
George Lois
Utah Mascoll
John Mazzola
John O'Keefe
Eleanor Perenyi
Joan Perlstein
Naomi Rosenblum
Roz Roose
John Russo
Martika Sawin

Carmen Schiavone
Paula Scher
Roger Schoening
Irving Schor
Robert Schor
Bernarda Bryson Shahn
Muriel Batherman Sheldon
Lou and Helen Silverstein
Babs Simpson
Gertrude Snyder Weinberger
Frank Stanton
Baron Stewart
Melissa Tardiff
Bradbury Thompson
Rochelle Udell
Jan Uretsky
Rose Warren
Kurt Weihs
Henry Wolf
Edgar Young

[Introduction]

Picture this: The year is 1932. The scene is a party in New York City at the studio of a design collaborative. The work of the collaborative is on display, and it includes model window displays with lively, colorful figures dressed in sophisticated cotton print fabrics. A powerful publisher attends the party and meets the young woman who designed the window displays. She is foreign-born and recently out of art school. He publishes fashion magazines. A man of decisive action, he invites her to meet his art director, who hires her as his assistant.

Thus began Cipe Pineles's apprenticeship with Dr. M. F. Agha, an apprenticeship that launched a career in magazines that eventually would take Pineles to the upper echelons of American graphic design. By the time of her death in 1991 at age eighty-two, Pineles had accomplished more than she could have dreamed during her art school days. She had assisted Agha, one of the major art directors of the time, at *Vogue*, *Vanity Fair*, and *House & Garden*, magazines published by Condé Nast, one of the most powerful men in mass-market publishing. Having won the trust and respect of both Agha and Nast, she went on to accept responsibility for another Condé Nast publication, *Glamour*. Pineles later was part of a powerful trio of women who shaped the new, innovative *Seventeen* and reconceived *Charm*, the first magazine to target a "working woman" audience. By the end of the 1980s, Pineles had won numerous design awards, been admitted to all the prestigious professional design organizations, enjoyed a long teaching career at Parsons School of Design, and worked on countless committees, boards, juries, conferences, and symposia.

Pineles gained recognition and respect for her pioneering role in the history of American graphic design. She became a "first" many times in her life. She began her career when the graphic design profession was still defining itself, its aspirations, and its standards—a period in which there were no other women art directors working independently. Directing several mass-market magazines through years marked by significant social change, Pineles occupied a position of authority and autonomy previously enjoyed only by men. The consistently high quality of her work and her innovative use of fine artists as illustrators brought her to the attention of her male peers. She became the first woman member of the New York Art Directors Club (ADC) and, later, its hallowed Hall of Fame, and she was among a handful of woman members belonging to the Alliance Graphique Internationale (AGI).

One of Pineles's important achievements was her equal professional and private partnership with two powerful, famous men also in design, William Golden and Will Burtin. Withstanding the pressures and strains common in such relationships, Pineles thrived on the shared enthusiasm and talent. In 1996, she was posthumously awarded the Gold Medal for career achievements by the American Institute of Graphic Arts (AIGA). As with her membership in the ADC's Hall of Fame, she joined Golden and Burtin, creating a "family" of three that continues to occupy a unique position in American graphic design.

That you may not have heard of Cipe Pineles, and certainly don't know how to pronounce her name, is part of the story of this book. The pronunciation is easy: SEE-pee pi-NELL-iss. She signed her work "CP," her initials being a homophone for her first name. How she got to the party at the design collaborative studio in 1932—and how she used her assistantship to spark an entire career—is the rest of the story.

You cannot even imagine
how beautiful it was
when the ship came
nearer and nearer to see
the port New York. . . .
The most beautiful place
is the longest street in
the world that is
Broadway, especially at
night. . . . From the
beginning we have hard
work, but I think that in a
few months, when we
will speak and
understand more English
it will be much easier.

(Cipe Pineles in 1923 essay)

[To America]

1908   Cipe Pineles born June 23 in Vienna, Austria
1920   family home in Gliniany, Poland, invaded by Red Army; family
               moves to Vienna, Austria
1923   family leaves Vienna and arrives in USA
1923–26 attends Bay Ridge High School, Brooklyn, NY
1926   wins essay contest
1926–29 studies at Pratt Institute, Brooklyn
1929   graduates from Pratt's General Art Course
               wins Tiffany Foundation scholarship; summer painting residency in
                   Oyster Bay, NY
1929–30 teaches watercolor in Newark, New Jersey Public School of Fine
                   and Industrial Art
1929   exhibits watercolors at American Fine Arts Building, NYC
1930   becomes naturalized citizen on September 2
               exhibits oil paintings at Brooklyn Museum
1930–32 takes first design job at Contempora, Ltd.

[N]ow picture this:

> It was on the 12 Oct. in the morning when we arrived to America. It was a very beautiful day and I was standing on the deck near the rail. The first thing that I saw was the horizon of New-York. But slowly the ship came nearer and I could just see the first buildings of New-York and the Statue of Liberty. Then we passed the channel leading to the port of New-York. There I could admire nearby the big buildings of New-York which I never saw before. When the boat stood just in the pier I saw a crowd of people which were waving with their handkerchiefs to the coming on passengers from Europe. But the greatest impression made on me the subtrain which led me to my home.

This description was part of Cipe Pineles's first high school essay, written in Brooklyn, New York, less than two weeks after her arrival.[1] She was fifteen years old.

Like many European immigrants in the early twentieth century, the Pineles family translocated to America in search of a better life. Although their situation was unique in many ways, they still experienced the same hardships of travel endured by other immigrants of that era. The move had a profound effect on young Cipe, and it remained at the core of both the private self and public self she created in later years. Pineles would always be, in part, European, and a member of a family that survived, and thrived, by leaving others behind. Cipe's new life challenged her and she responded with all her skills and talents. Throughout her long career and lifetime, she met difficult times with hard work and the determination to always look forward.

Ciporah Pineles (forever known as Cipe) was born in Vienna, Austria, to Hillel and Bertha Eichenholtz Pineles on June 23, 1908.[2] She was the second of three daughters (Regine was born in 1903 and Debora in 1910 in Poland). The sisters succeeded two sons, Sam and Jack (their American names). Much of Cipe's childhood was spent in Poland, as the family moved from spa to spa and from doctor to doctor, seeking help for Cipe's diabetic father before the days of insulin. In another school essay, she describes a town she must have seen during her travels:

> Early in the morning on the east side of the sky the sun rises slowly, higher and higher, beshining with its bright rays the little village. On both sides of the silent road are standing small cottages in a straight line. All they have white walls with the little windows in them in which are always seen beautiful flowers and the yellow thatched roofs they look very nice. In the front of every cottage is a small garden with flowers and on the back is a big orchard. In the yard are standing the sheds, the stables, the stalls, the styes and inbetween them is a kennel with a big dog. . . . The peasants take out the farming utensils to their fields

Cipe Pineles, c. 1918, probably in Poland.

previous spread: left, The Pineles sisters, left to right, Debora, Regine, and Ciporah in matching dirndl dresses including doll, c. 1913, probably in Poland; right, Book plate with self-portrait by Cipe, linoleum block print from high school.

meanwhile their wifes milk in a great hurry the cows because they must soon go to the fields. Also the children have what to do. . . . At noon time the young lasses prepare the dinner for their working parents and remain there until the evening helping something. At this time the village is as dead. . . . About six o'clock in the evening the life in the village begins again. The peasants come home at this time with full carts of corn on top of which are sitting girls and boys decorated with beautiful field flowers and singing many songs. The tired parents after eating their supper go to sleep but the peasants wifes make everything clean for the next day which is sunday. . . . After the divine service they all return home to eat the dinner which is on this day very well prepared. Afterwards the old folk go to visit their neighbors and there they speak about their households or about politics. . . . The peasants are a strong and healthy folk and are satisfied with their life although they must work hard all day."[3]

An orthodox Jew, Cipe's father was associated with Theodore Herzl, leader of the Zionist Congress. Though he had legal training, as a Jew Hillel Pineles had no court privileges and instead engaged in business. An intellectual, he was involved with the avant-garde and the Polish Jewish renaissance, in which philosophical and political discussions and hiking clubs were common. Though Cipe's father would die before his daughters reached adolescence, Cipe's mother, nicknamed Big Bertha, was a powerful matriarch and capable of heading the family. She was confident in business and would make sure her children were educated and trained for future work.[4]

The Pineles family was comfortable and middle-class. Theirs was the typical, idyllic country life enjoyed by many Jews in Eastern Europe before World War I and the upheavals in Russia. Their last home in Poland was in Gliniany, a small town located east of Warsaw. Here, the Pineles family lived in a large house with a garden and the two kitchens a kosher household requires. From this home, the family ranged over the countryside. In summertime the children ventured to the nearby forest almost daily:

All the trees looked straight to the sky and some of them were about hundred years old. Through the middle of the wood was flowing a river. On one side of this river was a big place full with branches and young trees. This was the secret place where we used to gather strawberries, which looked at us with the red caps through the green grass. I remember how delicious it was when we were already tired from gathering to sit down near the river with full cups of berries and to eat them. On the hot days my friends and I used to bath there and to learn to swim. Always when we returned home we made a great bouquet of the beautiful flowers which were growing between the berries.[5]

Village children in Poland, c. 1916; Debora and Cipe are in the first row in fancy dirndls, second and fourth from left.

On another occasion, Cipe tells of an excursion to more distant mountains on the border between Poland and Bohemia (then western Czechoslovakia):

About one o'clock we reached the frontier and there we were not permitted to go with the carts so we walked a great piece. We crossed also a river on small boats, which was very pleasant only very short. As we were on the opposite side, the first thing was to go into the inn and to eat something. We could get only black corn [?] bread and milk which we ate with great appetite, because we were very hungry. After the excellent dinner the elder people remained there and we went to climb on the mountains promising to be back in an hour. The mountains were very high and were falling steep down from one side. We chose one of the highest and went on. It was most fortunate that we all had big sticks, because it had rained a day before and the road was very slippery. With great difficulties after falling a few times we reached at last the top. There we rested for a few minutes and had soon to go down as we promised our parents.[6]

The political backdrop for young Cipe's life was complex, and exactly how the Pineles family was affected is not known. A land long subject to changing partition, Poland was, during Cipe's younger years, divided among Germany, Austro-Hungary, and Russia. The Pineles family was among the five million Jews living in Europe at the outbreak of World War I. Cipe's later enjoyment of food and memories of hunger suggest that the family endured some privation during this time. Cipe's brother Sam joined the Austro-Hungarian army, and the battles remained far away from the family's home. Then a different struggle moved closer.

The Pineles's relatively quiet and idyllic life was interrupted—and essentially ended—by the cataclysmic events to the east: the civil war in Russia. Gliniany was about 125 miles from the Russian border. In 1920, as part of the wide-spread nationalism stimulated by the war, the Polish Army invaded the Ukraine. In response, the Red Army attacked Poland's capital, Warsaw, where they were defeated in August. In a story titled "Bolsheviki," Cipe describes the most exciting event of her young life. Written in 1926, the eyewitness account won a national high school essay contest sponsored by the *Atlantic Monthly*.

"I wonder how they look!" "And what they wear!" "And how they act!" These were the questions asked over and over again while we awaited our guests—the Bolsheviki. We by no means desired their coming, but their visit was inevitable.

It was the summer of the year 1920 that the Bolsheviki, after a hard struggle in Russia, invaded the Ukraine and part of Poland. They came down in masses, overcrowding towns and villages, roads, and forests, spreading horror and fear among the people.

At this particular time my family and I lived in a little town very near the capital of Poland. Much interest and excitement centered in Gliniany, for such an invasion meant the invasion of the capital and consequently all Poland. Different reports, mysterious stories, new announcements, were heard every day. Rumor had it that the Bolsheviki were in the habit of killing men, women, and children—of destroying whole towns and villages. Others reported that the Bolsheviki were concerned with rich people only, that they confiscated their property and gave it to the poor. We heard also that the Bolsheviki came down to reform the world and the people; and, on the other hand, that they were against all humanity. Of course, with these stories came reports of the dreadful murders of mothers and children, accompanied with descriptions of terrible tortures of men, of bloodshed, of fire, and disease.

So we lived, week after week, in suspense, excitement, and uncertainty. Just such a thrilling life as is sometimes depicted in the movies. . . . [7]

The exact circumstances of the Pineles family's departure from Poland are unknown, but shortly after the Bolsheviks' invasion they returned to Vienna. The oldest son, Sam, was discharged from the Austro-Hungarian army where he had served as an officer (which was unusual for a Jew) and seen action in Italy. Bertha Pineles began organizing the next phase of the family's life. Sam got a job on a transatlantic liner, with the intention of emigrating to America. Cipe and her younger sister Debora began learning English, using a method that entailed memorizing Dickens's *A Christmas Carol*. Many years later Pineles still remembered the first words she learned in English: "Marley was dead, to begin with. There is no doubt whatever about that."[8] The only other information about the family's Austrian sojourn comes from one of Cipe's essays, in which she describes the six weeks they spent at a health resort in the snow-peaked Carpathian mountains, just north of Vienna, in central Czechoslovakia:

Every morning and evening we went to a beautiful garden, where music was played. Very often we made excursions into the mountains with a very pleasant and merry company. Sometimes it lasted a few hours and sometimes a few days. These excursions were very insecure because the mountains are very steep and every year many trippers find their death. We also visited all the beautiful places near this. When we came home we had for a few weeks also a very nice time. In the end of September, when we went to America, we traveled almost through a half of the world and could see all the finest countries of the world."[9]

By 1921, the two oldest children, Sam and Jack, were in America. Sam had paid for Jack's trip, and the men went into business. Regine may also have joined her brothers early; her mother arranged a millinery position for her. They settled in Brooklyn, where Sam, who had received army training in telephone and telegraph communications, had gotten a job with Semitone, manufacturer of hearing aids. Two years later, Sam began working for Westinghouse in Pittsburgh and was able to bring the rest of his family to America. The journey from Vienna to America lasted about two weeks; Bertha Pineles and her daughters crossed Europe by train and then boarded the SS *Berengaria*, a well-known "three-stacker," which took them across the Atlantic.[10]

Upon her arrival, Cipe was impressed by the harbor and ships, by Broadway at night, and by the "subtrain" that took them to their first home in Brooklyn. Bertha Pineles established her household in an apartment on 66th Street, where all the children, except Sam, lived with her. One week after their arrival, Cipe and Debora, age fifteen and thirteen, enrolled in Bay Ridge High School. Their memorization of Dickens served them well: it was almost the Christmas season and their vocabulary was appropriate and impressive. Cipe's essays illustrate her comfort with writing in the English language; speaking and understanding it, however, took longer. Throughout her life she retained a slight accent, which became a part of her style and charm.

"Ma," as everyone called her, was the center of the family. She organized the children's lives, sent them to school, and created a warm, generous, open home. Rose Warren, a friend who was welcomed into the family, said she "gravitated to their layers of culture . . . and relished their richness. . . . They were people who had been battered by the experience of loss of place, who maintained a high level of enjoyment." Like other immigrants, the Pineleses had "a way of seeking connections, either in terms of work or social well-being."[11]

Sam, who assumed a paternal role in the family, and Bertha Pineles insisted that Cipe and her sisters be able to earn their own living. During a conversation in which Sam urged Cipe to attend college, she replied that she would have a husband to support her. Pineles recalled him saying, "Marriage is not a full-time occupation. Did you ever hear of a doctor or a lawyer giving up his profession because he was getting married?"[12] Another time her brother said, "Marriage is not a substitute for having something to do in life."[13] His advice was reflected in Pineles's attitude toward work: "I didn't think of it as a career. When you're not married, and you're a young woman, you had a job—everybody did. Either you were a receptionist or you learned typing and shorthand so you could be a secretary. I never thought of having a job as unusual; I just thought that's the way it was."[14] Her brother was prescient: Pineles did not marry until she was thirty-four and was widowed twice; she was well served by his principles.

Bertha Pineles taught the daughters useful skills. Handwork was highly regarded, and they all learned to sew, knit, and crochet. Regine's creativity was focused early and perhaps not wholly voluntarily. Her millinery training, accomplished in Austria, was excellent, and she easily found work in America. Debora's talents led her into medicine; she

The Pineles sisters, left to right, Debora, Regine, and Cipe, late 1920s.

became a doctor. Cipe exhibited the most creative talent, which was cultivated in her new American high school through art activities, public acclaim, and supportive teachers.

Cipe thoroughly enjoyed her American high school and enthusiastically made friends with every girl in her class. At her graduation in 1926 she was chosen "best natured member" of her class, to which she responded, "This is what I love. That is the best thing that could happen to me. Of course I hope to become a great artist, and I want to write, too, in this free and good America, but more than anything else I wish to be popular with the Americans I meet."[15] Her outgoing nature, which helped her connect with new friends in her new country, would also play an important part in her professional success.

Having a clear mastery of the English language and having gained recognition with "Bolsheviki," Cipe considered studying journalism. For winning the essay contest she had received $50, which was not a small sum—a year's tuition at art school was $145. Cipe's artistic talents were also recognized; she had received a $25 Bay Ridge art scholarship to Pratt Institute and her artwork had been published on the high school page of the local newspaper.[16] Her high school literary and art monthly, where she served on the art staff, had published some of her poetry and illustrations. At that time, her illustration style was decorative and influenced by Art Nouveau examples. Beside Cipe's 1926 senior photograph were the words of her classmates: "She knows she draws well. A little Polish girl who won our hearts."

Choosing a three-year certificate program called the General Art Course, Cipe enrolled in Pratt Institute in Brooklyn in the fall of 1926. For Cipe it was an easy ride on public transportation from the Pineles home on Carroll Street. During her final year at Pratt, she received one of the sixteen scholarships available, the Katherine E. DeForest Scholarship of $25 for a student in the General Art classes.

The Pratt Circular of Information for 1928 states: "The courses are designed to educate teachers of art and industrial handwork, to train students thoroughly in drawing, design and color and as professional workers in the various arts and crafts, and in interior decoration, architectural construction and architectural design." The General Art Course was organized around a three-year curriculum, with an optional fourth year of advanced painting or illustration. The program offered many courses that presumably would have prepared Cipe for her future career, including drawing, illustration, painting, composition, art history, and even some courses with specific "commercial" and advertising intent. Her later apprenticeship, however, was a necessary addition to her education.

The Pratt catalog also says that the "design and commercial illustration class" included lettering and the design of posters, covers, and advertising illustration. The "decorative painting" class addressed magazine cover design, and the "composition" class covered book illustration. "Pictorial illustration" concentrated on costumed figures. "Commercial illustration" included exercises in creating newspaper

above: Cipe's drawing for a cover of her high school yearbook *Maroon & White*, 1928.
below: Cipe during Pratt years (photograph by Arthur Studios).

right: *Cactus* watercolor by Cipe, probably painted at Pratt.
below: Cipe, probably at Green Mansions, c. 1930.

advertisements, posters, and covers for publications. The senior "commercial illustration" class focused on photomechanical reproductive methods and the preparation of artwork for various engraving and printing processes. Much later in her life, however, Pineles could not specifically recall taking any commercial art classes or completing any assignments that required the combination of image and text. She did remember her life drawing and portrait classes, classical drawing from plaster casts, perspective exercises, and the encouragement of her female watercolor teacher. At Pratt she began experimenting with still-life painting, which led to a lifelong fascination with the subject, and at graduation her portfolio included food paintings: a chocolate cake, a loaf of bread, and a bottle of Coca-Cola.[17]

The school's 1929 yearbook, the *Prattonia*, indicates that Pineles played on the volleyball team in 1927, was president of the General Art class in 1928, and served as assistant photography editor for the *Prattonia* during her senior year. Next to her senior portrait is a comment from her peers: "The most remarkable water colorist in our class. Boys, it's too late; Cipe is wedded to her art—and they're both happy."

Pineles was already exhibiting her work during her final year at Pratt and in the years immediately following graduation. Her watercolors *Snapdragons* and *Tiger Lily* were included in the 1929 *Combined Annual Exhibition of the American Water Color Society and the New York Water Color Club*, exhibited at the American Fine Art Building. In November 1930, the Brooklyn Museum had an exhibition of oil paintings by Brooklyn and Long Island artists and included an oil version of Pineles's *Cactus*.

At graduation, the Louis Comfort Tiffany Foundation awarded Pineles a year-long fellowship, which included a three-month summer residency for painting at the Foundation in Oyster Bay, Long Island. The fellowship was an honor, and Pineles must have enjoyed spending

the summer with the group of resident artists. It did not, however, provide full financial support, and Pineles needed to find employment after graduation. Though she wanted a job in the commercial world and spent a year searching for one, her first position was in teaching. In the fall of 1929, she accepted a position as an instructor in watercolor at the Newark Public School of Fine and Industrial Art in New Jersey. Her salary was $10 a week.

While Pineles never commented on teaching in Newark, she did describe what it was like to be young, female, and looking for work in the months following the stock market crash and the beginning of the Depression. From the New York Public Library Pineles got a list of advertising agencies specializing in food accounts. She remembered, "When I left Pratt and began looking for my first job, I would drop my portfolio off at various advertising agencies. But the people who liked my work and were interested enough to ask me in for an interview had assumed by my name that I was a man! When they finally met me, they were disappointed, and I left the interview without a chance for the job. . . . Someone would explain, on a couple of occasions, that I would be working in a bullpen—a great big room with a lot of men—and they wouldn't like to have a woman around. So that was the first obstacle."[18]

Pineles's persistence and dedication paid off. During the years following graduation, she found employment positions that eventually led to projects directly related to her career. Within a year after graduation, she began working at Contempora, Ltd., and spent a summer working at Green Mansions, an adult resort/summer camp in the Adirondacks.

Green Mansions, with its intellectual and perhaps leftist political flavor, was a place frequented by young people from the city who were hungry for outdoor activities mixed with some culture. Pineles worked as a waitress (along with playwright Clifford Odets) and at one point tried to unionize the staff, prompting several friends to nickname her "Union." Later, and evidently in spite of her labor activities, Pineles was employed on a freelance basis to do promotional design work for the resort.

top row: Green Mansions brochure covers from c.1940, photocollages and lettering by Cipe. above: Green Mansions letterhead using French "woody" typeface.

The Art Editor fixes up a picture for the issue. She's responsible for the overall look of the magazine. She makes layouts, chooses illustrations and type. She has worked up through art jobs in an advertising agency, department store or magazine. She needs art training, taste, creative talent.

(*Glamour*, September 1946)

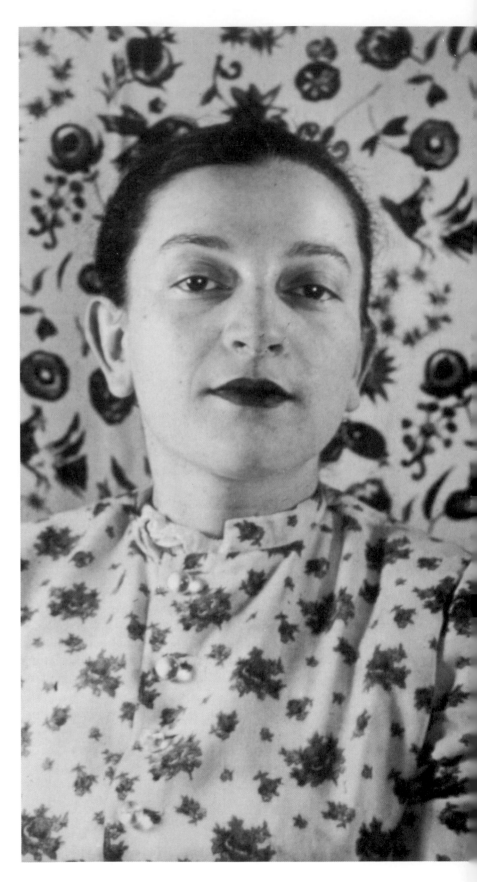

[Getting Started in Design]

[C]ondé Nast owned and managed the eponymously named publishing empire comprising *Vogue*, *Vanity Fair*, and *House & Garden* magazines. *Vogue* was his jewel. Started in 1892 as a weekly about fashion and society in New York City, it was bought by Nast in 1909. The magazine's editorial personality was the result of a collaboration between Nast and the magazine's editor, Edna Woolman Chase. She had been on staff when the magazine was purchased and would serve as editor from 1914 to 1952. *Vogue*'s visual style was developed and refined by Dr. M. F. Agha, art director from 1929 to 1943. From the beginning, *Vogue* and its close competitor, *Harper's Bazaar*, were the arbiters of fashion. *Vogue*'s "frankly snobbish" tone was exactly what Nast and Chase intended.[1]

Condé Nast was wholly and intimately involved with his publishing empire. He theorized that "class" publications did not need a large circulation to influence behavior and develop an audience. There was no fiction in *Vogue* because Nast believed it attracted a nondiscriminating audience. Any method that would filter out the "wrong" readers was employed; as Nast put it, *Vogue* was supposed to be a magnet that attracted only gold-headed pins. Nast and Chase saw *Vogue* in terms of its service function: it provided technical advice to women of fashion. They took this job of advising women quite seriously, even going as far as to use illustrations and photographs that provided enough detail that dressmakers could reproduce the fashions depicted.[2]

Nast was also a watchdog of statistics, and he closely monitored both circulation and advertising figures. He was constantly testing the market by keeping sales figures for different cover treatments. He controlled both the business and editorial sides of the magazines; he added features, he chose photographs. He insisted on using the best paper, the best photography and printing methods, and the most talented people. Nast kept up with trends in illustration and photography, championing those practitioners he admired and encouraging others to develop their talents more broadly. He credited cover artists as early as 1909, acknowledging the importance of their contribution.[3]

In 1925 Nast asked (Eduardo) Benito, a frequent contributor of art deco fashion illustrations and covers, to present a new plan for page layouts. Within the next two years Benito presented a dummy that proposed a radical shift from the use of decoration and eighteenth-century typefaces to the modern design the magazine retains today. Benito argued that instead of mirroring the established taste of the privileged readership, the magazine should reflect the changing times. The plan included the use of sans serif typefaces, new to American eyes, and the use of black rules and more open space on the pages. These changes referenced contemporaneous work from the Bauhaus school in Germany and from French architect Le Corbusier. There was now a "blueprint" for change, but no art director to effect it.[4]

In search of a new art director for *Vogue*, Nast traveled to Europe in 1928 and found Dr. Mehemed Fehmy Agha in Berlin. Previously the Paris studio chief of Dorland, an international advertising agency, Agha

previous spread: left, Portrait of Cipe Pineles, 1930s; right, Detail of sketch for Green Mansions brochure cover.

was working as the chief assistant and layout man for the German *Vogue*.[5] Nast was attracted to the "order, taste, and invention" of Agha's work, and he brought him to New York.[6]

Agha was a multitalented, widely respected man who developed a reputation for ironic wit and a sense of the absurd. He was also cynical, sarcastic, and outspoken. He was born to Turkish parents in the Ukraine and spoke several languages. He had studied art only briefly and had moved into advertising and publishing while living in France.[7] William Golden described him as "the man who knew too much to like anything."[8] Agha was quoted as saying, "Personally I might be inclined to [the view] that a fashion magazine conception of beauty, elegance and taste might be insipid and nauseating, but I firmly believe that a fashion magazine is not the place to display our dislikes of these things."[9] Nast found him perfectly suited for his publications.

Over time, Agha would be responsible for considerable innovation, both technical and artistic, in all the Condé Nast publications. He simplified and systematized the typography (*Vanity Fair* used a Futura variant for all display); he used photography on a larger scale and allowed it to take precedence over illustration; he removed all decorative dingbats and borders; and he opened the spaces of margins and gutters.[10] Agha began to implement many of Benito's concepts for layouts in *Vogue*. By the next year, he had introduced sans serif type to both *Vogue* and *Vanity Fair*.

Readers reacted negatively to the changes, as did Chase, who was inclined toward tradition. But Agha successfully argued that readers were, in fact, accustomed to the new look, pointing out that Intertype Vogue, the typeface in question, was being used by forty-two percent of their advertisers, by their competitor, *Harper's Bazaar*, and in trade journals.[11] Understanding the importance of synthesizing the editorial and design aspects of the magazine, Agha developed a close, equal relationship with both Chase and Nast. Nast had a great deal of confidence in Agha, though he continued to give final approval on all photographs and write long memos on all aspects of the art and covers. Agha essentially spent time massaging egos and communicating with his artists and photographers about the aesthetic and technical details of their work. Overseeing three magazines, *Vogue*, *Vanity Fair*, and *House & Garden*, he spread his time and energy throughout several offices.[12]

Among Condé Nast's favorite activities was scouting for new talent. He frequently invited people to work for him before he even had a position available for them. When Pineles went to meet Agha, there was hardly a question about hiring her, as she came with a reference from Nast himself. Upon joining Agha, Pineles instantly became part of women's fashion magazine publishing—and part of Agha's daily professional life. Pineles would later praise Agha as her employer, teacher, guide, and critic. She appreciated her unique position: "Fashion magazines were filled with women. A man was a rarity. The reason my job was so wonderful was that I was the only woman in the most brilliant

Dr. M. F. Agha, art director of all Condé Nast publications, 1928–1942.

Painting of Agha's office at Condé Nast by Cipe Pineles. He is hidden by lady editors in hats; Pineles is at far right.

man's office. I could listen to everything that was going on while quietly making sketches, layouts, paste-ups. . . ."[13] In addition, her salary was raised to $30 a week, and she was paid regularly, which was not a condition of her previous job. Pineles's salary seems fair in comparison with those of her contemporaries in the industry; in 1932, photographer Horst was paid $60 per week, and two years later photographer Toni Frissell, a woman, received $50 per week.[14]

Pineles's position at Condé Nast allowed her to develop her talents in a creatively stimulating environment. "By the time I was hired, there was no room in the bullpen, so my desk was wedged in behind some filing cabinets. . . . I was in on all the talk. [Agha] spent a lot of time talking with his creative people, going over ideas for them to develop. We talked about problems related to type; pictures and selection of pictures as satisfying an editorial concept or not. Agha gave us a lot of rope to hang ourselves. So we didn't do just one solution to a problem. I would try a solution two or three times. All those trials were the luxury of the job."[15] The staff was allowed to do as many photostats as necessary to explore different size relationships, and Pineles devised a way to save time. She loosely taped photographs onto her spreads, made a photostat, took off the photographs and moved them around, made another photostat, and so on, until she felt she had explored all the different possibilities. Using this method, she always had a whole spread composition recorded. She also saved money—and received a raise for her ingenuity.[16]

Pineles's comment about trying "a solution two or three times" was an understatement. Another veteran of Agha's methods, William Golden, described it this way: "Agha would present you with a problem, a little page. 'Bring me something with three variations.' He would then look at the work and he would say, 'Well, this is satisfactory, but I am sure that it is possible for you to do more.' We'd go out and do thirteen other solutions, straining ourselves, scraping the bot-

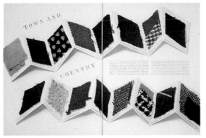

Spreads for *Vogue*, August 15, 1935, showing 3-D, textured **elements** and design crossing gutter.

tom of the barrel. Agha would look at these and he'd say, 'Well, that's much better, but I feel we need more.' We'd come back with another ten and he'd say 'Well, the second one you brought me was the best in the lot.'"[17] This was a hard training ground, but those who were learning the process appreciated it, and they often continued using the method later in their careers when they were working independently or were in charge. Lest any designer wonder how the magazines ever closed on time, Pineles also reported that it was the young designers who had this luxury of time and experimentation; the older designers worked on a schedule and were the ones responsible for getting the magazine out on time. Magazines in that era had large staffs who were paid at low rates. Pineles did not say how and when a young designer moved from experiments to responsibility.[18]

The rule-breaking innovations that Agha introduced were achieved by this method of constant experimentation. He was aware that young designers had meager knowledge of the use of type, so he provided his staff with a cabinet filled with galley type in a wide variety of sizes, leadings, and weights of Bodoni Book. The staff could cut up this dummy type for their "play." They tried headlines in all positions on the page; finally, Nast did object to having them at the very bottom. The effortless look of asymmetrical arrangements and "careless" scatterings of images was discovered through a meticulous process of trial and error. Photographs were used large and extended so they bled off the edge of the page. Other images expanded across the gutter to create a "landscape" on the double-page spreads. At times, visual elements from two related stories were allowed to span the gutter so that the division was no longer a straight line. This experimental activity also extended into the technical realm, where Agha, exploiting opportunities at the photography studios and printing plants also owned by Condé Nast, was able to supplant fashion illustration with photography, experiment with lighting and portraiture techniques, and develop greater control of color in duotones and full four-color printing.[19]

Cipe Pineles worked directly with Agha for about five years. She may have found her editorial design and fashion career accidentally, but she was well suited to it. She was trained by the best in the field, and Agha constantly challenged her. "But," she said, "I also learned from him to have a sense of pleasure in a job . . . a sense of fun. And I particularly remember his demand of me that I shouldn't become engrossed in the details, that I should look at the larger picture."[20]

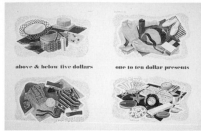

top right: Selected spreads for *Vogue* Christmas Primer, December 1, 1933, with illustrations by Pineles.
above: Christmas card for Condé Nast Publications by Pineles; shown closed and open.
below: Title pages for *Vogue* editorial wells, June 15, 1934; January 15, 1941.

Her duties at Condé Nast included work on all three publications: *Vogue*, *Vanity Fair*, and *House & Garden*. She was a talent scout for artists and photographers; she supervised experiments for *Vanity Fair* and designed at least one cover; and she planned and designed two covers and many features for *Vogue*. Beyond the serial publication work, Pineles was involved in designing many of the myriad service publications connected with *Vogue*: the seasonal supplements for shoes and corsets, the pattern books, promotional items for the publishing house, and even Christmas cards for Edna Woolman Chase. One year she was assigned to design a sixteen-page Christmas section for people bored with the holiday; another time she developed three different themes for an eight-page beauty section. Another project was to adapt the five key hues of red, yellow, blue, green, and purple of the Munsell Color System to color schemes for interior decorating.[21]

Pineles recalled that Agha "assigned me the task of selecting a different typeface for every headline in *Vogue*. I plunged into old type books, as well as into the advanced graphic publications from Europe, to gather inspiration. By the time you looked through five issues of *Vogue*, you had a hundred typefaces to work from including five versions of my own handwriting. I used to hate type. It scared me, but it was this process of being compelled to search for headlines that gave me my feeling for type. It made me see what makes one page look good and what makes the same typeface, specified elsewhere by another person, look poor."[22]

While she learned typography, page composition, and the use of photography, Pineles's previously developed talents in illustration were employed. She was given numerous small (and mostly uncredited) illustration assignments for both *Vogue* and *House & Garden*. Many of these were tiny black-and-white drawings that filled spaces and accented the service pages at the front and back of the magazines. More important were the spot illustrations that appeared on *Vogue*'s table of contents and the compositions for the editorial page that stated the issue's theme. The black-and-white pieces show a flair for the discipline of small-scale linework, a feeling for the contrasts of line, texture, and mass, and a love of decorative detail and pattern. The theme pages show a variety of media and approaches, including photography, line drawing, collage, gouache illustration, and playful typography combining several typefaces.[23]

Most important were the feature assignments. Here, Pineles was

far left: Pineles's painted sketch for *Vogue* spread using artist's work.

left: "Which of these great masters?" *Vogue* spread, November 1, 1940.

below: *Vogue* spread, February 1, 1933, showing combinations of 3-D materials.

able to combine active visual composition, typography, and illustration into a spread or series of spreads that expressed a complete editorial concept. At times these spreads revealed Pineles's interest in and knowledge of the arts and art history. Her spread "Which of these great masters would have chosen you as a model?" describes women's natural coloring and suggests which makeup and fashion colors they should wear by illustrating the various female figures and color palettes employed by the painters Derain, Laurencin, Lawrence, Goya, Renoir, and Lautrec. Other pages show beauty ideas in a tabular structure, which was a way of combining illustration, photography, and text with scientific overtones.

On other outstanding pages, Pineles used images of three-dimensional materials to enliven the otherwise two-dimensional surface. She used objects for themselves and for visual accent, and sometimes as literal punctuation. They were employed as illustrative elements to build a larger picture. Her abstract compositions of fabric swatches, photographed to heighten their textural and dimensional qualities, revealed her love of materials.

Though she found greater scope for its expression in later magazines, Pineles also began her professional food illustration at *Vogue*. Her food paintings were developed during the years she spent with Condé Nast, who commissioned the work on a freelance basis and published the illustrations in *Vogue*.

More often, Pineles employed her extensive illustration skills for editorial planning; there are numerous examples of full pages of image and type painted at about half-scale, showing layout, typefaces and typography, colors, and style of illustration. The multipage sequences were shown in small, bound dummies, some of which included recycled illustration or photography from previous issues to show the general tone or style proposed. In some cases, the final illustrations were not executed by Pineles, but they were often uncannily close to what she envisioned and sketched. (See next page.)

Condé Nast was well aware that covers sell magazines, and he retained firm control over this aspect of his publications. Over the years, he used a handful of artists whose work lent a general contemporary style and identity to *Vogue* and *Vanity Fair*. Pineles managed to break into this "club" three times. Her 1933 cover for *Vanity Fair*, "Return of the prodigal son," is for her an unusual example of political commentary: a fat-cat businessman represented in crisp newsprint greets a very

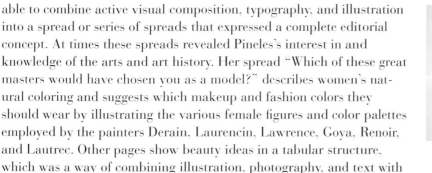

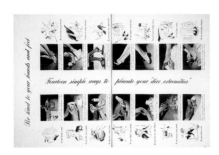
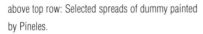

above top row: Selected spreads of dummy painted by Pineles.

bottom row: Matching printed spreads for *Vogue*, November 1, 1940.

below: Pineles at work at Condé Nast. Note the "old" materials of design: scissors and glue, ink and paint.

thin man on crutches who is down on his luck and "dressed" in rumpled newspaper. Her 1939 photographic cover for *Vogue* presents two hands and jewelry in an arresting way for the holiday season: the hands wear some minor pieces and gesture upward toward elaborate necklaces and bracelets arranged to spell the magazine's name. In both these cases, the surface is enriched by the use of dimensional materials or objects. Her strikingly simple 1940 photographic cover used tightly cropped women's heads and was an unusual abstraction for that time in women's magazine publishing. Pineles remembered how she developed the idea for that cover: "Once I was given a color photo and told to dummy as a cover. The photo was 8 by 10 and had black paper around it to show a section of the image [with the assumption it would be enlarged to fill the space]. I dummied the cover with the black around it to give the same effect of seeing a piece of the whole image."[24]

At some point in the early 1930s, Pineles, newly professional and financially independent, moved from her family home on Carroll Street, Brooklyn, across the river to Manhattan. She lived in several apartments in the East 30s. Though she lived alone for the most part, she occasionally shared an apartment with a man, in one instance living with the editor of a radical political magazine. Pineles had many suitors, and, according to a close friend of hers, she had a "European social ease with sexuality."[25] Marked by her Austrian background (and accent), she must have seemed more sophisticated than Americans. By this time, Pineles was developing her personal sense of style: a careful composition of a simple hairstyle (long hair pulled back into a bun or braided into a coronet), "classic" suits or dresses based on Austrian styles, simple jewelry, and minimal makeup. She emphasized the shape of her head and eyes, drew attention to the top of her body, and minimized the effects of her small stature. The impression was one of elegant smoothness and control.

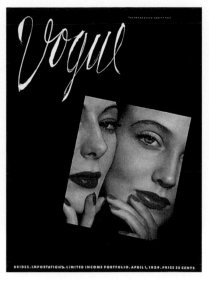

In what may have been an extension of her Green Mansions experience, Pineles became involved with the Theater Arts Committee (TAC) in New York City. The TAC was closely allied with the Federal Theater Project, which was funded by the Works Progress Administration (WPA).[26] The TAC published a magazine with the help of volunteers, and it was through this magazine that Pineles became acquainted with William Golden. As Pineles described it, "I first met Bill when I was working full-time at Condé Nast. He was working full-time at Hearst Publications. We met because in those days we gave time to interesting and needy avant-garde publications. We were both working at night on a magazine called *Theater Arts*."[27]

William Golden was a New York native, just back from California and working in the promotion department of the *Journal-American* newspaper. At some point in their early friendship, there was a job opening at Condé Nast and Pineles introduced Golden to her boss Agha. Golden was hired in the summer of 1936 as art editor for *House & Garden*.[28] Though he worked with Agha for only a year, it was a significant apprenticeship for Golden; Agha was probably the greatest single influence on Golden's design ideas and methods, and Agha's recognition of Golden was a turning point for his career.[29]

The significant friendship that developed between Pineles and Golden got off to a slow start, though there were some similarities in their backgrounds. Golden was an example of a self-made man—meeting obstacles and challenges with unusual energy and focus, he trained and educated himself to be a highly respected, even revered, leader in design and corporate circles. Born on the Lower East Side of Manhattan in 1911, Golden was the youngest of twelve children of Russian Jewish immigrants. He attended the Vocational School for Boys, where he learned photoengraving and basic commercial design. Forced by economic circumstances to leave the Vocational School after only a year, he moved to Los Angeles, where he did lithography and photo-

above left: *Vanity Fair* cover, October 1933, won an award from the New York Art Directors Club; in the *ADC Annual* Pineles is credited as designer, with Agha as art director.
center: *Vogue* cover, April 1, 1939 using cropping angles, by Pineles.
right: Proposed *Vogue* cover, using jewelry for letterforms, by Pineles. Printed cover, December 1, 1939, used only hands gesturing upward and slightly different jewel arrangement.

engraving at two printing plants and took evening classes at a trade school for another year. After creating advertisements for the *L.A. Examiner*'s promotion department, he transferred back to New York. He got similar work at the *Journal-American*, and soon thereafter met Cipe Pineles.[30]

By 1936, both Pineles and Golden were working for Condé Nast, but their friendship was almost immediately put on hold, as Pineles was offered an opportunity to work in England for seven months. Though Pineles had been at Condé Nast for only three years, the editors of *Vogue* showed their confidence in her by posting her to London to supervise the production of the special coronation issue of British *Vogue* (dated April 28, 1937).

The British *Vogue* editors had been quite successful in establishing a friendly relationship with members of King Edward VIII's circle, and later with Mrs. Simpson. The British and American public were spellbound by the romance, and both the American and British editions of *Vogue* were following the story and had used many of the same photographs. Ultimately, King Edward VIII's reign ended less than a year after it began, and he was married to Mrs. Simpson on June 3, 1937. Between the abdication and the wedding, on May 12, 1937, the coronation of Edward's brother, King George V, took place. It is difficult to know exactly what prompted the "home office" to think the British staff needed more help in covering the coronation. The coronation issue was larger than the regular issues, but the home office may have simply used it as an excuse to send Pineles on a scouting trip for talented artists and photographers. In any case, Pineles used the trip as an opportunity to make new friends and contacts, including Elwyn and Pearl Jones (later Lord Chancellor and Lady Jones) and British designer Robert Harling.

In the summer of 1937, Pineles was joined in London by her friend Rose Warren. Warren was a textile designer for Du Pont and was working on artificial yarns in their infancy. She was one of the few women in this field, and would become extremely successful in the 1940s and 1950s. Warren had known Pineles and her family since the early 1930s, when she and her husband, Norman, met them at Green Mansions. She felt a part of the family and considered Pineles her best friend. Warren and Pineles stayed in London for a few weeks and then began an adventurous, month-long trip through Russia.

Pineles's tour through Russia resulted in a beautifully executed, one-of-a-kind book illustrating their adventures. Created as a gift for Norman, it is titled *Dajte mne Vania, or Such is Life in a Big City* (the Russian translates as "give me a bath"). The subtitle is "an adventurous sketch of how two beautiful girls like us got in and out of Russia." In sixty-two pages, each painted and lettered in colored gouache, Pineles tells the story of two stylish ladies (they often wear hats, even in the bathtub) who try to maintain some level of style and personal hygiene in a foreign culture while fending off certain unwelcome attentions. Among other adventures, the ladies avoid the Left Book Club on their

below and facing page: Selected spreads from *Give me a Bath*, the painted chronicle of Pineles's 1938 trip to Russia with a friend.

Russian ship; sail through the Kiel Canal and see planes with Nazi insignia; discover that stockings are very expensive in Leningrad; arrive in Moscow to find no running water; learn that the ladies' room at the Culture Park is large and communal; dance at a diplomatic reception; shop for hats in Paris; and, thankfully, return to Brooklyn. Each illustration combines caricature with lettering to reveal, within the space of a double-page spread, the essence of the experience. There are some collaged elements: a photograph of the Commissar, a picture of Joseph Stalin. The paintings are done in Pineles's confident style and brushwork. Judging from lightly penciled notations in the corners, she planned out the sequence in the already-bound blank book and then created the scenes.

Pineles never explained why she went to Russia, nor did she talk about her experiences there. As a European (and someone who had come into direct and positive contact with the Bolsheviks as a child), she was interested in world politics throughout her life. She stayed abreast of current events, took part in political discussions, and was generally on the political left, supporting the ideals of the Soviet Union (and even Stalin for a while). Many of her friends were further to the left, advocated communism, and even may have been party members (this would become an issue during the 1950s). In short, all of this placed her in a very large group of professional New Yorkers who were socially and politically aware, involved, educated and intellectual, middle-class, and often Jewish.

Published articles have reported that Pineles returned from Europe in the fall of 1937 to become art director of the new Condé Nast magazine, *Glamour*, but the timing and her status have been exaggerated. In truth, Pineles resumed work with Agha upon her return.[31] She began working on *Glamour* two years later, when Nast purchased the magazine, but did not serve as art director until January of 1942.

Glamour was first developed as a pattern book featuring Hollywood-style clothes with mass market distribution in chain stores. Originally called *Glamour of Hollywood*, the magazine attracted an audience of young women, some of whom probably had jobs. This market appealed to Nast, who had become interested in developing a magazine for women without the attitudes and assets of the *Vogue* reader, and he bought the magazine in April of 1939. *Glamour of Hollywood* served women a breezy combination of fashion and beauty advice, sewing tips, and travel and career information. The magazine enjoyed an early newsstand success, but Nast thought the Hollywood connection too restricting and wanted to assure a "career girl" niche for the publication. He studied *Mademoiselle* (a competitor started in 1935) and upgraded the features to assume a more intelligent reader more useful to society than a Hollywood star.[32] In May 1941, the editorship changed and Elizabeth Penrose, who had been the editor of the British *Vogue*, was brought in. The magazine switched to a one-word title, jettisoning the Hollywood connection and becoming simply *Glamour*. In September the editors added the subtitle "For Young Women—the way to Fashion, Beauty and Charm."

above left: *Glamour*, July 1942 cover, brush logo-type, stencil lettering, and objects.

right: Painted page sequences by Pineles for November *Glamour* (no year).

Pineles worked on this new publication from its inception; she illustrated a double-page spread in the first issue. She does not appear on the masthead, however, until December 1941, when she is listed as art editor. In the next month's issue she is announced as the new art director. Though Agha had prepared her for the responsibility and she retained the position for three years, her experience and her feelings about the job were mixed. She was quite reticent about the experience in interviews and only one example of her *Glamour* work has ever been published (and that after her death) until now. Her silence is perhaps best explained by the few comments she made: "The magazine was supposed to appeal to the working girl who couldn't afford the clothes in *Vogue*. But *Glamour* was the wrong name. It is an archaic word and to me, seems to look down on the working girl."[33] Considering that Pineles herself was a "working girl," this must have been doubly offensive. Later she elaborated: "Condé Nast really had no interest in or respect for the young people they were addressing in this publication. Nothing was too good for *Vogue*, but the message was 'Don't put anything special in *Glamour* because the readers won't understand it or appreciate it.'"[34] It is possible, however, that the difficult working conditions she later encountered with the Condé Nast publications colored her memories of the *Glamour* experience.

Though she may not have appreciated the publisher's attitude, Pineles's employment at *Glamour* was an excellent opportunity for her to gain experience controlling an entire magazine, to try new things, and to develop working relationships with artists and photographers, many of whom became her friends and/or worked for her on all her magazines. For example, Pineles saw the narrative paintings of Lucille Corcos at the Grand Central Galleries and commissioned her work;

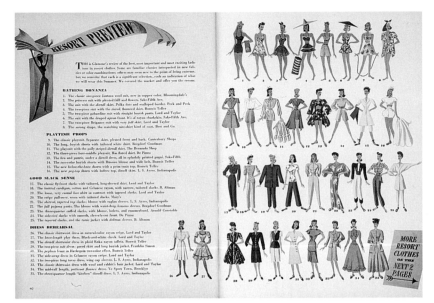

they became best and lifelong friends and colleagues.[35] Pineles ignored the publisher's condescension toward *Glamour*'s readers and used the best artists she could find, including photographers Andre Kertesz, Cornell Capa, Toni Frissell, Herbert Matter, and Trude Fleischmann; illustrators Corcos, Richard Lindner and S. E. Lindner (his wife), Burmah Burris, and Jacob Lawrence; and for information charts, Ladislav Sutnar, a Czech constructivist and one of the many European refugee artists and designers living in New York at that time. Women illustrators were always prevalent in fashion magazine publishing; women photographers had a harder time, though Pineles used several, including Frissell and Fleischmann.

Typographically, the magazine began as a less elegant clone of *Vogue*: Bodoni typefaces combined with brush scripts, stencil lettering, and various historical and display types. Later, the display typography became lighter weight, and in March 1943 the cover's logo changed from the brush-stroke style to an elegant tall and condensed Bodoni. The drop shadow was lost much later, and in 1945 italic was tried. Major design changes were slow, as Pineles was, on occasion, stymied and overruled by her new boss. Pineles was responsible for the noticeable addition of references to art and design: signs and posters (including a war poster series by Leo Lionni) are used in the backgrounds of fashion shots; models are shown posed in art galleries and museums. Pineles continued to find ways to bring more dimension to the page with object photographs, objects used as visual puns for letterforms, and complex photographic shots using dramatic scale changes in the picture space. By 1945 the typography and general layout were more often organized by a grid.

As she would do with all the magazines she controlled, Pineles found ways to include herself, her friends, and her family in *Glamour*. The first issue of *Glamour* that had Pineles as art director included a

above left: *Glamour*, January 1942, fashion illustrations by Pineles.

right: *Glamour* cover, January 1945; note Bodoni logotype.

below: *Glamour*, January 1942, spread about dirndls, photograph based on Pineles sisters photograph (see page 18).

bottom: *Glamour*, February 1942, fashion photographs showing Leo Lionni posters.

feature on dirndl dresses that used a fashion photograph based on an old family photograph of Pineles with her sisters. She claimed to have introduced the dirndl—the dress with a tight-fitting bodice and full, gathered skirt based on traditional Austrian and German styles—to the United States; she wore them, helped friends sew them for themselves, and saw the style picked up by New York department stores.[36] Another issue of *Glamour* includes a bedroom that Pineles's sister Regine, the milliner, had decorated. Lucille Corcos illustrated several features in one issue, including a story she wrote about her family's beach house.

The years between 1937 and 1943 proved life-altering for Pineles in many ways. They not only marked the establishment of her career as an art director, but also the blossoming of her relationship with William Golden. By the end of 1942, both Pineles's career and the relationship had undergone radical change, as she witnessed a major shake-up of the Condé Nast publishing empire and struggled with the stresses of being a wartime wife.

Pineles's new position as art director represented a considerable rise in professional status and coincided with the promising beginnings of Golden's career. By October 1937, when Pineles returned from Europe, Golden had finished his apprenticeship with Agha and was moving to Columbia Broadcasting System (CBS) to work in the sales promotion and public relations departments.[37] He soon became a rising star at CBS, establishing in the early days of his career his reputation for commitment to quality and integrity in design for business.

Though they both were involved in absorbing work critical to their professional futures, Pineles and Golden found time to continue seeing each other. By 1940, they had apartments in the same building on East 54th Street but would soon share one. The December 1941 attack on Pearl Harbor spurred Golden, like many men, to join the war effort. In August 1942 he applied for a short-term assignment and worked for three months in the Graphics Division of the Office of War Information (OWI) in Washington, D.C. In late November he was inducted into the United States Army and sent to Fort Belvoir outside Washington for basic training. Before he left, however, Pineles and Golden, accompanied by two friends, were married at City Hall on October 11, 1942.

For more than two years, while Golden was frustrated by army assignments that did not use his talents, Pineles went by train several times a month to see him at various bases around Washington. Between visits she wrote, and sometimes illustrated, dozens of letters that kept him in touch with family, friends, design colleagues, and her daily routines and work problems. The letters are funny accounts of friends' experiences in the armed forces; serious discussions about his frustrations and attempts to get better assignments; musings on the difficulties in their romance before marriage (when she was jealous of Rose Warren's attentions to him); descriptions of visits to their mothers; and frank discussions about their emotions, the joys of being together, the hardship of separation, her pleasure in being his wife, her longing for him.

above: Cipe Pineles and William Golden, probably on their wedding day, October 11, 1942.
below: *Christmas Play, The Golden Holiday*, painting for Golden by Pineles, about 1943.

By this time, Pineles was thirty-five years old and Golden thirty-two; they were well-established in their careers, newly married, and hoping for a short war. From the passionate letters, the many visits, and the monthly reports on her doctor appointments, it is apparent that they wanted to start a family immediately. Knowledge of their desire to have a child extended beyond the privacy of the family circle. Even Agha, the curmudgeon, upon hearing Golden had been granted a two-and-a-half-day leave, remarked that it was "enough for a pair of twins."[38]

Maintaining a long-distance marriage and trying to begin a family were not the only stresses Pineles endured during this tumultuous period. In 1942 Condé Nast died, leaving his publishing empire in the hands of Iva "Pat" Patcevitch, who was not fond of Agha. Within a year of Nast's death, Agha had left the company. In a letter she wrote to Golden, Pineles described her reaction to the event:

> This afternoon Patzewitze's [*sic*] office called me to come and see the boss. And I with all my sophistication have that same small fry mentality that expects a firing on every one of those occasions. So I go into his office with that in mind, and I am already renting a small room in Alexandria [near the base where Golden was stationed], when Pat announces to me that Agha has resigned. It was a good thing I was sitting down, and so I didn't have to faint because even though I knew Agha was thinking of something like it when he went to Washington job hunting, I didn't think he would pursue it after Nast's death. It's obvious of course that he did not resign—only was plainly eased out. Liberman became a great pal of Pat's the very first week he came to the company—whereas Pat and Agha have been for years rivals—their work overlapping in the case of finances, and contracts with artists, photographers, etc. What with Agha getting it from all sides that he is nasty to photographers, he inevitably talked himself out of a job. I am sure it must have come as a shock to him because only last week he called me down about a new campaign of his to try out 10 new photographers, and for the past three weeks he was knee deep in work compiling a new color book of all the old Vanity Fair color—Covarrubias' impossible interviews, etc. Well, I am shocked, and very sorry the old sour puss isn't going to be there, and I am very sorry for him and hope that the Turk doesn't feel collapsed. He hadn't been around much since last thursday—I haven't seen him at all. I also will miss the crook because after all he was real and I always felt he was on my side.[39]

Agha had always supported and promoted Pineles; as soon as she was eligible, he had proposed her for membership in the Art Directors Club (ADC); as a woman she was repeatedly rejected. Her letter indicated the depth of her emotion; she owed a lot to Agha and had learned to work well with him as well as respect and (grudgingly) love him.

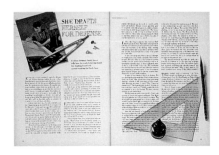

above: *Glamour*, July 1942, stencil lettering and objects.
below: Christmas card for Frank and Ruth Stanton, painted by Pineles.

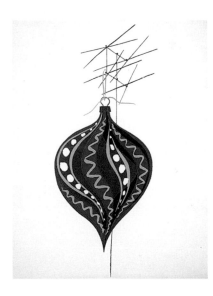

Agha's departure had major implications for Pineles's professional life—Alexander Liberman, Agha's replacement, was now Pineles's boss, and she probably shared Agha's opinion of him. Liberman had been hired, over the strong and futile resistance of Agha, by Nast during the last year of Nast's life. A Russian immigrant and war refugee who had done design work for some French publications that Nast bought, Liberman got on well with Patcevitch, who was also Russian and was then a financial manager for Condé Nast. Agha and Liberman played out a political game: though Agha had worked closely with Nast for years, Liberman encroached on what Agha felt was his territory. Now Liberman was consulting with Nast on *Vogue* covers. He even tried his hand at redesigning *Glamour*. His idea was not used but he was promoted anyway. Agha was fed up by this time; his authority had been undermined by Liberman's direct line to Nast. He gave Patcevitch the cliché ultimatum: He goes or I go. Though Agha had been with Condé Nast a long time and was highly respected, he commanded a high salary ($40,000) and had put off many people with his cynicism and intimidating manner. He lost the battle. Liberman was named the new art director for *Vogue* a month later (salary $12,000); he was thirty years old and would remain at Condé Nast for twenty-four years.

About a year after Agha's departure, Pineles complained about work in a letter to Golden:

> I was so bored all day in the office—screaming point boredom which ended with a very dull conference on the next issue—this is the third issue we are doing with absolutely not a day between, for catching your breath. My two girls and I are so sick of staying in every evening, we just left tonight at 5:30 and will worry to-morrow. To make matters worse I am stuck with some 10 layouts for pages, which don't seem to make layouts.
>
> I have always had a secret fear that some day I'll have a layout to do and I won't know how to do it—well, I have got it now—only it's 10 layouts.
>
> But who knows, with some good sleep tonight—I might be talented in the morning.
>
> Today at the office I really missed that magic touch of Agha's, when in a seemingly dull plan for an issue, he could with some well-chosen advice lift it out of mediocrity and put some sense and meaning into it.[40]

Even after he left, Agha would frequently call Pineles, ask about Golden, talk about his current activities, and ask her to recommend artists and designers for the consulting jobs he was working on at his home in Pennsylvania.[41] They remained friends and colleagues for many years.

During 1943, Pineles struggled with a new boss, overwork, the stress of seeing her husband only on infrequent weekends, trying to get pregnant, and a magazine she did not think was supported editorially.

In spite of these pressures, she continued to devote much time and creative energy to the magazine. At that time, Pineles was working with Isabel Johnson, *Glamour*'s beauty editor, who eventually became a very close friend of Pineles. Both Pineles and Johnson were frustrated with the magazine, as Pineles describes in a letter to Golden: "Isabelle Johnson, after the conference to which she sent a strong letter of protest over the lack of war consciousness in our pages, called me up to say that now finally she was giving up—that she is now fed up with the same old stuff and no war features. . . . But I still believe and I told her so, that the magazine cannot be brighter and 'awarer' than the people who work on it—and if she and I are the brightest people on it, we better wake up and produce more than criticism and personal unrest. We better sit down and propose some good features—No one ever turns down good stuff—so it's up to us. I really believe we have been too lazy and routine on the job."[42] In spite of Pineles's upbeat attitude, there was not a noticeable increase in war coverage and Johnson did not leave. The magazine continued to address "the girl with a job" and to run career features.

In what was probably a welcome break from the content and supervision related to *Glamour* and other Condé Nast projects, Pineles spent some evenings doing illustration and design work for CBS and Frank Stanton, William Golden's boss and mentor. She was able to be more inventive, display her sense of humor, and use her illustration talents. In a letter to Golden, she described the creative process for one of her pieces that worked as a flip book. She was stumped by the dry copy she was given:

> AND THEN I got an idea. In the little introduction it says you are to stick this questionnaire into the inside of your coat pocket and fill it out in the first time you find yourself waiting—waiting for any number of things these days, for instance the butcher. So I thought on that page I'll have the guy waiting on line, with ten people ahead of him, at the butcher shop.
>
> Then since there are ten questions—one on each page

above: *Believe it or not I am waiting for a pork chop* brochure for CBS, designed and illustrated by Pineles; selected pages; 3 by 6 in.
below: *Our Mr. Gallaher gets around* brochure for CBS, c. 1947, illustrated by Pineles; 12 by 10¼ in.

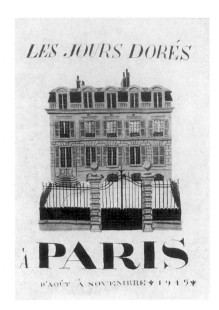

above left: *Les Jours Dorés à Paris* (*The Golden Days in Paris*), *August–November 1945*, cover for Pineles's painted book about her time in Paris with Golden.
right: Pineles's painting of the couple in front of Parisian bookshop, probably from *Les Jours Dorés.*

there'll be one less guy on the line—til finally when our friend has filled out the last question—the butcher will hand him a chop.

I telephoned the above to Frank who side-splitted himself with mirth at the whole idea—and told me to go ahead. He likes it a lot, but I told him I bet that meat will go off the rationing list just for spite. And Frank told me I don't have to stick to the copy—"KEEP OUT" on the cover, if I want something that ties in better with the inside stuff.

It would be good to have something else if I could think of it. What do you think of a guy all tangled up in a long question-naire with papers and pencils flying and a headline "BELIEVE IT OR NOT, I AM WAITING FOR A PORK CHOP."[43]

From February to September 1943 Golden worked for the Army Engineers doing publication layouts. In September he enrolled in a four-month course in Officer Candidate School at Fort Washington. Meanwhile, Frank Stanton was writing to all the influential political and military people he knew, trying to find a position that would use Golden's considerable abilities. Pineles also wrote letters describing his experience and skills and sent Golden "pep talk" notes. Finally, in April 1945, Golden was sent to Paris to work on publications for the United States armed forces in Europe. The opportunity was good— and frustrating. With the war in Europe essentially over and Paris lib-

G-EYE VIEW
OF PARIS
COLLECTIONS

erated, the military was in a clean-up mode. Most soldiers were waiting to be sent home and they were indifferent to others' energy and new initiatives; many used the time to travel rather than work. Golden's intensity (and, perhaps, pent-up energy) led him to make the most of the design and art opportunities, enthusiastically working on the publication *Stars and Stripes* and as art director for the new magazine *Overseas Woman*. Several of the artists and photographers he worked with on these projects became longtime friends and colleagues back home in the United States.

For both professional and personal reasons, Pineles was quite happy to take a leave of absence from *Glamour* and join Golden in Paris for three months. She helped him with *Overseas Woman* and was listed as "civilian advisor" on the masthead of the magazine's December 1945 issue. Started in April 1945, the publication was "dedicated to Women at War." It aimed "to be a link to the home-front, a channel of introduction to the people and countries in which we are stationed, a hand of friendship linking together all American women serving here."[++] American servicewomen included nurses, women in all branches of the military, Red Cross workers, dietitians, physiotherapists, and medical officers. In design terms, the magazine's early issues were an undisciplined collection of all the common layout ideas: a wide variety of display typefaces, good and bad illustrations and cartoons, available photography, "cute" frames and decorations, and chaotic compositions.

Pineles and Golden worked together on four issues of *Overseas Woman* (the last four, as it happened). Many changes appeared in the October 1945 issue; the format was enlarged to 8 by 10½ inches and the page layouts were toned down. In the hands of Pineles and Golden, all four issues had organized pages, some even highly structured; better reported and illustrated fashion and beauty features; a restrained variety of display typefaces; illustrations by Pineles; photographs by Golden; a much more inventive use of the second printed color; and an amusing final back cover by Pineles and Roy Doty that was inspired by a Norman Rockwell cover for the *Saturday Evening Post*. At the magazine Pineles met artists and photographers whom she would use profes-

top left and right: *Overseas Woman*, November 1945, pages 6–7 and 8–9, line drawings probably by Pineles; 8 by 10½ in.

above: *Overseas Woman*, December 1945, spread, building photographs probably by William Golden.

below: *Overseas Woman*, January 1946, back cover by Pineles and Roy Doty based on *Saturday Evening Post* cover by Norman Rockwell.

top: Letter from Paris, September 1945, self-portrait in uniform by Pineles.

above: Pineles buying botanical prints in Paris market (photograph probably by Golden).

sionally and with whom she became friends, among them *Vogue* photographer Arik Nepo and artists John Groth and Doty.

Pineles named these three months with Golden *Les Jours Dorés* (*The Golden Days*, pun intended) in her illustrated journal of the stay. She lived in his apartment next to the magazine offices and shared the same mess arrangements at the Hotel Champs Elysées nearby. By September she had a new suit based on a WACs (Women's Army Corps) uniform. She was responsible for a photo shoot of WACs at a fashion opening; she met Helen Brady, an American artist in Paris, and wrote a profile of her for the magazine. In addition to doing their work, the couple prowled Paris. Pineles indulged her love of old prints in the stalls along the Seine; Golden took lots of photographs.

Pineles wrote home to her mother and sister about meeting French women from the camps, about the lack of food, about fashions she saw on the streets. She described kitchen implements that reminded her of similar things from their days in Austria and Poland. She requested that they send food and clothes, which traveled very quickly across the Atlantic. She had tea with Agha's brother, an antiques dealer, and spent an evening with a colleague from *Vogue* watching a ballet and, later, scantily clad chorus girls at a night club. The Goldens traveled to London in October and reported on the devastation; they met the friends Pineles had made during her *Vogue* trip, the Elwyn Joneses and the Robert Harlings. Before leaving for home, Pineles could have joined others to see German conditions, but she refused to go. In December, just after Pineles had sailed from Le Havre, Golden was sent to Frankfurt. He left Europe in March and was discharged in April 1946.

The spring of 1946 was a very difficult time for Cipe Pineles: she still found her professional life unsatisfactory and her renewed married life required confronting their "family" problem. When Pineles returned to *Glamour*, the January 1946 masthead listed Liberman as art director and her as art editor. She was still unhappy with the publisher's attitude toward the magazine's concept and audience, and she found working with Alexander Liberman increasingly difficult.[45] Medical records showed that William Golden had a "normal" sperm count in March 1944. The problem appeared to be Cipe; of the five Pineles children, only one—Debora—was able to conceive children. The Goldens were at the stage in their lives when most happily married couples were starting families. The postwar climate in America was family-based and focused on a return to normalcy; for women this meant babies. Many of the Goldens' friends already had children, and Pineles would be an "old" mother according to the standards of the 1940s; there was no time to waste.

Pineles's family and friends were concerned about her emotional state that spring. Her mother apparently asked several of Pineles's friends to check on her on a regular basis. When Golden had to make a CBS business trip to California in late June, Pineles became extremely upset and begged him not to go.[46] He was planning to visit Norman and Rose Warren, who lived there at the time, and perhaps Pineles recalled her jealousy about Rose's romantic interest in Golden before he and Pineles had married.[47] Whether it was a result of her unhappiness about Golden's trip, pressures in her professional life, the stresses of trying to get pregnant, or some combination thereof, Pineles found her life too much to handle, and she threw herself in front of a subway train in the Times Square station. Fortunately, she fell between the rails, the train went over her, and she was not seriously hurt. A short article in the *New York Post* reporting the incident called it attempted suicide and quoted her saying in the ambulance, "I just wanted to die. I just wanted to die."[48]

Golden was still in California, and Frank Stanton called him to tell him the news (Rose Warren remembers him white-faced) and picked him up from the airport. Pineles was hospitalized for a short time and then returned to work at *Glamour*. For the most part, those few weeks were kept a secret; a few of her friends and colleagues knew and some of her family members were told much later. The suicide attempt did not change the respect Pineles's friends had for her, and eventually the event was forgotten.

Pineles's time at *Glamour* lasted only a few more months. Though she may have been exaggerating, Pineles later said, "I didn't leave. I was fired. They let Agha go, and the new art director Alexander Liberman got rid of the rest of us . . . in some situations and from some places it's an honor to be fired. If you are afraid of it you are allowing your employer to have the last word on your worth."[49] The masthead of her last issue in December 1946 misspelled her last name.

By the end of that year, Helen Valentine, a fifty-one-year-old grandmother and former colleague from *Vogue* with extensive experience in magazines and promotion, extended a hand to Pineles and asked her to join Valentine's recently invented magazine for teenagers, *Seventeen*. This new position, which offered Pineles complete artistic autonomy, was just the responsibility and challenge she needed to redirect both her professional and personal life.

Design is dealing with content. . . . Magazine design should never play second fiddle to advertising. If the editorial content is very interesting and has a reason for being, it attracts advertising. A fashion magazine should report on what the industry has to offer. We are journalists in our special field.

(Cipe Pineles in 1989 interview)

[At *Seventeen*]

Cipe Pineles, 1940s.

previous spread: left, Pineles dressed for the office (note three starburst pins); right, Detail of *Wild Rice* from Pineles's painted recipe book.

[D]uring the 1940s, women in American book and magazine publishing were usually restricted to working as writers or editors. Publishing was where many female English majors went to work for low wages. For women's fashion magazines, the controlling editorial vision was in the hands of women. Bradbury Thompson remembers working with twenty different editors on *Mademoiselle*, all women.[1] CBS had a few women working in its art department.[2] *Fortune* magazine had none at this time; in the early 1930s a woman art editor worked briefly on the magazine. Though work was available for female illustrators and photographers, the visual control—in contrast to the verbal control—was in male hands. In advertising there would be a few women art directors in the 1950s. Partly a result of the example Pineles set, magazine publishing began to change in the 1950s. Still, as Pineles moved on to new jobs, her old positions were not always filled by other women. During the 1940s, two women, Priscilla Peck and Lillian Bassman, also worked with powerful male art directors; both were struggling to achieve some independence and individual credit. They never would. At Condé Nast, Peck worked with Alexander Liberman at a fast pace, under onerous conditions, and "with Liberman's foot at her throat," as one sympathetic younger art director put it.[3] Before she became a fashion photographer, Bassman worked as a designer with Alexey Brodovitch at *Junior Bazaar*. Neither woman was given sole credit for her work when it won awards. A woman editor who worked on several of the Hearst and Condé Nast magazines at this time (but not with Pineles) recently realized with surprise that Pineles had been the only woman with sole control; the others had been in subordinate positions.[4]

The years 1946 and 1947 were hard ones in Cipe Pineles's life: she was ending an incompatible work situation, the resumption of married life brought with it new strains, and she had attempted suicide and recovered. Following her departure from Condé Nast, Pineles spent some months freelancing, but she found it unsatisfying, noting that "freelancing consists of having lots of second breakfasts, and lunches, and having to work at night."[5] As might be expected, she welcomed the invitation from Helen Valentine to join *Seventeen*. Finally Pineles had the freedom to shape a magazine according to her own creative integrity, without art directors or design directors looking over her shoulder. She could be on the front line, in equal collaboration with the editor-in-chief and other editors. Pineles later called *Seventeen* "the most enjoyable of all my magazine jobs. The editor . . . made me feel that on her magazine everything was possible . . . and I didn't have to wait forever between the time I presented an idea and the time I got an okay to go ahead" (a reference to working at Condé Nast).[6] "I was given great scope as an art director to express my own ideas and attitudes, and I worked with people who were very dedicated to the audience they were addressing."[7]

Seventeen created a unique niche between two other magazines for young women, *Mademoiselle* (Street & Smith) and *Junior Bazaar*

(Hearst). Begun in 1935 for "smart young women" (not a reference to their intellectual capacity), *Mademoiselle* was the more established of the two. It was pitched to women between eighteen and twenty-five years old. Some *Mademoiselle* readers had college or work experience but all were directed toward marriage and homemaking. Not distinguished by its design until the mid-40s, when Bradbury Thompson became art director, *Mademoiselle* was known for its fall college edition and its good fiction, which was often written by beginning female writers. (In fact, the magazine was ground-breaking in its publication of young writers who later became famous.) *Junior Bazaar* was quite new and lasted less than a year, when it was reincorporated into *Harper's Bazaar*. Directed toward a slightly younger audience than *Mademoiselle* and art directed by Brodovitch and Bassman, *Junior Bazaar* had a "modern" look, with hard-edged, strongly colored covers and a "constructivist" interior design. *Mademoiselle* continued to be *Seventeen*'s "competition" while the young magazine refined its attitude and message and carefully carved out its audience of thoughtful, socially engaged high school girls.

Seventeen developed out of a struggling, two-year-old movie magazine called *Stardom*, which was published by Triangle Publications. (Later known for *TV Guide*, Triangle Publications then published *Screen Guide*, *Official Detective Stories*, and *Gags*). After his dismissal from Condé Nast, Dr. M. F. Agha was hired as a consulting art director for *Stardom*. His proposal for the magazine was radical: change it to a book strictly about fashion and catch some of the advertising overflow from *Mademoiselle*, *Glamour*, and *Charm*. Agha knew Helen Valentine from their days at *Vogue* and suggested that Walter Annenberg, owner and publisher of Triangle Publications, offer her the magazine.

The premise of *Seventeen* was based on Helen Valentine's unique attitude toward young women. When Annenberg approached Valentine and asked if she would be interested in editing the struggling movie magazine, she commented, "There is nothing in the world I am less interested in than a movie magazine." When Annenberg asked what did interest her, she replied: "There's room today for a publication aimed at teenagers. They've been neglected by the established fashion publications. Everyone treats them as though they were silly, swooning bobby soxers. I think they're young adults and should be treated accordingly."[8] Valentine had observed that though *Calling All Girls* (circulation 556,330) and *American Girl* (202,752) existed (though with little cachet in publishing circles), there was room for another magazine aimed at young women. Further research showed that there were six million girls between thirteen and eighteen, the target audience for *Seventeen*. Annenberg was impressed. In September of 1944, *Stardom's* paper tonnage was reallocated to *Seventeen* (wartime restrictions were still in place), and, without a dummy or sample publication, Valentine launched her new magazine, which effectively killed *Stardom*.

By the time *Seventeen* celebrated its fifth anniversary in 1949, it claimed circulation of over one million. The editorial vision of the

Seventeen cover, June 1948, student illustration by Roy Head; 10⅜ by 13¼ in.

Seventeen's fifth anniversary luncheon with editors and publishers; the women from left, Eleanor Hillebrand, Fashion Editor; Helen Valentine, Editor-in-chief; Estelle Ellis, Promotion Editor; Cipe Pineles, Art Editor (photograph by Hugelmeyer).

reader as a young adult with interests beyond herself and her family was carried out faithfully in this "young girl's service magazine." There were feature articles on contemporary social issues, world events (*Seventeen* was well aware of the impact of World War II), community service, education, advances in science and technology, and career opportunities. Complementing the features were serious works of fiction and advice on fashion, beauty, and relationships.

In its first eight months, *Seventeen* was already a case study in success, though few could have predicted this. Initially, the industry was skeptical: the magazine's name was considered a mistake by some; its ancestry was lowly; its reader, the teenage girl, was regarded by advertisers as a "dubious, if personable, purchasing agent"; and Triangle Publications was described as "an outfit with a reputation more for velocity than stability, and one which has scratched magazines and race horses with the same apparent unconcern."[9] But *Seventeen* and its readers quickly proved their critics wrong. The magazine's circulation increased from the first issue's 395,000 to 694,000 for the eighth issue; advertising lineage increased from 29,969 to 68,283 in the same eight months; and advertising volume went from $26,000 to over $84,400. Advertising might have been even more extensive had wartime paper rationing not limited the amount of advertising pages.

Seventeen's early commercial success was due to Valentine's vision and to her collaboration with her editors, especially the promotion editor, Estelle Ellis. When Pineles joined Valentine and Ellis, a powerful trio was created. The combination of their intelligence, ambition, energy, and individual personalities ensured *Seventeen*'s editorial and visual success. Ultimately, the separate, complementary visions and talents of this troika would enable them not only to create *Seventeen*, but to reconceive and make successful another publication (*Charm*) as well.

Born Helen Rose Lachman to German Jewish immigrant parents in 1893 and a New Yorker all her life, Helen Valentine attended the Ethical Culture School and, an aspiring opera singer, graduated from Barnard College with a major in Italian. She started her career as a part-time copy writer for the Lord & Thomas advertising firm in the

1920s. She later went on to work at Condé Nast, editing the *Vogue Pattern Book* and doing promotion for *Vogue*, where she met Pineles. In 1938 Valentine joined Street & Smith and was the promotion manager for *Mademoiselle*.[10] Though she was happy with Street & Smith and its management and challenged by her job, Valentine was still tempted by Annenberg's offer to edit a magazine of her own.

Helen Valentine brought her love of the arts and her appreciation for education to her writing and editing. She was always seeking ways to expand her readers' experience of the world, even if that experience was only vicarious, and to broaden her readers' expectations of life, themselves, and their abilities, goals, and accomplishments. Her career in publishing was driven by her vision of what girls and women could aspire to and accomplish and by her commitment to the special audiences of teenage girls (*Seventeen*) and working women (*Charm*). Her ideas were partly the result of personal circumstances: she had always expected herself to work and she was an equal partner in her successful marriage to a businessman.

Estelle Ellis was just out of Hunter College with a degree in political science and journalism. With *Seventeen* from its inception, she was enthusiastic and very energetic. At *Seventeen* (and later at *Charm*) she was responsible for marketing the magazine to readers and potential advertisers. Her pioneering use of research on the readership of each magazine was instrumental in explaining newly defined demographic groups (with *Seventeen*, teenage girls and with *Charm*, working women) to those with products and services.

Ellis commissioned statistical studies on the teenage generation, making *Seventeen* the first women's magazine to do comprehensive, social-science-based market research. She taught the editors about the importance of quantifying the magazine; that is, of understanding their audience in terms beyond gender and age. Previously, advertising had been sold on the basis of a magazine's "coffee table prestige." In order to be taken seriously by advertisers and retailers and to promote the value of this new readership, *Seventeen* used statistics to prove its point.

David Hertz at Benson & Benson, Inc., in Princeton, New Jersey, conducted *Seventeen*'s first commissioned study, in which one thousand readers and their mothers were questioned about certain personal characteristics, their buying habits, and their future plans. Published in 1945 and called "Life with Teena," the study revealed that the composite, average reader—"Teena," as she was named—was sixteen years old, 5 feet 4.25 inches tall, and weighed between 116 and 120 pounds. Ninety-seven percent of the Teenas attended school, with eighty-two percent at public schools; they graduated at age seventeen. Fifty-two percent intended to go to college after high school, which was corroborated by the fifty-eight percent of mothers who echoed those plans. Socio-economic status was established through the fathers: fourteen percent were professional, twenty-six percent were business executives or owners, twenty-three percent were white collar workers.

"Life with Teena, II" was conducted by Opinion Research Corporation, also of Princeton, and published in 1947.[11] This study of 2,500 teenage girls and 800 mothers looked at Teena's brand awareness and preferences, her level of participation in food preparation and entertaining, and her plans for the future. Assuming that marriage was part of Teena's plan, the study indicated that sixty-nine percent wanted to keep house, thirteen percent wanted to work, and fourteen percent wanted to do both. The facts proved the contention that Teena had more concrete opinions and more economic power than anyone had previously imagined.

Information from these studies allowed *Seventeen* to argue for certain types of advertising and to wield influence over manufacturers and retailers. From the beginning, *Seventeen* urged its advertisers to tailor their campaigns to this narrow but deep audience. One special booklet called "Who is Teena—Judy Jeckyll or Formalda Hyde?" suggested Teena was leading a double life, as the editors saw her one way and the advertisers another. *Seventeen* cautioned advertisers not to use "jive talk" but rather regular English when speaking to her, not to try to sell her smaller versions of her mother's clothes, not to use overage models, and not to press "war paint" on girls with natural beauty. Regarding advertising lingerie, *Seventeen* remarked, "We'd be the first to admit our girl Teena knows all about the birds and the bees, we've been around her long enough to know she's not the kind of girl you can win with 'cheesecake.'"

Estelle Ellis considered herself a kind of missionary, convincing the nonbelievers that this new market existed and was sizable. Five years after *Seventeen*'s launch, the fashion industry and clothing manufacturers were vigorously responding to this new market. "Nearly every large department store in the country opened a high school shop—or enlarged the one it had. Teen-slanted fashion shows, windows, and ads all multiplied."[12] Finally, young women began seeing clothing styles and proportions suitable for their age and experience. Cosmetics were manufactured in special colors for teenage complexions. Reluctant advertisers were eventually convinced to develop separate advertisements for teens. Special events were organized, including a square dance in Central Park with a performance by Josh White, a popular black folksinger. The square dance was the first industry-sponsored event (by Pepsi) for teens; photographs show an audience of white and black girls, an integrated group unusual for the time.

The years before the 1960s were the golden age of magazine design—art directors had thirty pages or more of uninterrupted editorial "well," or sequential pages, in which to express their visual ideas. The visual style of *Seventeen* was still under development in its first years. Agha was listed on the masthead as "art consultant" in the beginning issues; three art directors would be listed in as many years before Cipe Pineles took over the position with the February 1948 issue. Agha devised the format and layout *Seventeen* used for its first three years; it followed the classical tradition of magazine and typographic design Agha had practiced at Condé Nast for so many years. A variety of column arrangements were available for feature articles. The main text type was Bodoni; headlines were presented in numerous display typefaces. For fashion sections where the photographs or illustrations predominated, text was minimal and subdued. For the fiction pages, quiet, booklike typography supported the prominence of the artwork.

As is often the case with publishing enterprises, the relationship between Cipe Pineles, Helen Valentine, and Estelle Ellis became similar to that of an extended family. When the three women joined forces, they spanned two generations and almost thirty years. In 1947, Valentine was fifty-four years old, Pineles was thirty-nine, and Ellis about twenty-eight. All three were married; Valentine had children and grandchildren, Ellis had children. The three couples and families became close, lifelong friends.

In addition to the difference in age, which brings with it differences in personal and professional experience, the three women were dissimilar in personality. Valentine was relatively quiet and private while Ellis was boisterous and open. Valentine, independent from an early age, was a consummate career woman: focused, logical, and inspired. Pineles, from a large, warm family, had been economically independent from her youth as well. She brought a different, partly European cultural sensibility to her work and relationships, and she had an open, intuitive approach common among creative people. Ellis, just beginning her career, was bright and eager to learn. In terms of culture, personal style, and professional behavior, she was both a blank slate and a sponge. Ellis had been taken in hand by Valentine. The younger woman saw "an incredible lady who was a generation older . . . a wonderful role model. Here was a very successful woman who had a successful marriage and a wonderful family."[13] All three were career women who had found work they loved and would retire very late in life.[14]

Personal friendship created an ease among the three that made working days pleasant and less stressful. They had begun with mutual respect and learned to trust one another. They developed love, devotion, and a dependence on their closeness. The three women supported one another when inevitable problems associated with their careers and the combination of a career and family arose. Valentine's daughter, Barbara Valentine Hertz (who wrote for the magazine under her married name and whose husband had done the statistical research) has said she cannot remember any problems among the three. Ellis described Valentine and Pineles as being private people, and she followed their model, though to a lesser extent. She shared her memories of their friendship: "We never gossiped about husbands or families. There was a saying that Helen was such a sweet person that flowers [in her office] never died; there was no venom. The whole world was wonderful. . . . We did what we had to do. We had each other; we enjoyed each other. We were fully engaged in what we were doing, and had no time . . . to

above left: *Seventeen*, October 1948, illustration by
Ben Shahn. ©Estate of Ben Shahn / Licensed by
VAGA, New York, NY.
right: *Seventeen*, October 1949, illustration by
Robert Gwathmey.

talk about what was not satisfying. . . . We were all young, [working
hard] at both levels [personal and professional]. Life was good."[15]

In addition to supporting each other, the three women received
moral and emotional support from their husbands. Ellis described
them as men who were "liberated early" and gave liberty to their
wives. Pineles had worked for over ten years when she married William
Golden; she was not "given" her freedom. However, according to Ellis,
"We were three lucky ladies; each husband was in a different [genera-
tion], but were [supportive of our working]. We did not feel guilty
[about work]; there was no stress."[16] Of the three husbands, William
Golden was the most prominent and successful professionally; he and
Pineles were equally accomplished and acclaimed. "Big Val" Valentine
was a businessman with a flexible schedule. When the Valentines' two
children were school-age, it was he who worked with the housekeeper,
picked them up from school, and was involved in their activities; the
couple considered this normal.[17] Ellis's husband was in business too,
and later worked as her business manager. All three women hired
live-in household help while their children lived at home (Pineles had
household help throughout her life); at that time it was common and
inexpensive.

All three women were unquestioningly committed to their professional world and comfortable with the ways they combined and inter-
twined their public and private lives. Their friendship strengthened
their ability to succeed, and they gave each other emotional support.
Their mutual trust enabled each to operate independently. They knew
they were lucky to have each other—this was "a barracuda time," Ellis
said, when "women who made it in our profession were mainly single.
They had fought [for their positions] and few women supported other
women. The idea of helping each other was a new concept; we loved
each other."[18] They also learned from each other, especially Ellis, who
was new to business, design, and culture. "She [Valentine] gave me a
sense of what a professional approach to business had to be, and that
was to reach for the best talents you could find and respect their ability
to do the job without being told what to do, to have a sense of trust in
your resource whether he was an artist or a production person."[19]

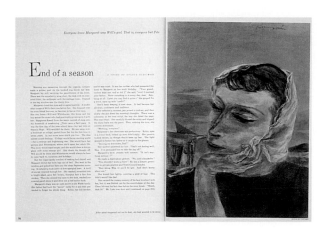

When Pineles joined the team, the "project" she took over already was familiar to her, as she had worked in Agha's mode before. Changes would be made, but they would always have his flavor, which was hers to some degree as well. However, as an artist and illustrator she brought a different perspective and creative agenda to the enterprise.

Pineles started the art/illustration program that would distinguish *Seventeen* from other publications and for which she would later win acclaim from the design world. For her first issue, she commissioned artist Richard Lindner to illustrate a fiction selection, continued to use some of the illustrators who were already working for the magazine (Jan Balet, Roy Doty, Bill English, Leslie Jacobs, and Al Hirschfeld), and even included one of her own paintings, of potatoes. Pineles had met Richard Lindner in London while she was working on the coronation issue of *Vogue*. It was then that she first decided she wanted to commission fine artists to illustrate fiction.

Pineles realized that the use of fine artists could increase the visual impact of a magazine and challenge the accepted standards of magazine illustration. *Seventeen* was a perfect venue; it strove to educate its readers and its readers took the magazine seriously. "I asked painters like Robert Gwathmey and Ben Shahn to contribute illustrations because I wanted to open the magazine to artists whose work the reader might not ordinarily see. I also wanted to engage artists who were not confined by the clichés of illustration. At *Seventeen*, under the pretext that young people aren't prejudiced about such things, and that they are interested in anything in print, I used such artists to broaden the visual experience of the reader."[20] It was a mutually beneficial setup: fine art and modern art were introduced to a young, mainstream audience, and it was an opportunity for many artists, some of whom were young or new to the country, to connect with a mass audience. Many artists' illustration work literally supported the time required for the work they placed in galleries.

During her first year at *Seventeen*, Pineles wrote to prominent art museums in the United States and to galleries in New York, asking them to name fifty important artists currently working in the States who could carry out a commission to illustrate a story. She received

above left: *Seventeen*, April 1949, Illustration by Kuniyoshi. ©Estate of Yasuo Kuniyoshi / Licensed by VAGA, New York, NY.
right: *Seventeen*, January 1949, illustration by Doris Lee.

above left: *Seventeen*, May 1948, illustration by
Lucille Corcos.

right: *Seventeen*, February 1949, illustration by
Mitchell Siporin.

lists and comments from five museums: Walker Art Center (Minneapolis, MN), Whitney Museum of Art (New York, NY), Santa Barbara Museum of Art (CA), City Art Museum of St. Louis (MO), and The Art Institute of Chicago (IL). It is difficult to interpret their comments
precisely; some curators sound a bit skeptical about her purpose. From
the Whitney Museum she received this reply: "A list of fifty of what I
consider the best American artists, I am afraid, would not be of much
use to you. Many of them I know would not or could not paint pictures
at all suitable for your magazine. I am thinking of such artists as
Marin, Weber, Stuart Davis to mention but a few. Your choices of
Shahn, Raphael Soyer and Gwathmey are excellent."[21] The director of
the Walker Art Center wrote: "I am attaching a listing of artists in our
last exhibition. I've checked the names I think most important. . . . I
would like to point out that I have checked some artists who I might
not normally put on a '50 Best' list, but they will be excellent for your
purposes. Likewise, I have listed some that will be useless to you, but I
could not ignore, because they are so important."[22] And from the Art
Institute she received this help: "It would be difficult to say who are the
fifty most important painters at work in this country today. I am, however, sending you a list of fifty artists whose work seems to me of interest and whose style covers a great variety of types and moods. I feel
sure that within this list you will be able to find painters who will meet
your requirements."[23]

Compiled into a master list, the names supplied by the museums
totaled 142 artists.[24] Pineles used many of the artists suggested by the
museums, including Carol Blanchard, Louis Bouche, Alexander Brook,
Lucille Corcos, Philip Evergood, David Fredenthal, Robert Gwathmey,
Yasuo Kuniyoshi, Jacob Lawrence, Doris Lee, Julian Levi, Reginald
Marsh, Waldo Peirce, Anton Refregier, Ben Shahn, Mitchell Siporin,
Raphael Soyer, Moses Soyer, and Karl Zerbe. She reported later that "it
was curious that the only person who refused to accept an assignment
was [Andrew] Wyeth. He said he was not an illustrator."[25]

Pineles was sensitive to the issues raised by approaching "fine
artists" to work for her magazine. Many were confused by the distinction made between fine and commercial art. "To label art that is

Cybernetics

Rising in Retailing

money
money
money

printed as 'commercial' has done and is doing an enormous amount of damage to artists and to everyone in the Graphic Arts," Pineles said in a speech to her peers in the design industry. "This label has kept some great talent away from us. It has been terribly confusing to the artist himself. Most American painters have worried about this horrible label to the point where they look on an assignment for publication in a mass medium as a fall from grace. Something to be done furtively, if at all. They don't want it to be confused with their 'real work' and as I have learned from my own experience [as an art director], their 'commercial' work is usually rejected because it is awful. And it's awful because they tried to make it commercially acceptable."26

Pineles used many other artists she knew personally or found through contacts and friends in the art and design world. Many were new to the United States, including Richard Lindner (and his wife, an experienced fashion illustrator), Xanti Schawinsky (ex-Bauhaus student), and Edgar Levy, the husband of Lucille Corcos. Corcos and Levy, artists who became close friends of the Goldens, are one example among many who made the transition from being Pineles's employee to friend. Pineles's friendships with her employees were always genuine; she never exploited or took advantage of the artists and friends who did work for her. The Goldens had an extensive knowledge of contemporary art and design; they frequently made friends with the artists they used, and they employed friends who were artists. Over the years, both Pineles and Golden used many of the same artists and photographers for their respective projects. Among those artists were Roy Doty, Joe Kaufman, Jan Balet, John Groth, Tom Courtos, Ben Shahn, William Helburn, David Stone Martin, René Bouché, Burmah Burris, Ben Rose, Leo Lionni, Jerome Snyder, and Doris Lee. The Goldens even used each other: Pineles did illustrations for Golden and CBS (Golden paid her exactly what he paid others, $125). Golden was the photographer for several of Pineles's projects, especially if the assignment needed a cat, his favorite photographic subject. What he was paid is unknown.

Other art directors had used and were using fine artists for "commercial work." Agha had on occasion, especially for *Vanity Fair*; William Golden was using fine artists as part of his plan for developing a corporate image for CBS; the Container Corporation of America was employing artists for its various series (the best known was "Great Ideas of Western Man"). However, all these audiences were limited (to business leaders, for example) or were elite masses (if that is not an

above left: *Seventeen*, October 1949, illustration by Xanti (Schawinsky).
center: *Seventeen*, September 1949, illustration by Edgar Levy.
right: *Seventeen*, March 1950, illustration by Jerome Snyder.
below top: *Seventeen*, January 1949, illustration by Bernarda Bryson. ©Bernarda Bryson / Licensed by VAGA, New York, NY.
center: *Seventeen*, April 1948, illustration by Burmah Burris.
bottom: *Seventeen* spread using photograph of cats, real and painted, by William Golden.

The Change

When a boys' club takes over

Of Dogs and Cats and Birds and Fish, Alarm Clocks and Careers

oxymoron). Pineles never claimed she was the first or the only art director to introduce the work of painters to mass publications. She did claim to have done it "on an important and consistent scale," and she did it in publications that reached the young and female masses—a more general mass audience than had previously been addressed. "These young people seemed to represent as nearly an uncorrupted and unprejudiced audience as one could find. I thought here was an opportunity to give them a new experience in seeing, that was spoiled for an older generation. It seemed to me, that if the magazine fiction pages were illustrated by painters and that no fuss or special attention was called to that fact, the readers would either accept or reject them without being challenged to judge them as Art. And maybe some young people would be moved by these paintings."[27]

Since she was an illustrator too, Pineles was the perfect art director: she left the artists alone. In a speech she delivered at the American Institute of Graphic Arts (AIGA) in 1948, Pineles described the common practice of the time like this: "The fiction editor would type out the specific passage to be illustrated. This passage was arrived at through conferences, and represented the best editorial opinion on just which morsel in the story was the most likely to lure the reader into reading the piece. My idea was to allow the artist to read as well as to illustrate the story and even to choose the part he wished to make a picture of. This was an unthinkable proposal, but I was new on that job, and insisted that the artist be allowed to make his own contribution, on the wild theory that he might have a more valid instinct about pictures than a fiction editor could have."[28] Later, she described the theory more fully: "I always tried to assign the artist to a story that I thought he would react spontaneously to, then let him go ahead on his own."[29] Participating in a discussion on mass media, Pineles commented that painters were better able to illustrate fiction because they worked with their own experience of the story; they did not depend on stereotypes as many commercial illustrators did.

She also thought the public possessed a more refined taste than it was usually credited with.[30] "When I commissioned the painting, I made a point of saying that, if it wasn't good enough for their gallery, it wouldn't be acceptable to me."[31] While this was some assurance of quality, it was also economically smart for both parties: she bought only reproduction rights to the work, which allowed the artist to hang the painting in the gallery for sale at a better price than the magazine could pay. In the galleries, the "illustrations" sold as well as the "paintings."

The mutual respect between Pineles and the artists she commissioned stemmed from her attitude and her experience and talent as an illustrator. Joe Kaufman, an artist and very good friend of Pineles, worked with her for more than twenty years, and Pineles gave him virtually complete freedom. She was a "terrific all-around artist," he has said. He also described the anxiety he felt during the preliminary discussions they had about projects. He always feared she would pick up a

Panel of *Seventeen* illustrators; from left, Cipe Pineles, unknown woman, Mitchell Siporin, Ben Shahn, late 1950s.

left: *Seventeen*, September 1948, celebrating fifth anniversary; illustration by Joe Kaufman shows staff united in song, each with visual metonyms of jobs, and publishers as cupids.
below: *Seventeen*, September 1949, illustration by Joe Kaufman.

pencil and begin sketching an illustration—and he would then be unable to see the solution in any other way. He told her to wait until he had done his research and completed his own sketches. [32] For the fourth anniversary group portrait of *Seventeen*'s editors, Kaufman was given a humorous rhyming text:

[for Helen Valentine, with glasses, a sharp nose, and on a
    platform]
With her we play in harmony—
The Maestro, Mrs. V
You think her teen-ideas are keen?
Well, frankly, so do we!

[for Estelle Ellis, holding a magazine as a megaphone]
"All teens and stores, meet SEVENTEEN."
Is Barker Ellis' shout.
She sometimes uses microphones—
You'd hear her, though, without.

[for Cipe Pineles, with a paintbrush bow on a T-square]
Art Director C. P. claims,
In laying out the book
The writing is irrelevant
But pictures make you look! [33]

He knew all the women well, and he discussed his idea for an approach with Pineles. His final paintings are sympathetic caricatures of his colleagues; the only males, the publishers, are present as cupids holding the curtains of the stage. The paintings are characteristic of Kaufman's work, which always has some metaphorical invention and humor of the most friendly kind. His other work for Pineles often required serious and sometimes historical research.

After seeing his *Harlem Series* paintings, Pineles chose to work with Jacob Lawrence, one of the few known African-American artists at the time. The magazine story she asked him to illustrate was called

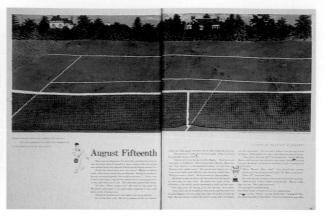

above left: *Seventeen*, December 1948, illustration by Jacob Lawrence. Courtesy of the artist and Francine Seders Gallery, Seattle, WA.
right: *Seventeen*, August 1948, illustration by Ben Shahn. ©Estate of Ben Shahn / Licensed by VAGA, New York, NY.
below: *Seventeen,* October 1948, composition with photography by Douglas Ebersole.

"The Fur Coat" and was about a young woman aspiring to be a social worker in a black neighborhood. In the illustration he submitted, Lawrence placed the young woman in the foreground and the black family in the far distance. Pineles wrote later that "It was the only instance where I had to ask the artist to do the illustration *over*. I bought the original . . . which is in dramatic contrast to what was used in the magazine."[34] In the published illustration, the foreground is dominated by a baby on a large bed, the family is in the middle ground, and the social worker is in the back.

Describing working with Ben Shahn, who became a fixture in her magazines, Pineles said:

> I remember the first story he did. It concerned a 14-year-old boy, a keen tennis player, who is ashamed of his mother because she is very pregnant, and he is determined to keep this fact from his friends. To do this he keeps them from using the family tennis court, which up to the time of the pregnancy had been the center of social activity. I gave Ben a two week deadline. He could do anything he pleased, in any shape and any number of colors. There was only one restriction. The hero and his friends must be clearly recognizable as youngsters in their teens. Three days later the finished job came in and it was plenty clear. There was no hero. There were no friends to be seen. Instead, stretching across two pages in a long, thin picture, was the most deserted, clearest, biggest tennis court in a brilliant color, marked with the sharpest, neatest, traditional white lines. It was a breathtaking beautiful shock of a painting to go with that story.[35]

The innovative, award-winning fiction illustration program was not the only notable aspect of *Seventeen*'s visual design. As art director, Pineles handled every section of the magazine. She was responsible for choosing artwork and photographs, page and spread compositions, and typography. In addition to the fine artists illustrating fiction, many artists, illustrators, and photographers were at work on the cover and other sections of the magazine. Feature articles showed the widest

range of visual material: narrative illustration in many personal styles, conceptual illustration that often combined a variety of methods, tongue-in-cheek and serious diagrams, humorous historical paintings, photography and photocollage, caricature, informal scientific illustration, information design (which was at that time just being developed) brought from Europe by several immigrant designers, antique engravings and etchings, fine art reproductions, and more.

Pineles also devised a typographic approach for each section of the magazine. The typography for the fiction selections was the quietest and most traditional in the magazine and was based on a typographic style associated with the best literary publishing. *Seventeen*'s artwork remained primary and was supported by two or three columns of text and simple headline type. The title of the story was set in a medium display size of Bodoni or a fine Clarendon, with variety in capitals, letter spacing, and position. Sometimes a smaller drawing would be close to or integrated with the words of the title. Larger initial letters occasionally broke up the text blocks. The materials at hand dictated whether symmetry or asymmetry was the organizing principle. If the illustration was not a full page, it ran horizontally across the gutter, usually with a defined edge creating a clear rectangle, in harmony with the rectangles of text.

The typefaces chosen for the feature articles and the ways they are used indicate that a much more inventive bent was allowed here. The text was arranged both in single, wide columns and in two or three narrower columns, which were usually reserved for fiction. Within the columns, many initial letters or phrases stand out in larger or italic forms. Subtitles and introductory decks tend to be in italic. Headlines get more expressive and playful; some decorative and connotative faces are used. Before they became associated so strongly with Herb Lubalin, examples of "graphic expressionism" and visual puns were used. An article about secretarial training uses two kinds of paper clips and staples to create letter forms and a human form. In another issue, the *o* of "money" has been replaced with a Christmas decoration. Infrequently, letter forms are distorted; in one case the thick strokes of a large "OLD" are literally broken. For all her love of lettering, her own inven-

above left: *Seventeen*, January 1949, illustration by Joe Kaufman and object letterforms.
right: *Seventeen*, December 1949, playful typography, photography by Ray Solowinski.
below: *Seventeen*, January 1949, by Leslie Jacobs using a combination of illustration and photography.
bottom: *Seventeen*, January 1949, "cinematic" strip.

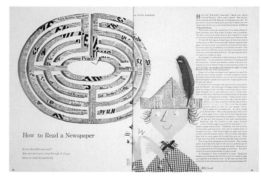

top left and below: *Seventeen*, February 1950, cover plus two spreads showing use of modern architectural settings and connection of interior to cover, photography by Dan Wynn.

top center: *Seventeen* cover, April 1948, photography by Francesco Scavullo.

top right: *Seventeen* cover, July 1949, photography by Francesco Scavullo. Look carefully; this is not a mirror image. Reproduced many times, it must have been one of Pineles's favorites.

tiveness with it, and her earlier involvement with it on the pages of *Vogue*, Pineles used very little hand-lettering in the pages of *Seventeen*.

Covers present special design (and marketing) problems. Throughout Pineles's tenure, the logo on the cover remained lowercase, bold, condensed, and italic Bodoni, though early on there was a subtle redrawing to sharpen the contrast and make the thin strokes into hairlines. Other text on the covers was limited to occasional single lines relating to the issue themes. The cover image was almost always a single female (except for the April "Girl Meets Boy" issues). Helen Valentine had wanted to use black girls as models (and on the teenage editorial board) but Annenberg would not allow either, according to Valentine's daughter.[36] Pineles tried to use girls new to modeling and to project a fresh, natural beauty through them.

Announced on the covers, different themes were repeated each year: home, (*Seventeen*'s) birthday, parents, back to school, career, and the popular "It's All Yours" reader-produced issue. The themes were carried throughout the magazine visually; for example, an issue sporting a cover with architectural grids in the background had fashion pages with construction-site locations. Covers for the teen issues used a photograph of a group of teenagers or a teenager's artwork, which broke the dominance of photography. Another cover used flowers under glass as props; inside, the fashion spreads reproduced insect prints and birdcages, which continued the nature theme. One Christmas cover's background included the collection of holiday greeting cards the Goldens had received the year before. Pineles was especially proud of a cover that used what at first glance appeared to be a reflection of a swimsuited model and umbrella. Of all of Pineles's covers, this one has been reproduced most often, a decision that was probably hers. It is among a number of covers and spreads Pineles marked with pink slips (sometimes bearing the artist's name). These may be the pages she was proudest of; many have been reproduced over the years in publications and catalogs.

The teen issues were quite a feat of coordination, as Pineles had
to work with a coed group of teenage writers and artists from across
the nation. These issues provided an unusual opportunity for teens to
have their work published and seen by thousands of people. In 1948,
Seymour Chwast had two paintings of a party included in the teen
issue. A year later, New York City's Downtown Gallery, with whom
Pineles had worked for years discovering new artists, exhibited the
work of twenty-six teenage artists featured in *Seventeen*'s May 1949
issue. One of the works chosen, *Peacock Dress*, was by Richard
Anuszkiewicz, from Erie, PA. Some of Pineles's assistants, like Tom
Courtos, who later went on to work with William Golden, were
teenagers Pineles discovered through this annual event.

The food and home pages employed many of the illustrators who
worked on the rest of the magazine. The food pages often had highly
structured, even abstract, arrangements of foods and objects on one
page and usually straightforward and restrained text on the facing
page. Even on the pages Pineles illustrated, where she might have
worked more loosely, the same double columns of type were only
slightly shifted up or down, and the standard headline was used. The
home spreads were more often combinations of smaller photographs or
illustrations and extended captions; their visual interest was provided
by the style of illustration or the content of the photograph rather than
by composition or typography.

In her first issue of *Seventeen*, Pineles served as both art director
and artist. Faced with what some considered an "ugly" subject, potatoes, she devised a fresh approach. "I had been as fed up as everyone
else with color photos of food and Bill goaded me into giving an assignment to myself. I had done a private cookbook for Bill's and my use
out of my mother's recipes and Bill was the greatest appreciater of my
food art, if not my cooking."[37] Later, she wrote of the potatoes: "I
thought they were pretty, so I dug out my kitchen tools, bought ten
cents' worth of potatoes, painted them on a double page size sheet of

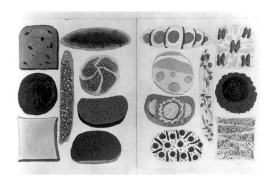

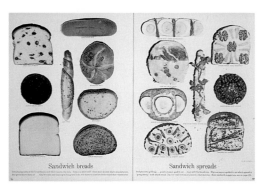

Sandwich breads   Sandwich spreads

right: *Seventeen*, February 1948, the famous potatoes illustrated by Pineles.

below: Pineles's painted sketch as art direction of photograph for *Seventeen* spread and *Seventeen*, October 1948, actual spread.

paper, indicated the type layout and left town. Total time 1.5 hours. Two weeks later, when finished art was needed, I went about the job more seriously. I nursed the potatoes, considered the type more carefully, and then tore the whole thing up. The rough was more fun. Total time 18 hours. As far as I know the feature didn't cause a run on potatoes, but made our food department, which had been weaned on color photography, happy."[38] The potatoes illustration won a gold medal from the Art Director's Club (ADC) in 1948. Over the years, Pineles created many food paintings for *Seventeen* and other magazines and even for her family and friends. In addition to painting the foodstuffs or the main dish, she enjoyed painting kitchen implements, containers, serving pieces, and linens. It is easy to see she liked the kitchen and cooking; false modesty and William Golden notwithstanding, she was an excellent cook.

The other illustrations Pineles created for *Seventeen* were for fashion spreads and two calendars illustrated with seasonal pictures. One of the fashion assignments even took her back to her cotton design and display days at Contempora. She was better at depicting objects than people, though when some caricature is appropriate, her figure drawings and paintings are sharpest. She said she always liked still-life painting because it didn't move.[39] She also liked things. Her pleasure in old objects, many of which she had collected, is apparent in her close observation, deft brush work, and lettering when it appeared in her work.

Just as she included her own family recipes and her own interests in her paintings, Pineles used props and locations related to her personal life in the photographs published in *Seventeen*. Her intent was not to reveal herself or her life; rather, it was a practical way of working, as she and William Golden owned many beautiful, evocative artifacts and their home revealed their passion for trying out interesting decorating schemes. Using the things and places already at hand was

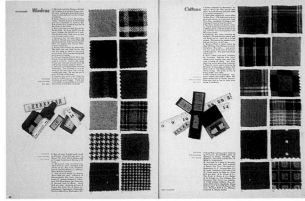

an easy way to save money, time, and effort. For years she had collected old prints of plants, flowers, fruits, vegetables, and fish, a hobby perhaps begun during her time in France. They were framed in a similar fashion and hung in groups of related subject matter. The wall of botanical prints from her bedroom appears in many photographs about home decorating, often with the antique, turned-spindle bed from the same room. She collected old china cups that were usually hand-decorated with various flora and sometimes lettering. The cups appear in paintings and in photographs. Golden's infatuation with cats is apparent in some photographs; their painted porcelain cat is in several layouts.

Following the imperative to be up-to-the-minute and exciting, fashion pages in *Seventeen* showed the greatest variety in form, typography, visual materials and composition. Here, in features that run in sequences of up to twelve pages, Pineles combined photographs, fashion sketches, and type. The type, though restricted in typeface, changed in size and form and moved around the page (but never off the horizontal). Some pages were filled with a light textural pattern of text and allowed small drawings to populate the paragraphs as if they were "sprinkled" across the space. Pages featuring fabrics, patterns, and colors were composed into loose grids, relieved by small collages of sewing notions or accessories. The photographs included the objects' shadows, which made the items seem to lift off the page, and stood in contrast to the flatter fabric samples.

To designers of the 1990s, these layouts may seem simple and flat in many senses. Printing technology and cost are the most likely causes of the lack of overlapping images: these pages are compositions of many rectangles, changing scales for limited dramatic effect. Another limitation that Pineles worked to overcome was the change between four-color and two-color pages (often in the middle of a spread) and paper stock (often within a single featured sequence). In these cases, she strove to integrate the pages by having some element straddle the gutter; the shape carried the eyes across the divide. Another strategy to disguise the visual break from four-color to two-color or between paper stocks was to print an object or graphic element in a duotone that suf-

above left: *Seventeen*, February 1950, bed and bedroom with framed prints from Pineles's house, photography by Dan Wynn.
right: *Seventeen*, July 1948, organized fabric swatches and 3-D objects.
below: *Seventeen*, February 1949, casserole illustration by Pineles includes one of her antique cups.
bottom: *Seventeen*, April 1948, fashion illustrations by Pineles.

above left: *Seventeen*, December 1949, spread
breaks from black/white to color; the easel bridges
the gap.

right: *Seventeen*, April 1950, photography by
William Helburn, who suggested the musical staffs
after seeing work by Saul Steinberg.

below: William Golden in CBS office, "eye" decorated birthday cake by Pineles.

ficiently maintained the color of a similar object on the four-color page.
A transition was effected that caused many readers to be unaware of
the technical changes between pages. The pages that had a theme or a
concept holding the pieces together (the raincoat spread using musical
staffs as rain, for example) are best. When the layouts were structurally
simple, the locations used for the fashion shoots became of more visual
interest. They also became part of the educational mission conceived
by Helen Valentine. The young women depicted were active and engaged in their surroundings. The out-of-doors was seldom used purely
as a backdrop for recreation; rather, the young women appeared in
open-air markets, in city construction sites, in historical places, and in
visually intriguing architecture. Indoors, they frequented bookstores
and flower shops.

Pineles learned a great deal about typography by watching
William Golden work, though they often engaged in friendly bickering
about, for example, when and how to use sans serif type. She recalled
the many weekends he brought his work home. He would spread out
all the materials for a CBS project, and she watched it take shape. "He
would work with each typeface as a kind of adventure; he didn't have
sheets of body type like those we used at *Vogue*, all printed up and
ready to be cut into columns. And he would sketch the titles in from
type books so that he could decide how to place the words to make
them more interesting or more readable. That was a very great revelation to me."[40]

Pineles and Golden worked with the beauty and elegance of
metal type composition—and also put up with its deficiencies. During
this period, in order to kern or letterspace or better lead lines, the careful typographic designer was accustomed to cutting up, letter by letter
or line by line, galleys of set type of all sizes. Designers often developed
their typographic arrangements by hand-lettering and/or tracing letters of the size they thought they wanted to use, line by line, to test
spacing, line breaks, and overall fit. This was common, tedious, and
necessary work. The typesetters continually set and reset the type to
get all the details in harmony. Golden was known for his fanaticism
about type and his careful measurements. According to a story told at

CBS about him, a typesetting job was off by a point. He sent it back for correction, but the returned galley was still wrong according to his ruler. Realizing all the rulers in the art department were different, Golden collected them and had new ones made to match his. Later, as a joke, his staff had a bronze one made for the boss.[41]

Like many couples who work in the same field, Pineles and Golden enjoyed discussing similar issues that each encountered. They were fortunate that, because they were not in any direct competition, there was no reason not to share all they experienced and knew, and, for the same reason, they could draw on each other's strengths:

> It wasn't always easy and we had lots more things to quarrel about than most couples, like "why does that artist do a decent job for you and never one as good for me?" . . . Or, "How come they invited you only to be a judge at this show and are relegating me to socialize with the other wives by the pool?" But seriously, we supported one another . . . each of us respected and admired the other's work. Though we held very different jobs we liked to compare daily disasters, to talk shop and often come up with better solutions to problems just by letting off steam. I learned a lot from Bill. . . . It was during those three day weekends [offered a raise, Golden had instead negotiated a four-day week] that I learned even more about our craft from Bill. He often brought work home and I looked on with awe at how he transformed what looked like a deadly dull job into a thing of beauty and importance—a CBS rate card for instance. I would watch him sketch type pages, trace each word of a headline and combine the elements in different ways on a page. . . . His room was a mess of cut papers, drawings, photos in layers on his desk and at the end of the day he would emerge with . . . a book recording a radio play in which fourteen characters from various times in history talk to each other in fourteen different typefaces.[42]

Their deep commitment to design quality and their long hours and attention to detail allowed both Pineles and Golden to gain respect from their peers. For some years, Pineles won awards from the ADC of New York, a membership-by-invitation-only professional group. With her work on *Seventeen*, she would become a regular winner, particularly for her art direction of the artists commissioned to illustrate fic-

above: *Seventeen*, February 1949, complete fashion story, photography by Carmen Schiavone.
below: *Seventeen*, April 1950, illustration by Dong Kingman.

above left: Pineles and Golden with individual New York Art Directors Club Gold Medals, 1948.

right: Pineles on design jury.

tion. In the 1951 show, she received eight awards, including those for art directing Dong Kingman, Ben Shahn, Arnold Blanch, Symeon Shimin, and Doris Lee; the artists received medals as well. Pineles also won medals for her own illustration: in 1948 the potato painting won a gold medal. Golden won a gold medal for his CBS radio and television promotional work that year; it was the first time both a wife and a husband won individual medals in the same year.

In those days, the ADC was a typical male bastion and was satisfied to remain so. For years Dr. Agha proposed that Pineles be granted membership, but he got nowhere. In 1948, when the club asked William Golden to join, he declined on the grounds that it was not a serious professional organization if it would not admit his wife, a well-qualified, award-winning art director for many years. According to the story, the club extended an invitation to both Pineles and Golden the very next day, and they accepted. Bradbury Thompson, art director of *Mademoiselle* at the time, remembers the excitement he felt when she was voted in. He was on the board of the club and spoke out in her favor, which was unusual because, as he said, he did not usually have the courage. This time he thought change was needed, and he was sympathetic to women's ambitions.[43] Cipe Pineles was the first woman member of the ADC of New York; she would later become the first woman admitted to its Hall of Fame.

Though hardworking, the Goldens had a active social life involving good food, many of their artist friends, and holiday celebrations with family and friends. For well-deserved vacations, they gravitated to water: they enjoyed the pedestrian way of life on Nantucket (it may have reminded them of their days in France), and they spent more and more time with friends on Fire Island, a seaside community originally settled by vaudevillians and long popular with members of various creative worlds. A narrow barrier island just off the southern coast of Long Island and (until 1959) without cars and reached by ferry, Fire Island is organized by a boardwalk "spine" connecting a succession of towns. Transportation was by foot and red wagon. Pineles and Rose Warren had shared a house on the island in 1938; the Levys had discovered the island before the war and bought a little house there. The houses were small "shanties" built on stilts so the ocean could swell without damaging them. In the late 1940s, the Goldens bought a house in Ocean Beach, the Valentines and the Ellis/Rubinsteins rented houses in the neighboring town, and the three women extended their office friendship into a more relaxed atmosphere. Weekends were filled with sailing, reading on the beach, taking photographs, picking beach plums for jelly (a specialty Pineles enjoyed giving to friends), cooking, and playing with each others' children.

The children of Pineles's friends found her house and its objects strange and enchanting. She was also known to give idiosyncratic, unusual, or unexpected things as gifts. She would wrap them in a variety of materials and add tags with her inimitable lettering. One year she gave mystified children books about and the supplies needed for taking up calligraphy (one of her passions); another time it was Schiaparelli shocking pink stationery for a young girl. Another year, known as the "year of the white-headed pins," she gave friends boxes of artfully arranged and packaged white-headed dressmaking pins. Everyone was amazed that such a simple, utilitarian thing could be considered a gift, but all were wholly appreciative of its uniqueness and her perception that the pins were valuable in their beauty and interesting to own.[44] She always chose the best for herself and for others, whether it was a simple bowl or the perfect champagne glass. Her vision and taste were highly developed and all her own.

It is possible to see how Pineles's discerning eye and eclectic appreciation of beauty in every aspect of life led to her creation of fascinating personal environments, welcoming and stimulating parties at home, and strange and wonderful presents. She could pull together people from different places and philosophies to create an exciting evening as well as she could orchestrate 150 pages of a magazine. It was this same ability that allowed her to call upon the talents of a disparate group of artists and photographers and make their work part of her whole vision, to arrange her illusionistic and tactile pages with two- and three-dimensional objects and type, and to conceive and harmonize the amazing melange that comprises any magazine. She was a natural "art director"—a collector and organizer of things—in some essential part of her intellectual and emotional being.

By 1950, her eighteenth year in the publishing industry, Cipe Pineles had proven beyond doubt that her abilities in art direction were not dependent on any supervisor. For the first time she was truly independent and in control, and through her work on *Seventeen* she earned the admiration and respect of her peers. Her many awards and her membership in ADC proved she could be "one of the boys" beyond the niche of women's magazine publishing.

above: Pineles and Golden on vacation, probably on Fire Island, late 1940s.
below: *Beach Plum Jelly*, illustrated recipe by Pineles, used as family Christmas card; 16 by 11½ in.

As Art Directors go, she was one . . . we called "civilized." . . . In a category I would call "uncivilized". . . there are types of art directors who feel they know more than the artist does . . . types who would start telling you what to do. Others just take everything as a matter of fact. A really civilized art director is one who really knows what you are doing and appreciates it.

(Bernarda Bryson Shahn interview)

[*Charm* and Family Life]

1950–59 Cipe Pineles works as art director of *Charm*
1950   article in *Studio News*
           visiting critic at Parsons
1951   boy baby is born on March 30; named Tom Golden, he is adopted
                 by Pineles and Golden
           ADC awards for *Seventeen* and *Charm*
           AIGA awards for *Charm*
           William Golden now creative director of advertising and sales
                 promotion for CBS TV
1952   AIGA awards for *Charm*
           ADC awards for *Charm*
1953   ADC awards for *Charm*
           work in *Graphis* magazine
1954   ADC awards for *Charm*
1955   Golden family moves in May to Stony Point, NY
           article in *Print*
           ADC awards for *Charm*
1956   ADC awards for *Charm*
1957   ADC awards for Green Mansions
1958   ADC awards for *Charm*
1959   leaves as *Charm* art director
           ADC awards for *Charm*
           becomes art director of *Mademoiselle*
           William Golden dies on October 23
1960   ADC awards for *Charm* and *McCall's*
1961   leaves publication design to become independent design consultant
           ADC awards for *Mademoiselle*

[B]y 1950, America was well into its postwar recovery. Wartime industrial developments were being adapted for a society at peace. Products given up or rationed during the war were being reintroduced and new products were becoming available. Wartime had necessitated improvement in communication media, which were primed to play important roles in a culture spreading across the countryside. Commercial television was poised to be taken into every home, and print media were about to fight for (and lose) visual supremacy. Companies were back in competition and spending time and money on promotion. Advertising agencies and design firms were populated by European immigrants with "modern ideas," and American designers, some of whom already had been following the avant garde, were eager to employ them. Magazines played an important part in both communicating culture and new ideas and providing a vehicle for the advertisement of new goods. Families were moving, new homes were created, and there were many new products to acquire. While women were certainly not new to the marketplace, they were more visible now. Money was being spent, much of it by women proud to have earned it themselves.

Impressed by her success with *Seventeen*, *Mademoiselle* publishers Street & Smith invited Helen Valentine back to the company in 1950, hoping she could effect a turnaround on their publication *Charm*. Started nine years earlier, *Charm* was a fashion magazine targeted toward women working between school and marriage. These readers were called "business girls," and over the years they had slipped away. Valentine accepted the offer to revamp the magazine, and several editors who had worked at *Seventeen* moved to *Charm* with her, including managing editor Andrée Vilas and fashion editor Eleanor Hillebrand Bruce. Most importantly, Cipe Pineles joined as art director and Estelle Ellis as promotion editor. In an April 1950 memo "To all whom *Charm* concerns" (who were most likely the advertisers), Valentine wrote:

> All of us . . . are agreed the Magazine for the Business Girl should become, by intent, content and subtitle, the Magazine for Women Who Work. *Charm* will be edited for the nation's 16,500,000 working women—not just the girl behind the typewriter.
>
> We envision the magazine's readers as the millions of women who are contributing to the nation's wealth and welfare in hospitals, banks, schools, stores, government and industry offices. These women comprise the country's most alive, aspiring people. They are working because they want to . . . because they find it stimulating . . . because they want more things, better things—and their incomes can help them get what they want. Many are single and on their first job; many are married and trying to do *two* jobs successfully. *Charm* will help the girl just out of school get her first job and *Charm* will help the woman leading the "double life" balance her time and energies between home and office.

. . . Its fashion pages will acknowledge the working woman's need for a seven-day-a-week wardrobe—this is no pinafore, Sunday-dress-up consumer.

She goes on to mention the necessity of looking one's best and its affect on the paycheck, and the need for products directed toward housekeeping efficiency. Valentine ends the letter by noting that she is "looking forward to the opportunity of editing a magazine for America's business and professional women."[1]

Charm recognized that working women held two jobs—the obvious one in the workplace and another at home—decades before the latter was dubbed the "second shift." Statistics indicated that women had constituted a large part of the workforce during the war; Helen Valentine maintained that these women were seen as working only temporarily. By 1950, however, there was a permanent class of working women, the majority of whom were married and therefore represented a double consuming potential. In 1951, figures indicated that 19 million women were working in the United States. Of these, 4.5 million worked in offices and earned a total of $11 billion; 1 million taught school and earned $3 billion; 1.5 million were saleswomen earning $3 billion; 350,000 were nurses earning $850 million; and 1.5 million were professional and executive women earning $5 billion.[2] Thus, office workers and nurses earned $2,400 a year; teachers earned $3,000; saleswomen were paid $2,000; and professional and executive women brought home $3,300. The audience Helen Valentine perceived included all these women; it was an "interest" group, not an age group or "class" of women. These career-oriented women needed a service and fashion magazine that could help them fit their jobs into their lives.

The reinvented *Charm*, subtitled "the magazine for women who work," was launched in August 1950. The first issue began with Valentine's editorial "We Work Too," which was accompanied by sixty small photographs of women with different occupations (some were identified as *Charm* staff; the doctor was Dr. Debora Pineles Schor, Cipe's younger sister). Six stories by members of the *Charm* staff explained how the staff were also part of *Charm*'s audience. One essay, "I want my wife to work," was written by a bachelor. An illustrated spread titled "They too love(d) wives who work(ed)" provided short descriptions of twelve women ranging from contemporaries Clare Boothe Luce and Helen Hayes MacArthur to historical figures like Helen of Troy and Marie Curie. It ended with Eve, "unemployed . . . and look what happened." Another piece, "Men you can't live without," was about the reader's hairdresser, tailor, grocer, etc., and ended with "your own," which was illustrated with a photograph of a man behind a newspaper (the model happened to be William Golden reading at his breakfast table).

The staple contents of the magazine included profiles of women working in different professions, cultural reviews, fiction, and job-related articles about career and financial planning, new career oppor-

above: *Charm* cover, August 1950.
below: *Charm* cover, July 1951, photography by Ernst Beadle.

above: *Charm*, August 1950, six-page introduction to new magazine and staff; large photograph by Robert Frank.

below: *Charm*, August 1950; *Wives* illustration by Joe Kaufman.

tunities, childcare, equal pay, tax laws, and men's reactions to working wives and women employees. Housekeeping advice was based on the needs of time- and energy-strapped readers, and fashion advice was practical and covered clothing for both work and after-hours. The attitude was serious, the language was straightforward, objective, informative, and supportive, and the tone was frequently light and humorous. *Charm* saw working women not as drudges but rather as a group of curious, intelligent women who needed a little help to keep going. The editors were their friends who happened to be paid to research, write about, and show the new ideas and products that could make the dual life, a life well known to the editors, easier.

The first magazine specifically to address a "working woman" audience, the new *Charm* was launched twenty-two years before *Ms.* magazine and twenty-six years before the publication named *Working Woman*. As Pineles said in 1976, "*Charm* was really the first feminist magazine. There would have been no room for *Ms.* magazine if *Charm* had not been dropped."[3] Championing the magazine that would later be called both the "spiritual mother"[4] and "forerunner"[5] of *Ms.*, Pineles, Valentine, and Ellis joined forces once again.

The three women were models of the new working woman: they were serious, inventive, and hardworking, were committed to their families and jobs, and dealt with the stresses and strains of the life they chose. This role for women was new to America; it was still in development and would later become more radical, with far-reaching economic, political, and social consequences. The three could be called "proto-feminists"; they communicated an ideology, a social and political agenda that we would now call feminist.

Seeing the three women as "trailblazers" is only possible in hindsight. In 1985, Ellis said of *Charm*: "It was the articulator of the needs and aspirations of working women, and we were criticized for taking ourselves too seriously. But we had a vision of where things were going and we were ready to blaze the trail."[6] Ultimately, their vision was realized. But at that time, their actions were based more on intuition and less on politics (in an activist sense) than their later statements suggest. As Barbara Valentine Hertz said of her mother, "She was a 'feminist' but did not think or talk in these terms; she was wholly unself-conscious [about this issue]."[7]

At *Charm* Valentine, Pineles, and Ellis were mainly concerned

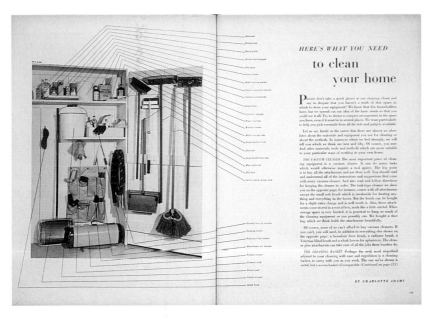

left: *Charm*, October 1951, organizational advice in a diagram, photography by Ben Rose.
below: *Charm* cover, January 1952.

with being professional and getting the job done. They took working for granted and did not see themselves as "women" accomplishing these tasks. Nor did they use the magazine as a means for public, political action. Valentine lectured widely to industry groups, where she was able to be somewhat more straightforward than she was in the magazine. In a 1954 speech to the Washington (D.C.) Fashion Group entitled "How to keep more of the money you earn," Valentine talked about change for women in economic, political, and social terms. She discussed needed changes in childcare, maternity leaves, tax laws, and social security benefits. In the penultimate paragraph she said: "Surely there is no reason to be shy about asking for the things that are so important to our happiness and our progress today. The thing that holds us back, doubtless, is the fear of being called feminists. Nonsense. What's wrong with recognizing our power as women who work and using it to get ourselves—not special privileges—but merely consideration as human beings."[8] It is important to recognize the difference between Helen Valentine's use of the word "feminist" and her daughter's perception of its meaning. In the mid-90s, the word has become so weighted with the struggles of the women's liberation movement and its backlash that it is not the same "feminist" of the 1950s, when Valentine equated feminist goals with basic humanity and simple equality.

The changing nature of political language and definitions over time makes interpretation difficult, and hindsight is not always clear. What friends and coworkers do recall is three very dedicated women who lived their vision for all women and who did not seem to spend much, if any, time and energy in debate or self-conscious appraisal. Muriel Batherman, who worked on both *Seventeen* and *Charm*, recalled that "Cipe was not happy with the connotation [of feminist]. To them [Pineles, Valentine, and Ellis] it was their spirit; it was natural to them. They were confident in their abilities. They had no sense of defending

right and opposite, top: *Charm*, December 1956, eight-page feature working around printing changes from full-color, duotone, and black/white, photography by William Helburn.

women's rights, it was the natural thing to do."[9] Carol Burtin, daughter of designer Will Burtin, presents a more complex picture of Pineles, saying she "never used the [feminist] rhetoric. . . . I don't think she actively said we should promote women; she had her eye for quality, for talent, for enterprise. . . . [On the other hand] she was not above using being attractive as a woman, she didn't lean on ability only, [and] she flirted in a way that was not unpleasant. . . . She could use being adorable as well as being very talented."[10] In the late 1970s, almost twenty years after *Charm*'s reconception, Pineles would say: "At first, I was against women's lib. I felt it was diverting us from the real issues of the time. Perhaps I felt that way because I didn't know I needed to be liberated. I had a husband who introduced me with pleasure as a working wife and took pride in my work."[11] This is the key: they didn't need liberation. They forged ahead, supporting each other.

    Charm was a quiet and subtle and therefore more subversive force for change. It provided a place of resistance within a set of cultural forces that celebrated the return of the woman to the postwar home, encouraged the nesting activities in the growing suburbs, told women they were happy, and created the culture of "Ozzie and Harriet." It was evident to the trio how much enjoyment, satisfaction, and self-worth they derived from their work. An assistant who knew the troika when they were in top form commented: "[They] gained tremendous support for each other. . . . [They] understood their struggle, each individually to be the perfect wife, perfect mother as well as career woman, but never talked about having it all; they just did it. . . . They did not see themselves as pioneers—did not understand how unique they were—and yet there was a consciousness of it, because [there was] an attempt to bring that concept to American women in those publications . . . they had a mission in terms of their own work."[12] They believed in their model of combining private and professional lives. They could provide information and encouragement to their readers—but they could not more openly advocate social and political change for women in a mainstream magazine that was operated as a profitable business. However, through the examples and alternatives shown in the magazine, the three clearly argued for different goals for all women: to successfully combine the professional and private, to make work fulfilling, to be more knowledgeable about and independent with finances, to take active public roles, to develop one's talents. All of this was accomplished without using the buzzwords favored by the

coming revolution. Valentine, Pineles, and Ellis were not radical and did not foresee the wrenching social and cultural consequences of the full expression of the ideas they communicated. Unaware that the developments they fostered would also require fundamental adjustments among men and institutions, the trio continued to focus on women. During the same years that produced the distressed, depressed, unfulfilled women of Betty Friedan's 1963 *Feminine Mystique*, and when other women's magazines were claiming that "happiness is life in the suburbs with appliances" (and refusing to publish Friedan's articles),[13] Valentine, Pineles, and Ellis were showing alternative paths to professional achievement, personal fulfillment, and happiness.

Less than a year after *Charm*'s reinvention, Cipe Pineles fit the magazine's reader profile even more perfectly. After years of trying to start a family, William Golden and Pineles decided to adopt a child. The adoption agencies, however, were hesitant to accept working parents and believed the Goldens were too old (in 1950, Cipe was forty-two and Bill was thirty-nine); they turned the couple down. The Goldens decided instead to adopt privately. Through friends, they found the woman for whom they would care and who would give birth to the baby, whom they named Thomas Golden, in March 1951. Brought home from the hospital to the apartment on 54th Street, the baby was welcomed by designer and friend Will Burtin, his wife Hilde, and their daughter Carol, who held a large white teddy bear.[14] In time, several of this group would be more than friends.

Comments Pineles made in hindsight about parenthood sound nonchalant: "A lot of my colleagues had more than one child and were managing too. . . . I was five minutes away from my office and so was Bill. I could be home for lunch two or three times a week. And we were lucky to find Roslyn, who not only took good care of Tom, our son, but also kept the apartment tidy, shopped and cooked dinner, and took care of us too. I didn't think I was doing anything unusual."[15] At the beginning, however, she was anxious. She was an older mother surrounded by younger friends and colleagues who were having babies and continuing to work. Mothering was a new experience for Pineles, and, though it was something she had desperately desired, it did not come naturally to her. With live-in help it was easy for Pineles not to be involved with mundane tasks, but she learned caretaking skills nevertheless. In some ways, a friend remembered, William Golden was more comfortable with the idea of a baby. Having finally achieved

above: Pineles and baby Tom Golden at home; note variety of framed scientific illustrations of shells.
below: Golden family, about 1952.

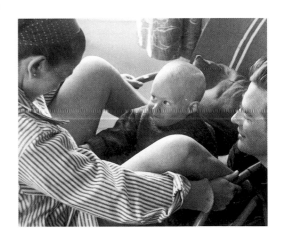

their wish, they enjoyed their family life and shared it with many friends.[16]

During Tom's early years, Pineles made daily visits home but still kept reasonable and regular hours at the office. The arrival of a child did not change her commitment to or involvement in her work. Nor did it change Golden's. The four-day work week Golden had negotiated with CBS allowed for more flexible family time on Fire Island and later at their country house. "It was a wonderful arrangement. . . . Bill worked with incredible concentration at the office Monday through late Thursday night, and then took a jam-packed briefcase home and worked all weekend [at home]."[17]

Pineles integrated her jobs as mother and career woman with her unique style and flair, as this description from a former young assistant illustrates: "She always wore a suit and in the office took off the jacket. Underneath was usually a cream silk shirt, sometimes with a bow. An accessory she usually wore was a gold safety pin with about eight or nine smaller gold pins attached to it. [She started buying these] at Tiffany when her adopted son was a baby. If she was going to have pins pinned to her shirt for diapering, as was the mode at the time, they were going to be nice pins. Her skirts were simple and her shoes flat and comfortable. She was a short and sturdy woman, with sturdy legs."[18]

In 1955 the Golden family joined millions of Americans and many other New Yorkers in the postwar exodus to the suburbs. Pineles remembered her husband "yearning to go to the country."[19] Many of their friends were already established across the Hudson River and high on its cliffs in Rockland County. One of these friends described the area as the "closest unspoiled countryside to Manhattan . . . a pastoral landscape."[20] Though now the town of Stony Point is just north of the Tappan Zee Bridge, in the mid-50s those commuting to the city were limited to the George Washington Bridge or the Weehawken (New Jersey) commuter train. The Goldens moved within a few miles of Lucille Corcos and Edgar Levy; architect, preservationist, and editor James Marston Fitch and his wife, Cleo; and designer Will Burtin and his family. These families were the Goldens' closest friends and would play a variety of roles in Pineles's life.

Lucille Corcos and her husband, Edgar Levy, were primarily products of New York City. Members of the first generation of American artists to be educated in the United States rather than in Europe, they both studied at the Art Students League. In the 1930s Levy and Corcos were full-time painters working and living in Brooklyn Heights. A small artists' community grew in the then-"undiscovered" neighborhood; their neighbors were Adolph Gottlieb, Mark Rothko, Louis Shanker, David Smith, and Dorothy Dehner (one of Lucille Corcos's closest friends, who was often in disagreement with Pineles about the equality of art and design). Levy and Smith were good friends and did not participate with the others in what would later be called Abstract Expressionism.

Pineles in *Charm* offices.

The Levys were the first of a growing group of people in the arts to find the countryside above the Hudson River in Rockland County conducive to creative family life. Lucille, Edgar, and their two sons, David and Joel, left the city in 1941 and moved to South Mountain Road in New City. Edgar Levy continued to paint. Some themes focused on their lives in Brooklyn, while other work was based on his anatomical studies, the automobile, and the airplane from his service in the Army Air Corps. Corcos was a successful painter and illustrator by this time. In the 1930s, fashion, culture, and home magazines published her work, and her popularity continued into the 1960s.

Cipe Pineles's close friendship with Corcos had begun when Pineles commissioned Corcos's work for *Seventeen* and *Charm*. Her humor in personal interactions and in her art made her an engaging collaborator. Corcos's paintings were densely packed with many small stories and commentary. The compositions had detailed, multiple subjects; perspective and scale were distorted for practical and expressive purposes. This new modern primitivism was considered part of a native tradition in American art and its "unacademic" nature was celebrated. Corcos's subjects included rural landscapes and urban scenes, ranging from *Christmas Eve, Rockefeller Center* to *The Oyster Party* to *Everybody Meets to Boat*.[21] In addition to doing commissioned illustration, Lucille Corcos built her career as a fine artist and was a steady participant in New York gallery shows and annual exhibitions at the Whitney Museum of American Art from 1936 to 1954. During the same time she was part of major exhibitions in Chicago, Pittsburgh, Philadelphia, Washington, D.C., and other institutions in New York.

In 1952 Will Burtin and his family also moved to South Mountain Road. The Burtin house, built three years later, was designed by James Fitch and Burtin. A comment William Golden made about the home reveals both men's obsession with precision (and, one hopes, their sense of humor). When Golden saw the Japanese-like arrangement of boulders in the garden, he remarked to Burtin, "You know, you should really move that big boulder one pica over to the left."[22]

Burtin's daughter Carol remembers the time and the place:

It was the first migration out of New York City by a number of artists, lefties. It was the McCarthy period, the HUAC (House Un-American Activities Committee) period; and we knew the Levys, we knew the road. Jimmy Fitch was the architect [of our house]. Everybody on South Mountain Road seemed to be something in the written or drawn arts, actors: John Houseman, Alan Jay Lerner busy writing *My Fair Lady*; there were sculptors; Ernie Kovacs, Lotte Lenya, everybody lived on the road. So many everybodies lived on the road that when we built our house, and I went to school for the first time, word seeped out that my mother's name was Hilde and they figured out we must be Hildegard of the Liberace Show. Boy, did I get respect—briefly. . . . The road, the community, became a self-nurturing thing. The

politics of the time, the Korean War, the Cold War, everybody was hunkering down amongst the friendly ones. I know that people on the road lost their jobs; one was a Swiss neighbor and foreign correspondent for the *Toledo Blade*; the newspaper was identified by McCarthy's committee as a left wing journal because it carried Herblock cartoons that denigrated GIs. I know people brought food, left money in the door. Everybody was helping each other; there was a real sense [of attack]; I was only ten to fourteen years old before that stopped; it was a pretty formative time.[23]

During that same time, CBS, like many organizations, required employees to sign loyalty oaths. A colleague recalled that Golden, whose politics were certainly liberal if not radical, refused to sign, and the whole art department supported him by refusing to sign as well.[24] Frank Stanton, Golden's boss, said he "might have been, don't know for sure, a member of the communist party . . . [but] I never knew who signed and who did not." He collected the papers and simply put them away. "That was a dark period in our [country's history]."[25]

Having sold the Fire Island house to friends, Pineles, Golden, and Tom settled into a ten-room Victorian house high above the Hudson on ten acres of land in Stony Point. They chose it, Pineles said later, because "it looked like a good Paris apartment."[26] The house's architectural style was Second French Empire; it was built around 1860 and had a brick exterior, a simple, rectangular plan, fourteen-foot ceilings, narrow, tall windows and doors with curved tops on the first floor, and a mansard roof. Originally, the house had a porch overlooking the boats on the river about five miles away and iron ornaments around the entire roof. The Goldens did extensive renovations, "purging the house of frivolous aspects"[27] and painting the interior all white and the exterior yellow-beige and gray-blue. It was gradually furnished in an eclectic style held together by their good judgment and taste. In the living room were large period mirrors, modern teak shelving, original Thonet chairs, glass-topped tables, elegant, lightweight sofas, paintings by

Pineles and by friends, and three original Toulouse-Lautrec posters from Golden's days in Paris. The dining room held a wall of framed botanical prints, a tall epergne with a constantly changing display of interesting *objets*, and tables arranged to enjoy the view and light. Golden enjoyed the pleasure Pineles derived from the evolution of the house project; he found his pleasures outdoors.

William Golden was able to indulge his passion for gardening here. He spent the winter reading, discovering no two books agreed on how to till the soil.[28] He grew both vegetables and flowers in large gardens; his friends remember his dirty, long fingernails, his sun-bleached, ash-blond hair, and his tanned body.[29] He balanced his devotion to his work at CBS with gardening, reading (he sought to mend his interrupted education), and spending time with his family. With characteristic intensity, he continued to demand high standards of himself and those around him. This, combined with a personality that allowed few emotional outlets and limited physical exercise, would eventually take its toll.

No matter what the constraints of the environment, Pineles always indulged her love of family gatherings and parties with friends and colleagues; she enjoyed both the preparations and the event. The new house provided an extraordinary stage for occasions that were memorable for everyone—"a reaffirmation of the aesthetics of life" is how one guest described them.[30] She loved to cook and present her food beautifully, and she always decorated for the season, holiday, or occasion. Her very personal and idiosyncratic style was lavish, not in terms of the monetary value of the objects and materials she used, but rather in terms of her attention to detail and to the physical and visual qualities of her objects. Carol Burtin remembered visiting the house during the holidays and commented on the sense of luxury: "It wasn't the size of it, particularly, but the things that were in it; our house was big although modern; there was a different feeling, a greater sophistication [at her house]."[31]

While Cipe Pineles was an extrovert who sought and nurtured friendships, Golden was closed and serious, with few close friends and a low threshold for boredom and family parties. She was understanding: "Bill was interested in every aspect of living fully. He didn't make small talk, but he could talk very comfortably. He was a person who would have the most marvelous time at a good party. When I would feel a party coming on, sometimes he'd say 'Please don't make any parties next month,' because he was going to be busy. Two weeks later, he'd ask, 'That party we're talking about . . . whom are you inviting?' I'd give him the guest list, and he'd say, 'I like the party. I don't like the guests.' He might not cross out anybody, but he would add names to make it a party he felt he'd have a marvelous time at."[32]

Tom Golden remembered the parties, the weekends filled with visits from friends who lived in the city, and the more common, regular visits among the three families that grew together: the Goldens, the Burtins, and the Levys. He was the youngest child among them; David

above and opposite top: *Charm*, December 1956, selected spreads from multi-page Christmas feature sequence using the Golden's Stony Point house; note scale of architecture, eclectic furnishings, Toulouse-Lautrec prints. Illustrations by Lucille Corcos and Edgar Levy; photography by Carmen Schiavone.

and Joel Levy were about twelve and eight years older than he, and Carol Burtin was about eight years older. Tom learned to play chess from Dr. Agha; he considered Lou Dorfsman (later Golden's successor at CBS) almost a godfather; and he received fabulous gifts from his parents' friends, as this was an easy way for them to repay the Golden's generous hospitality. He was the same age as the son of Kurt Weihs, Golden's associate, who remembers Golden playing with the boys and driving them around the countryside in his jeep.[33]

As she had done at *Seventeen*, Pineles worked her interests and environments into the pages of *Charm*. The whole house in Stony Point became a stage for the December 1956 issue: the large curved doors and neighborhood youngsters (including her son) introduced the holiday theme; the massive doors and eclectic furnishings of the living room served as a backdrop for holiday clothes; a Toulouse-Lautrec poster featured prominently in the fashion shots; and one bedroom's ivy-print walls and antique spool bed became a setting for lingerie.

Tom Golden and his friends (paid in stuffed animals) were used as models in many of the fashion shoots that used the Stony Point house as an elegant location. He remembered one occasion as the realization of every boy's fantasy: "I was about seven or eight years old, just off the school bus at the end of the road and raced home to use the toilet. I ran up the stairs and burst into the bathroom where I found it filled with beautiful models in various states of undress." He finished the anecdote, "Thank you, mother!"[34]

All *Charm*'s offices were on one floor. The editorial and art offices were next to the promotion office, which provided easy access and fostered collaboration. The office where the assistants worked was next to the art director's office; the door was always open. They could even overhear Pineles chatting on the phone with Golden. One morning, in an intimate sharing of their successes, she itemized her just-received awards as he did his. Pineles employed young assistants, some of whom later became magazine art directors and designers in prominent design offices. Tom Courtos, whose high school artwork had been published in *Seventeen*, came to see her after he graduated from Pratt. She remem-

bered him and offered him a position. They worked together for about five years, after which she sent him to see William Golden, who hired him. Courtos remembers the collaborative planning sessions of the four "amazing ladies": Valentine, Pineles, Ellis, and fashion editor Eleanor Hillebrand Bruce. Working the standard three months in advance for a monthly publication, they would plot the issue around the seasonally based main subject and combine fashion, accessories, manufacturers, fiction, and feature articles, decide how many pages would be allotted for each section, and choose which photographer would get the cover. Pineles often wrote copy, inventing good phrases and inspiring the others.[35] The relationship among the four women was so close that once, after Eleanor Bruce and Pineles had crossed views, Bruce brought her flowers after lunch.[36]

Using preprinted sheets with tiny double-page spreads laid out in a sequence, Pineles planned the number of four-color pages, two-color pages, and the general pattern for the issue. Later, to explain her ideas to the editors, she made full-size dummies that suggested a particular mood or special effect for the issue. The dummies used pasted-up, already-existing art and photographs, accompanied by dummy type and written comments about ideas for photographers to use. In this fluid process, words and pictures gradually combined to create a message. The "portfolios" (the six- to eight-page sequences on one subject) were displayed on the bulletin board: the design stayed loose and plastic while different possibilities were explored (shades of Agha's method). Many editors, assistants, and designers were involved in the collaboration, and the sequences underwent many changes.

"I stood beside her and helped when she did major fashion layouts," Pineles's former assistant Roger Schoening recalls. "Layout sheets came printed with a big margin. She always cut the margin off and worked to the direct size of the page. She used frames that were spread-size and put the photostats beneath the frames, moving both about until she achieved the effect she wanted. When she was finished she would ask me to paste it up. She worked on a big cherry table in her office."[37] At other times, she allowed the assistants to work inde-

Pineles in *Charm* office, Joe Kaufman's *30 Moderns* illustration at right.

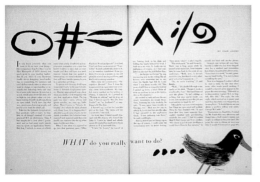

pendently on their sections; all work, however, was shown to her before it was released.

Critical to Pineles's success in working with artists and photographers were her talent and experience as an illustrator and her outgoing, generous personality. Constantly on the lookout for new people, she visited galleries, watched the press, and reviewed portfolios. She introduced less-experienced artists to her readers by keeping a file of small spot drawings and using them as filler when needed. She discovered new talents, developed others, and encouraged all with whom she collaborated. She developed friendships with the people who worked for her, and they admired her. Though Pineles's work paid less, photographers often did projects for her before completing the advertising work they did to pay the bills. They even brought her gifts.[38] Like Agha, Pineles would spend hours in her office talking with artists and photographers about their existing work and about projects she had for them. She warmed people up; her charm was extraordinary and her slight accent delightful. One colleague described her look as "Flemish," like a classical painting with an ageless face and flawless complexion.

The photographers Pineles routinely commissioned included Francesco Scavullo, Carmen Schiavone, and Louis Faurer, "a great photographer who could not take an ugly picture of a woman."[39] She used William Helburn for fashion and Ben Rose for still lifes. Pineles was an important contact for any creative person at that time. One photographer recalled a story Faurer told about himself: He was very nervous about meeting Pineles for the first time, and, wanting to make a good impression and knowing he naturally perspired a lot, he had covered himself with talc. At some point, in a friendly gesture, she patted him on the back, surrounding them both in a cloud of powder.[40] Robert Frank was Pineles's discovery for magazine work; he had strong ideas and was a difficult person to give an assignment to. For *Charm*'s first issue, Pineles assigned him to photograph "a cross section of our audience"; after two weeks he brought in a photograph of movement in a crowded street, with the focus on a single female figure.[41]

Pineles rarely went to the studios or the location for the shoots.[42] She probably had practical reasons for remaining aloof from the creative photographic process, but essentially Pineles trusted her assistants and collaborators. Photographer William Helburn called her "terrific; not an obvious art director type, not heavy-handed," which is an intriguing comment on her peers. He considered her more an "editor," or an intellectual art director, than a personally expressive director who might have more "amazing graphics" on the page. He liked to work with her because she would explain her concept for an issue; he had a higher regard for her than for her magazines. They would discuss an issue over lunch in the office, and she trusted him to be inventive within the parameters of her concept.[43]

Cipe Pineles continued to use fine artists as illustrators for both fiction and feature articles in *Charm*. Many were the same artists she had used at *Seventeen*: Doris Lee, Joe Kaufman, Jan Balet, David Stone

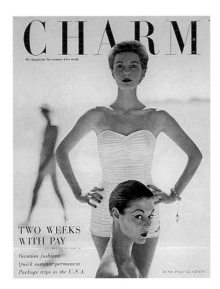

Martin, Richard Lindner, Jerome Snyder, Leslie Jacobs, Ben Shahn, Lucille Corcos, and Edgar Levy. New artists included Robert Osborn, Tomi Ungerer, and R. O. Blechman. Her assistant, Muriel Batherman, often contributed drawings, just as Pineles had done at the Condé Nast publications when she was working with Agha. She allowed the artists, especially those with whom she had a longstanding friendship, like Joe Kaufman and Ben Shahn, free rein; they understood each other well, and there were seldom changes. Because they appreciated her attitude and the opportunities she afforded them, the artists would often offer a two-color "extension," or secondary drawing used later in an article or story (perhaps after the story had jumped to the back of the magazine), to tie in with the four-color, primary artwork at the front. Or they would do their own color separations for printing.[44]

Initially, *Charm*'s format design bore a general resemblance to *Seventeen*'s, though the trim size was smaller. Over its nine years, the magazine design changed with the times. Influenced by changing design and advertising ideas, the typography moved away from the book tradition and became more dynamic. While Pineles was not as consistently playful or dramatic as other designers were, she did make visual puns with letters and objects and experimented with a variety of typefaces for headlines (another legacy from Agha). Conscious of typographic "color," Pineles did endless tracings to see what color value different sizes and weights would provide. She liked contrast, especially between text and headings. A classicist of sorts, she originally used the Bodoni type family, from Bodoni Book for regular text (which *Vogue* and *Seventeen* had used) to Ultra Bodoni for headlines.

By the mid-50s a modernist visual vocabulary had been adopted by many corporations: sleek, straight skyscrapers for headquarters; industrial materials and geometric shapes for products; bold, dynamic sans serif typography for their messages. Mathematical grids in buildings and on pages expressed objective and rational purpose. *Charm*'s

above: *Charm* covers for June 1952, November 1954, September 1959 showing changes in logo; photography by William Helburn for 1952, 1954, Carmen Schiavone for 1959.
below: *Charm*, January 1957, typographic puns.

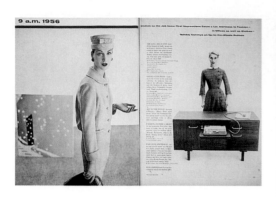

above and right: *Charm*, January 1956, ten-page fashion sequence about different jobs (and the modern furniture or equipment associated with them), photography by William Helburn.
below: *Charm*, April 1956, painting by Raphael Soyer used as sidebar.

interior type reflected these changes in American graphic design. Probably more noticed by readers, however, were changes in the cover logo: it went from an indifferent, high-contrast serif face to an elegant, slightly condensed Bodoni. In 1953, the logo was enlarged half-again; in late 1956, it was changed to a smaller, solid sans serif (Franklin Gothic capitals, boldface, italic, and extended), which was used until 1959, when new editors were hired.

Charm's articles about artists, inexpensive collecting, and decorating with reproductions helped educate the magazine's readers. Some articles sought to inform readers about a single artist, while others were introductions to a whole style or period of work. Readers were encouraged to become more observant of their surroundings and what "art" might be found there. Part of Pineles's aim was to break down the barriers between the public and its perception of Art as "fine," "high," and "not for me" and to educate and sensitize her readers about bringing art into their homes and lives. Occasionally a reproduction of a work of art from a museum was used to complement the theme of a feature article. The reproduction was not an illustration that had any literal connection to the article, but was rather a visual "sidebar" with commentary that bridged the two forms of expression.

The new editorial vision was best revealed in the presentation of fashion, as this was the biggest break from traditional notions of fashion reporting and presentation. *Charm* fashion was a challenge, Helburn recalled, because *Charm*'s editors had not chosen the "fantasy flip" attitude found in other women's magazines.[45] Instead, they limited themselves to realism, responding to women's need for fashion that fit real life. *Charm*'s clothes were for women who worked. They allowed women to look attractive, professional, and be comfortable on a reasonable budget. *Charm*'s time- and expense-conscious readers eagerly welcomed this practical wardrobe that required little ironing and dry

smooth office routine: the jersey dress

cleaning. *Charm*'s models were presented in a workday context: at the office, in the city, commuting, or shopping during lunch hour. As Pineles put it, "We try to make the prosaic attractive without using the tired clichés of false glamour. You might say we are trying to convey the attractiveness of reality, as opposed to the glitter of a never-never land."[46] Her most frequent advice was to "get a picture of an attractive girl wearing America's most popular clothes . . . make the models look normal."[47]

Photographers used a variety of city locations for fashion shoots, including streets, public buildings, art galleries, storefronts, shop interiors, train stations, and cab stands, as well as recreational areas in the country and interesting vacation spots. The latest modern American architecture and industrial design became backdrops and settings for the latest fashions for the modern American working woman. These included buildings, urban spaces, modern furniture, and office machines and equipment. The spaces were treated like stage sets, and the machines and furniture became a form of sculpture. Sometimes the machines and their products were reduced to abstract patterns. The primary theme remained: these clothes are for working women. The spaces chosen and the machines used were often signs of specific occupations. To our late-90s sensibilities, the career choices represented in these images appear limited to traditional "women's work": clerical, nursing, retail, teaching, and occasionally executive positions. However, one must bear in mind that those were the majority of opportunities open to women in the 1950s.

The editors remained realistic in their portrayal of readers' lives in the fashion pages. It was in the images connected with feature articles that their higher goals for women could be expressed. However, their total message was constrained to some extent, particularly by advertisements, which reflected the prevailing views of women at that time. This was (and is) the condition of mass market media publishing in capitalist America: the message reflects the status quo. *Charm* was a successful commercial product in the booming postwar economy and could not obviously stray very far. That is why the editorial team can

above: *Charm*, September 1957, part of six-page sequence using office machines as indexes of jobs, photography by Carmen Schiavone.
below: *Charm*, January 1957, part of sequence using constructed International Style architecture, photography by Gerald Hochman.

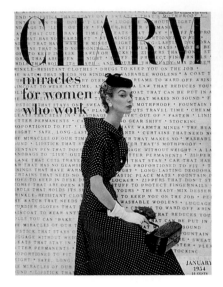

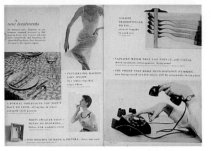

Charm, January 1954, cover and complete sequence on *Miracles*; cover photography by William Helburn.

be seen as "subversive": the alternative message was there to be read by those who looked for it. Valentine, Pineles, and Ellis were working as best they could to counteract the standard construction of the role of women.

Charm's January 1954 issue was subtitled "Miracles for Women who Work" and featured a long sequential compilation of foods, household appliances, clothing, accessories, new materials, new fabrics, and beauty products. The issue informed readers about the "miracles" that made the second shift possible and easier: washable fabrics, convenience foods like frozen orange juice, commuter trains, improved telephones, cleaning products, and better medical testing during pregnancy. "Panorama of Progress" was the theme for the January 1956 issue. It included "profiles" of the three machines (the telephone, the typewriter, and the sewing machine) that significantly changed women's public and private lives, an eight-page sequence about women's progress in a wide variety of fields (from medicine to publishing), a four-page historical panorama of women and office machines, a history of the two-week vacation as a benefit, and an article on the consequences of automation in the office. Visual materials consisted of historical line cuts and photographs and several contemporary works, including a photocollage, drawings by Ben Shahn, and a full-spread

Joe Kaufman illustration titled "30 Moderns," which featured portraits of active, successful women from the last one hundred years. The portraits were presented decoratively and diversely framed and they appeared to be hung in a home setting. The illustration's composition was reminiscent of a wall arrangement in Pineles's apartment, which Kaufman knew from his visits. In fact, the artist claimed, "Unconsciously, it must have been in the back of my mind; she had good taste."[48]

A highly successful series of feature articles about women's contributions in various cities across the country widened the geographical distribution of *Charm*'s readership and furthered the magazine's "working woman" agenda. Called "She Works in [city name]," this series was the result of a concerted research and promotion effort by Estelle Ellis. Over a period of four years, week-long celebrations of working women were organized in nineteen cities. In each location, city fathers, chambers of commerce, department stores, corporations, and women's groups were brought together to show and celebrate women's contributions to the city's economic life. Opened with a well-publicized speech by Helen Valentine, each event was reported on and presented as the theme for a specific issue.

In April 1956 the series featured Detroit. Suitably introduced on the cover by a car in the background, the city theme permeated the issue and focused on the city's automotive industry. The issue reported on living and working conditions in Detroit and profiled a textile designer. Design in Detroit was explicitly described in captions, which identified sculpture at Cranbrook Academy of Art, the architecture of Eero Saarinen for General Motors, a new traffic plan, an auto assembly line, and other examples of new, modern architecture. The city was used as a backdrop for the fashion pages, which combined photographs of models with images of architecture, sculpture, automotive assembly lines, and expressways. New cars formed the backdrop for "commuting" clothes, and "vernacular" typography—in the form of parking garage signs—added a three-dimensional quality to the page.

Cipe Pineles and her collaborating artists and photographers consistently won awards from the Art Directors Club (ADC) and the AIGA

above: *Charm*, January 1956, *30 Moderns* illustration by Joe Kaufman based on the Goldens' apartment; framed art includes *Vanity Fair* Modern Art "family tree" from 1933 in upper right, possible Pineles painting in upper left, reproductions of botanical illustrations.
below: same issue, six-page sequence with illustrations by Ben Shahn. ©Estate of Ben Shahn / Licensed by VAGA, New York, NY.

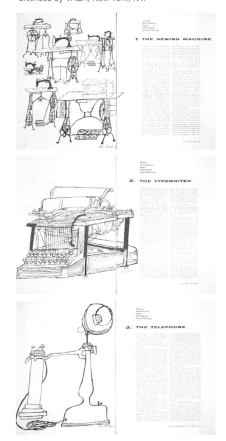

this page and opposite: *Charm*, April 1956, "She Works in Detroit" issue. Cover photography by William Helburn.
Fourteen-page fashion sequence in city with photography by Louis Faurer.
Eight-page fashion sequence using vernacular garage signs with photography by William Helburn.

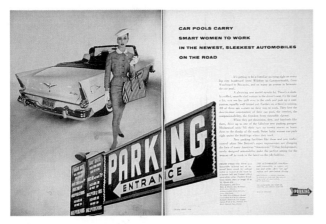

for their work on *Charm*. The ADC presented Pineles with awards for *Charm* every year that she art directed the magazine, and she won awards at AIGA magazine exhibitions for two consecutive years. The first year was 1951, when she was on the jury with Alexey Brodovitch and her friend Jimmy Fitch, and Will Burtin was on the advising committee. At that exhibition, Pineles received three Certificates of Excellence for three issues of *Charm*; a cover and three spreads were cited, one of which included William Golden's photographs of cats. The next year, when Dr. Agha was on the jury, she received two certificates for two issues of *Charm*. The fact that many jurors were Pineles's friends and colleagues illustrates how small the New York design world was at that time. Holding competitions would have been impossible if the design community had let potential conflicts of interest preclude individuals from entering or judging.

   Unbeknownst to those entrusted with the magazine's care, the glory days of *Charm* were to be followed by a quick fade. What the magazine might have become as society changed around it and as more women acted on their vision can only be imagined, because in late 1958, Street & Smith's young publisher and champion, Jerry Smith, died suddenly. It soon became apparent that Smith had been defending *Charm*'s editorial group against the advertising department. The gender and ideological conflict was that the women were publishing for their peers in the workplace, thereby promoting their increasing empowerment in American society and their participation in the economy, while the advertising department, composed of men, was trying to sell a more traditional magazine to advertisers. Without Smith, the "bottom line" prevailed. Overall, the management was weakened, and *Charm* was bought by Condé Nast publications. Without support for her ideas, Helen Valentine stepped down (or was eased) from the editorship. And the changes began.

Apparently, not everyone (even from the old team) had seen the value of *Charm*'s message. When former fashion editor Eleanor Hillebrand Bruce became *Charm*'s new editor-in-chief, she decided to make the magazine, in Roger Schoening's words, "less stern and single-minded about working women and more up-to-date in its fashion coverage."[49] Another editor, who worked at *Charm* just before it was discontinued, joined the publication solely because it offered her a higher salary. "It had no prestige," she comments, and, dismissively recalling its special audience, she remembers it as "a ghastly thing, [that had] organized [a conference] on the 'two-paycheck marriage.'"[50] Given these conditions and coworkers, Pineles reluctantly continued to work at *Charm* for the new editor and even developed a new design for the October 1959 issue. That summer, however, the issue (in both senses) became moot: Condé Nast bought Street & Smith just months after S. I. Newhouse had acquired control of Condé Nast's *Vogue, House & Garden*, and *Glamour*. Though *Charm* and *Mademoiselle* had coexisted happily for years at Street & Smith, it was now believed that, as Pineles explained, "*Charm* and *Mademoiselle* were in competition, so *Charm* ceased publication."[51] This also ended *Charm*'s competition with Condé Nast's *Glamour*.

Charm's demise marked the end of the close collaboration between Valentine, Pineles, and Ellis. By then a grandmother of four and great-grandmother of seven, Helen Valentine moved to *Good Housekeeping* magazine and worked as a columnist until her retirement in 1963. Her monthly column, "Young Wife's World," was for the generation of women at home during the space race and the cultural, social, and political upheavals of the 1960s. She continued to write against the prevailing messages to women, and she encouraged women to become independent, educated, and involved with their families, their communities, and the world. One of the memorable lines from her column is "Your life does not revolve around the whiteness of your wash." In 1989, Helen Valentine was posthumously inducted into the Publishing Hall of Fame for her "lifelong commitment to consumer magazine publishing." The accompanying statement in the program said: "By acknowledging magazine publishing as an art as well as a science, we recognize Helen Valentine as a practitioner of both. . . . [She] stood as the consummate role model, and a symbol of the emergence of women as a force to be reckoned with in the marketplace."

As *Charm* was "folded" into *Glamour*, Estelle Ellis continued her promotion work for the older magazine, and in time, for the rest of

above left: Pineles on a panel about magazine art direction (photograph by Tom Milius).
right: Pineles on 1951 American Institute of Graphic Arts magazine design jury; juror on her right is James M. Fitch, editor of architectural magazines.

Condé Nast's properties. She operated her own consulting practice, serving businesses and educational and cultural institutions by identifying signals of social change. Over the years, her projects provided a basis for continued collaboration with Pineles as a designer.

Cipé Pineles stayed on with the new owners through the many changes in editorial direction, and then, along with most of the *Charm* staff, she moved to *Mademoiselle* magazine after *Charm* ceased publication in the fall of 1959. Within months, and with appalling synchronicity, her private life would be severely ruptured as well; she would lose her main supporter, confidante, and foil.

As creative director of advertising and sales promotion for the CBS Television network beginning in 1951, William Golden valued his staff (at different times made up of Lou Dorfsman, George Lois, Kurt Weihs, Mort Rubinstein, Tom Courtos, and others). He stood up for their work in the face of criticism; he never took undue credit for their efforts. Though he was a tough boss, he was liked and respected. Jack Cowden, an associate, recalled that those who worked with Golden agreed "he had a greater impact on their careers than almost anyone they ever met. He was a constant source of speculation, a favorite topic of conversation." In fact, there was "one occasion when a group of us sat down to lunch and someone said: 'Shall we order first, or start talking about Bill right away?'"[52]

In addition to developing the well-known CBS "eye" service mark, Golden and his staff created a successful and greatly admired corporate identity and promotional practice.[53] From the lowliest black-and-white newspaper advertisement to elaborate program kits announcing new shows, through the use of the best artists and illustrators for large newspaper announcements and special commemorative publications, Golden kept his eyes and hands on the details of design, art, and typography, and demanded the highest standards from himself and others. He also refused to be pretentious about design. For example, Philip Johnson, curator of a small graphic design show at the Museum of Modern Art, asked Golden about his use of two rectangular maze forms in the piece exhibited and suggested that he was influenced by Mondrian. Pineles, who was standing nearby, reported that "William Golden, who stood for no nonsense, replied 'Not at all, influenced by looking at mazes.'"[54]

Unlike most art directors, Golden was interested in the management's policy decisions and was concerned with and involved in the content of some of the television programming. During the McCarthy period he was criticized for using Ben Shahn as an artist and instructed to stop using him because CBS had received letters threatening that advertisers would pull out. Bernarda Shahn remembers her anger that he gave in. "Bill said, 'You know I could resign, but I could do more good staying at CBS than I could if I resigned in protest.' Ben loved Bill and didn't take offense, but I did. . . . When Leo Lionni, the art director of *Fortune*, heard about this, and he heard it right away because the grapevine in those days was very active, he called Ben immediately and asked him to make the next cover of *Fortune* magazine. And Ben did."[55] This was a way for the art and design community to support each other and may even have been a subtle slap on the hand by one corporation to another. *Fortune* was the premier business magazine, published by conservative Henry Luce.

CBS's corporate lines of authority could be breached; good ideas could come from many sources. Golden was interested in all aspects of the business. Frank Stanton and others valued his involvement, even if his position did not warrant it, and Edward R. Murrow and Fred Friendly of the news division respected him. The televising of the McCarthy hearings prompted much internal debate at CBS, with Golden in favor of airing them.[56] When the network later got nervous about Murrow's show on McCarthy and pulled the advertising budget, Golden independently designed and placed the *New York Times* advertisement that Murrow and Friendly paid for.[57] After the influential show was aired, and so well received that CBS was no longer so scared, Ben Shahn "resumed work for CBS. It was a great day for art, CBS, and America."[58] Later, during the heyday of the quiz shows in the mid-50s, Golden tipped off Murrow and Friendly that there was cheating, and, hoping to clean up the problem (at least for CBS), he suggested that the network do an investigative show. That show was never produced, and the stage was set for the public uproar when the scandal was revealed.[59] Later, as a participant in the (failed) face-saving negotiations, Golden was outraged at having to deal with the same lawyers who had earlier quashed his show idea, stating it "would be in bad taste."[60]

The design perfectionism, the hard work, the corporate politics, and his heavy smoking, a habit prevalent in the 1950s, were not prescriptions for good health. William Golden apparently knew he had heart problems but did not share this with his wife. On a fall day, at lunch with Fred Friendly, Golden recalled the shame of the quiz show

Jury for the 1949 AIGA *Printing for Commerce* exhibition included Ladislav Sutnar, far left, Will Burtin, center, and William Golden, far right (photograph by John Hlinka).

scandals and bemoaned that the good name he had fostered for CBS had been diminished. "Like Murrow, he was one of broadcasting's last angry men, and like Ed, he loved CBS. . . . Bill's anger turned to sad despair about where the industry and CBS were headed. The last thing he said to me that afternoon was 'You guys should have done that show.'"[61] Late that same day, Kurt Weihs found him "with arms and head on his desk. He said 'I don't know what's wrong, my arms hurt.' He was perspiring. He asked me to walk with him to get his car. I offered to drive but he said no, Cipe would worry. She was waiting at [her magazine] on Madison Avenue, got in and they drove off."[62] On the ride home, Golden continued to voice his despair about CBS and, perhaps too subtly, his concerns about his current health. According to a friend of theirs, "Cipe and Bill were driving home from the office to Stony Point and he asked her 'if someone became ill, do you know what you would do, you know, about stopping the car?' The next day he was gone."[63] It was October 23, 1959; William Golden had a heart attack during the night and died, age forty-eight. Pineles called the Fitches in the middle of the night; they were the closest friends.

For Pineles and their son this was a devastating blow—an adored husband and father was dead in the prime of his career, and their developing family was interrupted. Eight-year-old Tom had to face a loss from which he would never recover—his whole world changed. The Golden years had ended.

Just as each perfor-
mance in Lincoln Center
is produced under the
direction of a "designer"
in one or more of the
performing arts, so it is
essential that each
message emanating
from Lincoln Center be
produced under the
supervision of a designer
in the communication
arts.

(Cipe Pineles in 1966 Design
Program for Lincoln Center)

[New Lives]

1961   Cipe Pineles marries Will Burtin on January 28
1961–72   works for Will Burtin, Inc. as consultant designer
1962   begins teaching at Parsons
1964   work in AIGA's "American Magazine Show"
            works on Illinois pavilion with Burtin for New York World's Fair;
            Will Burtin designs Kodak pavilion at World's Fair
            freelance illustration for *Ladies' Home Journal*
1965–70   designer for Lincoln Center
1965   freelance illustration for *House Beautiful*
            Carol Burtin marries Robert Fripp
            Will Burtin organizes Vision '65 conference
1966–69   Pineles serves on executive board of national AIGA
1967   named design consultant to Lincoln Center, Inc.
            Family Service Association mark in Society of Typographic Arts
                    trademark book
            Will Burtin organizes Vision '67 conference
1968   Pineles's Lincoln Center work in *Graphis Annual*
            Russell Sage Foundation work in *Print Annual Report Best*
1969   Tom Golden graduates from Rockland Country Day School
1970   Pineles becomes director of publications for Parsons
1971   Will Burtin creates Chromosome Puff exhibition
            Will Burtin receives AIGA Medal

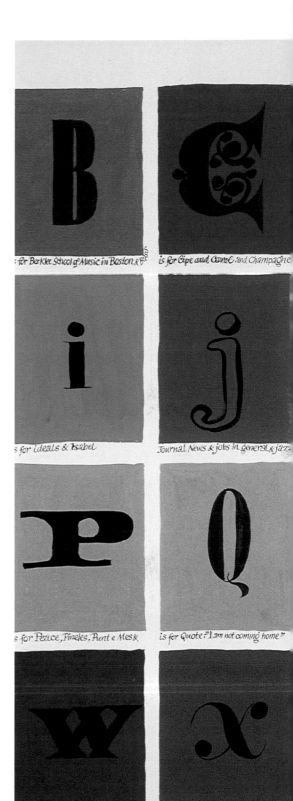

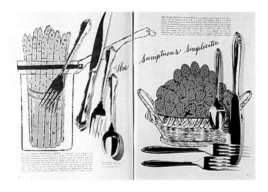

above top: *Mademoiselle*, October 1960, photography by Carmen Schiavone; 8½ by 11¼ in.
center: *Mademoiselle*, July 1960, photography by William Helburn.
bottom: *Mademoiselle*, June 1960, illustrations by Andy Warhol, photography by James Viles.

previous spread: left, Will Burtin and Cipe Pineles; right, Detail from birthday card for Tom Golden by Pineles.

[B]y the end of 1959, William Golden had died, *Charm* was defunct, and Cipe Pineles was again reporting to Alexander Liberman at Condé Nast. Faced with this rupture of both her private and professional worlds, Pineles persevered, as she always had. One of the few times that she publicly referred to her troubles, she said, "I like my work, and in hard times in my life I could forget myself and everything around me by getting deep into a job."[1] In September 1959, when Pineles began her appointment as *Mademoiselle's* art director, press releases were sent to twenty-three newspapers and fashion trade publications, with more to follow to the art trade press. The January 1960 issue was the first for which she was responsible, and she appears on the masthead as Cipe Pineles Golden, in some tribute, as this was the first time she had professionally used his name.

Though Pineles may have intended to dedicate herself to *Mademoiselle*, she and the magazine were not a perfect match. The autonomy on which she thrived was gone, and working for Liberman was not any more comfortable for her the second time. Roger Schoening, the assistant who had moved from *Charm* with Pineles, described her time at *Mademoiselle* as "not a great success. I don't think she really cared about the magazine nor did she really have any fresh ideas on how to rejuvenate it."[2] Ultimately, Pineles would spend only a little over a year at *Mademoiselle*, leaving it to launch her own design consulting practice and for a new relationship with longtime friend Will Burtin.

Though her time at *Mademoiselle* was brief, Pineles was able to make some changes to the publication. She succeeded Bradbury Thompson, the friend and colleague of Pineles's who had championed her membership in the Art Directors Club (ADC). Thompson had worked for *Mademoiselle* since 1945, when he changed it from a publication undistinguished in design to a well-regarded consistent award winner. When Pineles took his position, she changed the cover logo to a smaller Bodoni, round and regular in form, with greater contrast between the thick and thin strokes. Inside, the headlines contrasted more with the text type. Initially, compared to Thompson's, Pineles's pages had more design elements and fewer photographs extending to the page edges, which gave a more obvious structure to the page. Toward the end of her tenure, the overall design became bolder and more colorful, the latter due in part to improving printing technology. Illustrations for fiction were not a primary interest as they were in *Seventeen* and *Charm*, but Pineles continued to use artists from her "stable," such as Joe Kaufman, Lucille Corcos, Doris Lee, Robert Osborn, and Richard Lindner. For drawings of shoes and of food, she continued to use a young Andy Warhol.

Pineles was able to change *Mademoiselle* to some extent, but, compared to the independence she had previously enjoyed, she was simply going through the motions of art direction. She and the art department had to contend with a circulation director's statistics for cover approval, statistics that favored large, friendly faces and little fashion.

They also had to contend with Betsy Blackwell, editor-in-chief since 1936, and not in favor of the changes proposed, even though she had barely survived the shake-up. Other personnel left the magazine, among them Eleanor Hillebrand Bruce, who had moved from *Charm* hoping to be Blackwell's successor one day. Many years later, after a discussion with Pineles, an interviewer would present the events in diplomatic terms, making it sound as though she chose to leave: "The autonomy so necessary to her own creative spirit and to her relationship with her stable of contributors was threatened, and so was the four-day week she had negotiated in lieu of a raise some years before."[3] Actually, she was fired, and she recommended Schoening to succeed her.[4]

It was not easy for Pineles to leave the life and routine she had begun with Dr. Agha in 1932. Great changes had occurred in magazine publishing during the almost thirty years Cipe Pineles had been involved in the industry. There was now a growing group of young women who were working in magazines. Some, like assistants Joan Fenton and Sara Giovanitti, were women Pineles had helped directly, while others, like Ruth Ansel and Bea Feitler, had been brought up through the ranks at Hearst and Condé Nast. The paradigm of male art director had certainly been broken; women in the field were increasingly independent and were receiving notice and some acclaim for their work. Though women's participation in art direction still did not equal that of men, Pineles had played a significant role in changing attitudes and opening doors. Leaving the industry to which she had contributed so greatly must have been painful. Pineles may have foreseen and even been relieved by her dismissal, but she was more upset than she revealed to most people.[5] The last issue with her name on the masthead was for December 1960.

Her decision to leave magazine publishing was based on several factors. Perhaps Pineles realized she had run out of new ideas for magazines; perhaps taking on one more magazine, one more editor, and one more publisher was too much. She was at an important juncture in her professional life. At the same time, her friendship with Will Burtin had turned into something even closer; they decided to marry in January 1961. Hilde Burtin had died in October 1960 after a long illness that was hard on her husband and daughter. Many of their friends in the area, the Levys and Pineles in particular, had been supportive during and after this lengthy period. Pineles could readily sympathize, as she was feeling lost in this first year after Golden's death and was faced with the upbringing of eight-year-old Tom. She and Burtin started spending more time together after his wife's death. Pineles knew him and Carol very well, as he knew her and Tom. They had shared family lives, friends, neighbors, and colleagues for years. In an objective way, their merger made a lot of sense, as each was yearning for a return to a stable and family-oriented personal life, and as Pineles was struggling through the year at *Mademoiselle* and having to make decisions about work. The decision also had a subjective dimension, as Carol Burtin

Pineles and Burtin on the same panel, probably for *AIGA A Critique of the Magazine Show* in 1953; others from left are Ernst Reichl and George Samerjan.

told it: "It was a very numbing time for a lot of us. [My father said he] felt the need to make a straight line; everything was done in graphics terms, but in some way [marrying Cipe] sort of continued normalcy. I think they came to love each other. I mean there certainly was attraction there, they liked each other, and they both realized it was a good idea. In some ways, the real love only grew as opposed to what there was [at the beginning]; there was enough love to do it, but a lot was like and respect."[6] Pineles mentioned to a friend that she was surprised she could fall in love again at her age.[7] She was fifty-two years old.

Will Burtin was as different from Cipe Pineles as William Golden had been. While Pineles was warm and gregarious, Burtin was quite the opposite. He was in many ways one stereotype of a German: tall, stately, quiet, and precise. Some found him a bit authoritarian and exacting. He was fascinated by technology and science, and committed to perfection in design. For example, the art staff at *Fortune* had the saying "There's a pica; there's a point; and there's a Burtin."[8] Differences in temperament and design sensibilities aside, Pineles and Burtin made a marriage based on mutual respect for each other's abilities and accomplishments. Theirs was a deepening love. A note on lined paper, dated July 1964, reads: "CIPE DEAR: We must consider ourselves very lucky people. Our troubles are merely troubles of life and not of happiness and health. We must remind ourselves of this when we are busy and when we are not. There is no worse status than not being, or not being aware of love when being. The universe means nothing but what we are doing for each other is everything. —Big words? Perhaps. Foolish words? No. One gets merely into an age when things make a little more sense. Love, Will."[9]

Pineles compared her husbands and said about her marriage to Burtin: "I look back on this time with gratitude. Though they shared the same profession two more dissimilar temperaments I can't imagine. Both of these men had rigorous standards of design. Will Burtin, perhaps because he was born and trained in Cologne was more rigid, less flexible in his decision making. Bill Golden, who was equally diamond sharp in his philosophy, was more fluid in his approach to a design solution."[10] Burtin's predilection for order could have come from his training in traditional typesetting combined with a mind attracted to the scientific method and applied technology. Born in 1908 to a Catholic couple in Cologne, Germany, Burtin grew up poor. His mother was German, and his father, to whom he credited his ability to reason, was a Flemish-French chemist. Burtin's formal education was permanently interrupted by World War I. After the war he was an apprentice to Dr. Knöll, a typesetter and typographer, for four years. He continued his education with evening courses in design at the Cologne Werkschule, where he also taught. He married Hilde Munk (1910–1960), one of his students, in 1932. They became design partners and worked in graphic design, exhibition design, and motion pictures until 1938.

The Burtins' practice was successful, and they had clients from several European countries. Noticed by the Nazis, Burtin was recommended as a designer to Hitler in early 1938. He met with Hitler twice. There was pressure for him to accept a commission but he was reluctant, in part because Hilde was Jewish. "I was asked, as a non-Aryan, to design an exhibit on the effects of Nazi culture and civilization on the non-Aryan mind. They were insidious. I couldn't refuse and stay in Germany."[11] On the second visit he asked for a visa, explaining that he wanted to take a short Mediterranean cruise that would allow him to "consider the offer without the pressures and interruptions" of his practice and teaching.[12] As soon as the visas arrived, the Burtins packed two bags and took the first ship for the Mediterranean. They got off at the first port, applied to enter the United States, and were sponsored by a cousin of Hilde who was already in residence. In June 1938, Will and Hilde Burtin arrived in the United States.

Burtin made contacts easily in New York and got work almost immediately because he was known in the United States through publication of his work in *Gebrauchsgrafik*. Cipe Pineles remembered him appearing at Condé Nast; she helped with some translating while he interviewed with other art directors.[13] One of his early commissions was a cover for *Architectural Forum*; he also designed exhibits for the New York World's Fair. Within a year of his arrival, Burtin also began teaching at Pratt Institute, where his students helped him learn English. In 1959, he became head of Pratt's Advertising department, changing it into the Visual Communication department. The new name was a sign of deep changes in American graphic design and design education, occurring in large part due to immigrating European designers like Burtin.

During World War II, Burtin worked for the newly organized Office of Strategic Services. He designed teaching manuals for soon-to-be aerial gunners who were teenage boys, often semiliterate, whose lives depended on understanding and operating complex guns in the context of flight mechanics and battle. After the war, Burtin was art director of *Fortune* magazine for four years. In this premier business journal he was able to fully develop his ideas about the visual presentation of complex processes and natural and mechanical relationships. The graphical displays with charts, diagrams, maps, and the use of the best illustrators and photographers of the time were a revelation to *Fortune*'s business audience and to other designers. These displays were part of larger presentations that contained text and images organized as counterpoints to each other. "One could get the sense of a story by simply following the layout with the text acting as a clarification and reinforcement," reported Ezra Stoller, photographer and collaborator.[14] Such treatment of the "text" did not always endear Burtin to the authors; he was concerned with the totality of the communication and presented it in the precise typographic form he had learned in Cologne.

Burtin's small American studio, opened in 1949, did work for several major corporations, including pharmaceutical and chemical

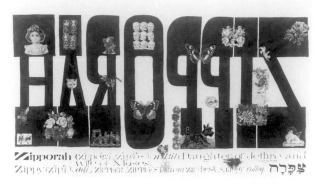

Name pictures for friends and relatives painted and lettered by Pineles; flowers, angels, animals are stickers added by Will Burtin from the collection of his first wife.

companies. His major client of many years was the Upjohn Company, for whom he designed *Scope*, a quarterly publication for doctors, and for whom he produced large-scale models of parts and processes of the human body. Finding American designers "insular" when he first arrived, Burtin showed them both the totality of the corporate identity concept (that corporate identity is created by all visual and verbal messages rather than simply by a single logo or service mark), and how to use design to educate the public about scientific and technological facts, processes, applications, and issues that were invisible, complex, and difficult to understand. Burtin said, "What took years to discover should not take years to communicate. Einstein spent years developing his theory of relativity; it should take only weeks to communicate. The role of design is to make technology available, accessible. And in turn there is a need for humanistic values in the application of technology."[15]

After arriving in the United States, the Burtins did not continue their joint practice, though Hilde may well have continued to assist Will as he got started. Within five years, their only child, Carol, was born. When the family moved to the country, their simple and modern house was gradually filled with the mechanical gadgets Burtin enjoyed and a variety of museum-quality American pieced quilts the couple collected on their frequent weekend trips around the rural Hudson River Valley. As his companion in both their escape from Germany and their new life in America, Hilde was Burtin's only tie to his roots and the past they did not discuss. This was lost at Hilde's death.

Upon his new marriage, Will Burtin and Carol moved willingly into Pineles's house in Stony Point. Her style and the house comforted them; their house was, now, too much Hilde's house. They brought with them the antique American quilts, many of which would grace the walls, and Burtin's collection of mercury glass, huge glass balls coated inside with the silver-colored metal. They suspended one of the balls above the dining room table.

Burtin and Pineles's union created a new family with two children several years and many experiences apart. Tom and Carol had known

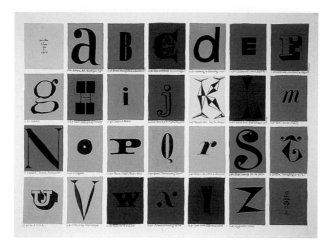

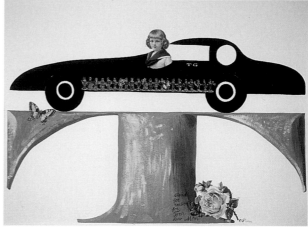

Birthday cards by Pineles for Tom Golden's nineteenth and twenty-first birthdays; 24 by 18 in. The car was delivered separately.

each other since they met over a teddy bear; he had been a much younger "pest" when they were still visiting each other's homes. Now Carol was attending Barnard College/Columbia University, and she visited Stony Point on weekends. For most of her life, Carol had known Pineles as part of the close-knit group in Rockland County; she had memories of the elegant house and the wonderful parties. Since she was about eleven years old, Carol had been receiving the gold safety pins from Tiffany's that were Pineles's mark, and she appreciated her stepmother's fine taste and constant energy. Over the years, Carol became somewhat of an advisor to her father and Pineles as they tried to help Tom develop his interests and skills and find a career.

As an only child, Carol had developed a close relationship with her father; she was interested in his work and good at languages. When she was about five, he used her handwriting for an advertisement for Upjohn. Another time, she rearranged some circles in a layout he had on his desk. Hilde said that Carol's arrangement was better than Burtin's, and it became a cover for *Scope*.[16] Twice as a teenager Carol went to Europe to help interpret her father's exhibits for government agencies. She also helped him edit his writing—he loved words and was profligate in their use—and developed skills that were useful when she became a television producer in Toronto. Through her parents' contacts abroad, she was able to teach in Great Britain, where her fiancé, Robert Fripp, was finishing his degree.

Tom Golden was almost ten when his mother remarried. Again he had a family; he had even acquired an older sister. While his mother was inclined to be indulgent, his stepfather provided more discipline and stability. Though Burtin was a caring and constant parent for him, Tom remembers being less than enthusiastic about his new stepfather and refusing to change his name because he did not want the initials T. B. In hindsight, he acknowledges that it was difficult for Burtin to deal first with a "liberated" ten-year-old boy and then with a teenager during the 1960s, but he now understands that Burtin meant well.[17] The intense focus of the household and its members affected Tom both positively and negatively. Tom's artistic talent was nurtured and appreciated; at the same time, the surrounding standards and expectations were incredibly high. Not a natural student, Tom developed several areas of interest that his parents supported. He considered art school but felt the legacy was too strong to pursue that direction. After graduating from Rockland County Day School, he studied music at the Berklee School in Boston and pursued a musical career for many years.

At one point during his difficult high school years, Tom had a problem typical during the 1960s—school regulations about hair length. Perhaps as a way to show her sympathy for his problems and to find a way to communicate with him, and perhaps because she, too, was frustrated by the narrow views of the school, Pineles decided to create a book called *Hair Apparent* (pun intended) in 1967, and dedicate it to Delilah. She researched famous American founding fathers and other prominent and significant men who had sported long tresses, from Jesus Christ to Albert Einstein and John Lennon, to name a few. Similar to the yearbooks she would create for Parsons School of Design in later years, *Hair Apparent* was a combination of text (written by Ed Zern) and historical images from wide-ranging sources. The format was a seven-inch square. When she wrote to a publishing friend thanking him for encouragement, the book was called *Male Hair—Malheur*;[18] a bilingual pun, the French means both "bad luck" and "unhappiness." She showed the prototype to several publishers but there was no further interest and it remained an amusing dummy.

Pineles's new life with Will Burtin radically changed both her lifestyle and her design practice; she started to travel and moved into areas of design other than magazines. Through William Golden, her professional affiliations, and her work at Condé Nast, Triangle Publications, and Street & Smith, Pineles had been among the small group at the center of the New York art and design world. Until the late 1950s, New York defined both the east coast and American creative worlds, but during the 1950s, film innovations in Hollywood and new opportunities in postwar industries began to draw designers to California, creating two design hubs. Though she had a few English friends from her *Vogue* work in 1937, it was through Will Burtin that Pineles joined the international group of creative people that represented Europe's design center. By the early 1960s, Burtin had been in the United States for twenty years and had maintained an international network through projects and conferences. In addition, he was a member of the small, prestigious Alliance Graphique Internationale (AGI), where membership was (and still is) by invitation only. Now that she was not tied to a regular publication production schedule, Pineles had the freedom to travel: "His commissions required frequent trips both here and abroad. I went along with pleasure. Will felt it was urgent for designers to communicate not only with other designers but also with writers, scientists, architects, and philosophers all over the world, and he soon found himself a central figure in international design conferences."[19] They began making annual summer trips to Europe, planning projects, and maintaining their friendships.

Now Pineles had even more friends and colleagues to entertain. While William Golden turned his wife's parties into gatherings he enjoyed, Burtin had another approach. "They kept him from thinking," Carol explained. "My father's defense, if it was summer, was to go out and lie in his Barwa chair. He would remove himself, with his yellow legal pad, if necessary with a flashlight. . . . He preferred not to have his time interfered with."[20]

If privately the Burtins had come to live with Pineles, professionally, the opposite happened: Pineles moved into his studio, Will Burtin, Inc. ("Visual research and design") on East 58th Street. From that office, she worked on illustration commissions and a proposed magazine project, completed design work in association with Estelle Ellis's Business Image, Inc., and launched her independent design consulting practice, which serviced Lincoln Center for the Performing Arts, Russell Sage Foundation, Family Service Association, and the Museum of Early American Folk Arts, among others. She also began teaching at Parsons School of Design.

One project, which spanned Pineles's widowhood and the first year of her new marriage, was *The Visual Craft of William Golden*, a book edited by Cipe Pineles Burtin, Kurt Weihs, and Robert Strunsky, and designed by Pineles and Weihs, "with Mr. Burtin serving as consultant."[21] Dedicated to Tom Golden, it was a tribute in the form of a compilation of Golden's work for CBS, the text of three of Golden's public statements, and essays by Burtin, Ben Shahn, Feliks Topolski (an artist who worked with Golden), and Jack Cowden (a colleague at CBS). Frank Stanton wrote the preface. Its publication was followed by an April 1962 exhibition of Golden's work at the AIGA gallery in New York. The exhibition traveled across the United States and to several sites in Canada; it was held at typefounders' and publishers' venues and at art and design schools, colleges, and universities.

When Pineles and Burtin decided to work in the same studio, they had intended to collaborate on projects. They did work together on a few Lincoln Center projects and a slide program on Abraham Lincoln for the Illinois State Pavilion at the 1964 New York World's Fair, but ultimately they found working independently easier. As Pineles described, "We only got in each other's way. He felt that my attitude to type was too capricious, even frivolous. The scientific data that stimulated Will into designing a walk-in [model of a human] cell and other breathtaking structures merely put me to sleep."[22] Ellis thinks "work-

above: *Eight Recipes for Summer* an eight-page sequence for Italian magazine *Panorama* illustrated by Pineles.
below: Cover of 1962 book on William Golden edited by Pineles.

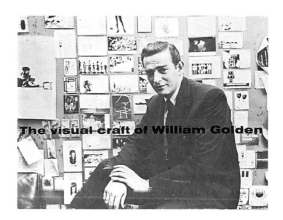

The visual craft of William Golden

above: Cover of catalog for folk art museum, designed by Pineles in 1962; 10 by 8 in.
below: 1969 letter to Ken and Wanda Garland written and decorated by Pineles.

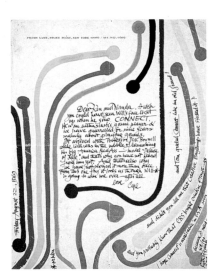

ing in his studio was difficult for her; he was the master of all he surveyed . . . he had run the studio [his way] for a long time. . . . [Cipe never complained] she was realistic, tough and non-self-pitying."[23] Just as she had been influenced by William Golden's work habits, Pineles received type lessons from Burtin. "I was pretty good at type specifications, but now and then Will would look over my shoulder, sit down beside me and without a word redo them properly—after all, he had been a typesetter. It made me furious every time, but just the same, I do them now only the Will Burtin way."[24] Later she recalled that their "most heated marital quarrels were about spacing and Helvetica type; he didn't think there was any reason to use any other typeface."[25] Carol remembers the debates over typefaces but points out that they helped each other quite a bit: "He was helped by her in a kind of person-oriented sense; she brought that warmth to it. She was helped by him because of his cleanness, the purity of the principle—she could be a little slapdash. They both had a good sense of humor and a lot of respect for each other; these things never became major arguments, but they certainly became animated discussions!"[26]

Pineles's extraordinary force of personality and social skills were also employed to support her relationship with Burtin, even in professional settings. Ken Garland, a British designer and author, told a story about when he was an invited presenter and first met Pineles in New York at the Visions conference. Will Burtin had organized the conference, and it unfortunately had gotten off to a bad start. With her characteristic willingness to help, Pineles did her part to get the conference back on track:

> If it hadn't been for Cipe's steadying presence I don't know what might have happened. Though I was fond of Will, I felt something more like love for Cipe, and when she quietly took me aside and said, "Ken, you're the first paper tomorrow morning. If there's any way you can think of to pep this conference up, Will would be so pleased, and so would I," I moved heaven and earth to please her. Will never knew that Cipe had spoken to me as she did, though I'm sure it wasn't the first or the last time that she had supported him in this fashion. In our later contacts over the years, this paradoxical awareness that this tiny person was the strong partner and even protector of her vast husband was reinforced often.[27]

Working out of Burtin's office, Pineles began developing her own practice. In February 1967, Lincoln Center for the Performing Arts, Inc., officially appointed her design consultant. A nonprofit institution, Lincoln Center was created in 1956 to coordinate the community of artistic organizations and bring the arts of music, dance, and drama to the widest public audience possible. Begun as part of a 1955 urban renewal plan and financed through public and private means finally totaling $185.5 million in 1969, Lincoln Center comprised several constituents, some of which were well-established before the Center was conceived of and its building program begun (the Metropolitan Opera and the New York Philharmonic Orchestra, for example) and some of which were created after its conception. Its collection of buildings sits on fourteen acres at the southern end of Central Park on the west side of New York City.[28]

From its inception, Lincoln Center's activities were communicated and promoted through the usual variety of print media, including advertisements, posters, programs, and brochures. Given the number of organizations and the number of events, this produced an avalanche of materials, the design and coordination of which were criticized from the beginning. Critics had difficulty determining Lincoln Center's role and who its audience was supposed to be. This confusion was mirrored by the Center's overall graphic image, which *Print* magazine described as "confused and bland, and wildly uneven in quality."[29] in part because it was handled by several different designers. In a 1967 press release, Jack deSimone, vice president for public information, said, "We believe that consistent design of the highest quality . . . is essential. A unified, strong identity graphics program will be of great value."[30] The press release noted that Pineles was stepping into a new position and that she would supervise Lincoln Center's entire graphics program, "creating a uniform communications environment for the full range of the Center's activities." Pineles also would advise on development of all other visual material. She was taking on a formidable client and her work would have high public visibility—a different kind of visibility than her magazines had.

Though the press release indicated that Pineles began working at Lincoln Center in 1967, she actually started designing for the organization in 1965, when she was recommended by Frank Stanton, who was on the board of directors. In her first year she arranged a retainer for two days per week, but in review she discovered she had worked three. For the year 1966–1967 she was retained as designer/art director for two days per week for a total fee of $10,000. This arrangement would undergo changes over the years as budgets were diminished in times of financial hardship. The agreement outlined that Burtin's office would be engaged for presentation and production services and paid monthly, and that direct expenses for photography, illustration, typesetting, printing, etc., would be charged directly to Lincoln Center. Pineles was to oversee all activities and keep time and expenses to a minimum.[31] Later in the year she had to defend her level of supervision over the design process, from concept through final printing; she argued that her work was distinguished by a particular kind of craftsmanship and that this quality standard was only possible through her direct and personal control.[32]

Pineles was an active and insistent voice for coherence within this large institution that initially had unclear communication goals, later was unable to afford promotional and communication materials, and always was unable to fully coordinate its diverse communication activi-

Cipe Pineles and Will Burtin.

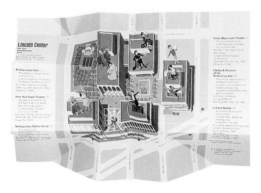

above: Lincoln Center foldout map by Joe Kaufman. below: *Calendar* for Lincoln Center, August–September 1967; 8½ by 11 in. All Lincoln Center materials used by permission of the Archives of Lincoln Center for the Performing Arts, Inc.

ties. When she took the job, Pineles had made it clear that a designer could not produce quality work if he or she was made to work with a committee (this arrangement had previously cost Lincoln Center some fine designers). She worked with two designated representatives, the director of public information and the director of development.[33] For an interview in a prominent graphic design magazine, Pineles described how she saw the job from the beginning: "The differences in quality between existing printed materials were so great and the new needs so pressing, that it was possible to proceed only by solving one problem at a time. The underlying aim on my part, however, was to strive for clarity, simplicity and unity. I wanted to project the feeling that this was a new kind of organization which was in the process of exploring its potential. . . . One of the limitations of the job which I accepted was that the Lincoln Center's printed material should have a quality of understatement and simplicity. Luxurious annual reports, elaborate brochures would have no place in the Center's promotional budget."[34]

After one year of collaboration, Pineles presented to the officers of Lincoln Center an extended "memo" that outlined "A Design Program for Lincoln Center for the Performing Arts, Inc." In her letter to the ghostwriter, who was to "put into better form and better English" Pineles's ideas for design, she explained the points she was trying to make with this group of businessmen and arts administrators:

> Where I give the costs of Will Burtin, Inc., I am really trying to tell them that we don't make any money on commissions nor other deals. Nor are we on salary. L.C. people have been so impressed with the need to use their funds responsibly that they often forget that there are other ways of being "lavish." Like with peoples' time. (And that goes for their own time as well). Neither do I want to be scolding them. L.C. people also have been spoiled by having others offer their services for nothing, just to get in; they have fallen for this gag. But again, I don't want to talk with them about that either. However, I do need to make this memo educational, and I need to make them aware that they must organize themselves in a more businesslike manner and employ my services in a more businesslike way.[35]

Pineles began her "Design Program" by describing the function of design at Lincoln Center; she allied the Center with progressive corporations that had the same obligation to provide effective communication through design programs, as well as to deliver high-quality goods and service. To bolster her arguments she quoted an unnamed corporate executive who asserted that quality communication materials reflect positively on institutions.[36] She spoke of connecting with an audience that suffers from media overload and of the necessity for Lincoln Center pieces to be readily identified so that they would not be discarded before the message was read. She explained that the role of the art director/designer is similar to that of the performance director; both must take responsibility for communicating a meaningful message that is consistent with the ideas of the institution and is presented through quality materials. Pineles then listed immediate design needs (a new letterhead, calendar of events, newsletter, guided tour folder, Philharmonic Hall book, and Lincoln Center picture souvenir book) and long-range needs (a symbol or emblem, a flag, a poster program, gift shop design, house programs and refreshment-related items, a plaque honoring John D. Rockefeller III, the first president of Lincoln Center, a Book of Friends for individual constituents and the Center as a whole, an exhibit program, a Teachers' Guide, and stationery and materials for the Student Program).

Pineles first redesigned and coordinated Lincoln Center's letterhead and stationery system, which helped bring unity of identity to the Center's many parts and programs. She used a condensed Bodoni typeface for the Center's name and a Grotesque sans serif typeface for less important information. The latter typeface, in condensed form, was also used as the primary face for special program identification and publications. Later, various forms of Helvetica replaced the original sans serif typeface. All these materials continually required new variations, as various programs were always being added.

Next, Pineles reworked the Calendar of Events, a monthly mailing that was the main connection between the Center and its constituents. The old format provided a straightforward chronological listing of events in each building, as well as a calendar display that showed the daily events and programs at the Center. Small photographs filled in the empty calendar spaces. Pineles's newly devised format kept the 8½-by-11-inch size (which could be folded in half and mailed) but added illustration and provided variety by using a different colored paper stock and printing ink each month. Pineles hired Joe Kaufman for the illustrations, most of which were of the different buildings. Photographs of performers and performance scenes broke the grid of four columns. For a short time Pineles used illustrations of performers, but some of the performers saw the illustrations as "caricatures" and complained.

Though some of the first work Pineles did for Lincoln Center involved explorations of a mark, symbol, or logotype to identify the Center and its programs, this work was not officially shown until other needs, like the stationery and calendar, had been addressed. Sketches reveal her research into existing marks she admired and a variety of sources for new images. She also examined the Center's architecture and furnishings, experimenting with ideas based on the repeated arches of the Metropolitan Opera House, the central fountain and paving patterns, and some interior lighting clusters. These shapes and patterns were combined with the Center's initials, *L* and *C*. Other sketches explored various typefaces and form relationships between the letters. Several ideas show the influence of new technologies in the early 1960s, when phototypesetting liberated designers from the constraints of metal type and launched a wild period of experimentation with form, espe-

Lincoln Center stationery, 1967.

logo dropped out of a high-contrast photograph of dancer José Limon, and it was used as a dingbat to signify the end of articles in the journal's interior. In fact, the *Journal* covers became the primary site of the mark. The monthly publication was projected as moving "away from the parochial newsletter kind of thing to a publication of rather more general interest."[40] The 16-page, 8½-by-11-inch journal included a re-designed calendar, feature articles, news items, and photographs, and it could be folded in half vertically and mailed. Thirty thousand journals were mailed monthly; an additional seventy thousand calendar sections were mailed separately. The format and typography showed how the newest typographic ideas influenced Pineles's work. She was using a grid structure as an organizing device for type and photographs more strictly; strong contrast existed between the sans serif Aurora Grotesque headlines and the serif Aster text type face, and a simple hierarchy organized the calendar's program listings. Pineles was moving beyond the classical typography she had used on the early magazines (though later issues of *Charm* had shown signs of this change) and was responding to widespread changes in publications and advertising at that time. In addition, she was working from Will Burtin's office, where she learned many typographic lessons. Carol Burtin has commented that the Lincoln Center projects were the one area where they collaborated most. Ultimately, however, the *Journal* was another victim of the stringency that would be required in 1968, and it folded that year.

Lincoln Center periodically reported on its building and fundraising progress in small publications. The first, printed in 1964, was a tall, 124-page booklet that presented the Center's history to date through photographs on the left-hand pages and text on the right. Pineles confined the text to the lower two-thirds of the page and set it in several weights of Helvetica and very condensed Grotesque. The concept and organization of the Center were explained, as was the Center's fundraising program. The architectural plan and its phases were presented with photographs of the construction. Interrupting the small-

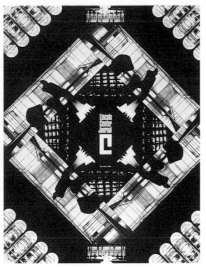

scale rhythms dividing the left-hand pages was a three-page, heroically scaled photographic mural by Arnold Newman with collaged images of the architects and John D. Rockefeller III with models of their buildings. (See page 120.)

Pineles's work for Lincoln Center received design awards and other positive responses, and Pineles developed many close working relationships.[41] But she was frustrated by the continuous squeezing of budgets and her lack of control over certain areas. Pineles considered the Center's use of student designers for theater posters "exploitative" and she disagreed with several of the constituents' independent direction of their own promotion strategies and hiring of designers. She did not think most of the hired designers' work met the standards set by the Lincoln Center work, nor did it have any visual relationship to her work, the result being a fragmented identity for the organization. She also was denied involvement in the well-publicized List Poster program, which was based on the widespread and largely erroneous assumption that famous painters can produce effective poster designs. Furthermore, she was criticized early in 1967 by the trade press for not being vigorous and provocative and given only faint praise for her "skilled and practiced eye" and her "professional" dependability.[42]

In 1968 Lincoln Center was clearly spending more than it was raising, and the offices were reorganized. This restructuring moved individuals with more business than arts experience into positions of control. The communication program was curtailed, and Pineles's arrangement underwent a revision that took her off retainer and paid her separately for each job. After a few months she complained and outlined the personal philosophy that had led her to work for Lincoln Center in the first place:

> I consented at that time to give you my services for exactly half the going professional rate. I turned down an offer for twice that sum by an agency with good project advertising and high design standards.

You were decidedly on the winning side of our former arrangement because in addition I was also generous with my time allotments. Since the concepts you have to sell are the kind of concepts I naturally prefer to spend my energy on, I found it not necessary to be too strict a clock-watcher, or to consider when to stop thinking about your problems to turn my attention and skills in the direction of a more lucrative client.

It has been stated more than once—and not by me—that I am uniquely qualified for a client like Lincoln Center. I have only a limited time to give (three days at the most) and I prefer to give this time to a client of my choice: A client with more to sell than a product—a client who vitally needs my experience and skills—a client who benefits visibly by my efforts on his behalf. Such a client is Lincoln Center.

Now that you are entering a year of austerity you need more than before guidance, support, and the professional authority, as well as the continuity that I bring to your printed image as your designer and consultant.

Pointing out that they did not make changes in fundraising and program directing that required hiring the cheapest people available or dividing up similar tasks among many less-experienced people, she continued:

I suspect that a wrong decision was made in my case because no one at Lincoln Center quite understands and appreciates the importance which design has today in bringing your message compellingly and consistently to your audiences, to establish your image in their minds and memory.[43]

She asked to return to the retainer arrangement, suggesting one day a week if the Center could not afford more. Her wishes were granted, but only temporarily. By May 1969 she had agreed to cancel

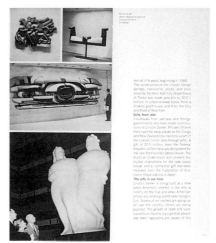

the renewed two-day-a-week retainer contract and again was working on an ad hoc basis.[44] Discussions with Lincoln Center were reasonable and amicable; the organization was in difficult straits and needed to drastically reduce its spending.

Probably the last large project for Lincoln Center was the Summary Report 1956–1969, which was called the "red book" and designed in 1970. The forty-eight-page book was, in part, a celebration of the completion of the capital campaign and the building program. Pineles used one of her favorite formats, the almost-square, with the text, mainly tables, positioned in the bottom three-quarters of the page. The Times Roman type family provided a strong weight and contrasting italic. The scale of the type was small and the effect elegant. Marginal notes were printed in red, as were the thin rules. Full-bleed photographs showed the buildings in use: some pictured crowded public spaces while others depicted quiet scenes of artwork being contemplated by a few people. The cover was typographic: "Lincoln Center for the Performing Arts" in large Times Roman capitals, closely spaced to fill another almost-square and printed in white on the front and in black on the back. The same configuration of words appeared on the mailing envelope. Edgar Young, the Rockefeller staff member most closely connected to the Center's development and the author of the report, wrote of his pleasure with the final result. He mentioned the book's "visual impact" and the "human quality" imparted to the text by the photographs.[45] More recently, he has commented that he enjoyed working with Cipe Pineles and had "great confidence in her ability. She had a knack to anticipate problems and [she produced] a clear and forceful presentation to the public via this design. [It was] attractive, brief and readable."[46] Another Lincoln Center staff member remembered the book as having "good tactile qualities. . . . One would readily pick it up. It said 'read me,' and it was legible to donors who tended to be people over forty-five."[47] (See next page.)

With the exception of the troubled logotype, Pineles successfully established a visual structure and typographic identity for Lincoln Cen-

opposite and above: 1964 *Lincoln Center for the Performing Arts, Inc.*, selected spreads from booklet; 5 by 11⅝ in.; photomural by Arnold Newman; illustration by Ben Shahn. ©Estate of Ben Shahn / Licensed by VAGA, New York, NY. All Lincoln Center materials used by permission of the Archives of Lincoln Center for the Performing Arts, Inc.

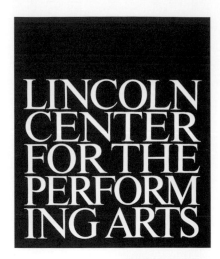

*Lincoln Center for the Performing Arts, Inc.
Summary Report 1956–1969*, cover and selected spreads; 7¾ by 9 in. All Lincoln Center materials used by permission of the Archives of Lincoln Center for the Performing Arts, Inc.

ter. She was constantly mindful of the subtle messages of images and materials. She used a wide variety of colored paper stocks and colored inks (low-cost effects) to achieve interest and variety; formats were limited and standardized when it was practical to do so. Impact was created by bold typographic treatments, strong images, dramatic photographs, unusual colors, colored and printed envelopes for special events. Her working relationship with the top management was close and friendly; several remember visiting her Stony Point house. She educated her appreciative clients about the value of design. Most of her work for Lincoln Center was done during a period of management transition and financial difficulty. She brought communication order for a brief time. However, when her regular retainer agreement was terminated, there was no longer centralized control of the design program, and the cohesiveness she had achieved was not maintained.

The 1960s were an extremely busy decade for Pineles. Her professional time was divided between consulting design for several clients in addition to Lincoln Center and her teaching at Parsons School of Design, which began in 1962, the year after her marriage to Burtin. Pineles's private life was divided between a teenage son and a husband with whom she often traveled. This rich mix was accented by her customary party-giving, the occasions she made to maintain friendships and help younger people in the field, and her commitments to professional organizations. Through her accomplishments and contacts from her own years of practice, and now the addition of Burtin's network, Pineles had developed a reputation that was widely respected and admired. This respect was wide enough to attract the notice of Icograda (International Congress of Graphic Design Associations), which must have been gratifying for Pineles. In response to a colleague's offering the position of president-elect of Icograda in April 1966, Pineles declined, saying (the spelling is hers):

> Anyway, you would not want to concider anyone who has not put away Christmas decorations nor window screens. . . . And now I can go back to my job of parttime wife, mother, stepmother, mother-in-law, organic gardener, plain type cook, fancy hostess, lax and beigel party maker, AIGA director, Rockland Country Day School trustee, Parsons School of Design instructor, amateur plumber, design consultant to Lincoln Center, dressmaker extraordinary, collector of gold safety pins, plant-a-tree charter member conservationist, Sunday painter of recipes, free-lance graphic expert to The Child Welfare League of America, Mental Health Institute, House & Garden, Business Image, Inc., Russell Sage Association, The New York Public Library, Family Service of America, and contributor to The Cook, the new bi-monthly newsletter for gourmets . . . and vice-president of Will Burtin Inc.[48]

Now in her fifties, Pineles was also beginning to receive acclaim for her design beyond the narrow annual awards system that had always recognized her magazine work. Her art editorial work was included in the AIGA's *American Magazine Show* in 1964/5; the Society of Typographic Arts book *Trademarks USA* (1967) included the mark she created in 1963 for the Family Service Association. In 1968 the *Graphis Annual* included her logo for Lincoln Center, and *Print's* "20 Best Annual reports" reproduced her work for the Russell Sage Foundation. Her projects to promote Parsons began to collect awards, too.

Pineles was an invited juror and speaker for many professional design organizations over the years. In the fall of 1970 she spoke about "The Visual Craft of William Golden" (she had edited the book in 1962) as part of the *Heritage of the Graphic Arts* lecture series at Gallery 303, organized and sponsored by Dr. Robert Leslie and The Composing Room. In 1976 the Society of Publication Designers presented a lunchtime program with slides and four speakers on "Jerome Snyder—as I knew him." Pineles spoke, along with Milton Glaser, Richard Hess, and Herb Lubalin. Snyder had been one of her illustrators for *Seventeen*; his wife Gertrude had briefly been her assistant at *Charm* and later interviewed Pineles for her *U&lc* profile. For the same group in 1981, Pineles discussed her early magazine work and innovations in illustration. In 1976 and 1977 she served on the selection committee for the National Magazine Awards given by Columbia's School of Journalism. Here, she recommended that future committees comprise more individuals representing the typographic and pictorial side of the judging in order to foster parity in attention to both the visual and verbal parts of a magazine.

Earlier, when the ADC asked on which committees she would like to serve, Pineles had answered, "Only the committee to admit more women." This remark was flippant rather than an enunciation of principle: in addition to being on the boards of several other design organizations, Pineles was a willing participant on ADC committees. In 1958 she awarded the President's Medal to her old friend Ben Shahn. In her memorable speech about him, she discussed the unnatural separation of fine and "commercial" art and working with Ben. She commented on her trust in his judgment and on the liberty he took in interpreting the text, even to the point of ignoring, in one case, the simple bit of instruction she gave him, which ultimately produced an effective, award-winning piece. (The full text is in the Appendix.) Following her own induction to the ADC's Hall of Fame, she served on its committee twice, the first time as chairman.

Through the 1960s, while Pineles was engaged with Lincoln Center and Parsons, Will Burtin organized several international conferences, continued as a consultant for the Upjohn Company, and worked for Eastman Kodak and other corporations. For Upjohn, Burtin had conceived and designed three enormous, walk-in-sized models, The Cell (1958), The Brain (1960), and The Chromosome Puff (1971). These were first developed for medical conventions but soon traveled to museums in the United States and Europe. The Cell required a year of research, design, and construction. As part of his research, Burtin vis-

STRENGTH
TO FAMILIES
UNDER STRESS

Identity mark for Family Service of America.

ited with scientists. "I have taught myself to speak to scientists. I understand their language, their systems. Now I am trying to convey the essence of this understanding as it applies to other areas."[49]

These exhibits made an enormous impact because of their size and the complexity of information they imparted. The Cell was a generalized human cell, magnified one million times the size of a blood cell, that measured 24 feet in diameter and 11½ feet high. The model was positioned on a metal mirror; a visitor walking through the model had the impression of being wholly inside the organism. The illusion of pulsating movement in a living organism was produced by a blue light that moved around the base at a controlled frequency. The plastic materials drew the light, and the cell appeared luminously alive in the surrounding blackness. Based primarily on medical slides and photomicrographs, the model was a visualization of something never actually seen, and its forms evoked a surrealist world.[50]

Two years later, Burtin's Brain exhibit was an early example of what we now call multimedia. Not about anatomy, this model showed how the brain works in receiving, articulating, and responding to experience. As Burtin put it, trying to understand brain activity by its anatomy "is as inadequate as trying to evaluate sculpture by looking at the sculptor's tools."[51] Limited, for demonstration purposes, to the functioning of the sensory mechanisms of sight and hearing, the model's eyes and ears were the starting points, connected by light-carrying tubes (the neural paths) to aluminum forms representing the essential functional parts of the brain. In the center was a "consciousness screen," where "becoming conscious of a sensation" was shown by various representational images. A stationary audience watched and listened to several sequences of moving, colored light and sound, as the "brain" registered normal activity during both sleeping and waking states.

In 1971 Burtin returned to the walk-in model concept for The Chromosome Puff, an 18½-foot-tall, 289,400-times-life-size model built of aluminum and plastic. Using red and blue balls, the model showed a chromosome in two states: dormant and "puffing," when it produces a chemical that is part of protein production. Again, a complex process difficult to see even in microphotographs was clarified through a visualization real enough for a visiting geneticist to claim, "It's as if I've been here before."[52] Among Burtin's assistants on this model was Edgar Levy, who had done graduate work in mathematics.

The Eastman Kodak exhibit at the 1964 New York World's Fair was the culmination of Burtin's work for this corporation. Here, reminiscent of Eero Saarinen's TWA terminal in New York, Burtin arranged the photography exhibits to flow through a freeform pavilion that surrounded a tower where changing images were presented through rear projection. The pavilion's roof line was to give the impression of a floating and curling magic carpet.[53]

Throughout his career, Burtin traveled to consult with scientists and then to accompany his exhibits. As the president of the American

The Brain, 1960 exhibition designed by Will Burtin (photograph by Ezra Stoller © Esto).

section of AGI, he was in contact with designers throughout Europe and with many other members of international design organizations, of which he was a frequent officer. He collaborated on several conferences that sought to bring together designers with scientists, philosophers and other thinkers. His vision was always broad and searching. He developed programs for the Aspen Design conferences, for two international typography conferences held in the United States in the late 1950s, and two world congresses on communication, Vision '65 and Vision '67 "Survival and Growth." His last project was an exhibition for a United Nations' Human Environment conference.

Pineles appreciated the differences in their thinking processes and design interests. She was a largely intuitive designer who responded to her surroundings in a sensory way and employed color, texture, and form in her design to describe and enliven the subject matter. She loved pattern, decoration, the tactile, and the mistakes caused by human endeavor. She was an expressive designer. Burtin, on the other hand, approached his design projects through research and logical problem-solving, making form analogies for invisible processes, exploring new materials. He was intrigued by any kind of machinery and the latest scientific discoveries. He was interested in the communication of fact and the change of data into information for understanding. She benefited from the exposure to the interdisciplinary nature of Burtin's work and to the individuals involved. Pineles's work experience had been in a rather narrow and circumscribed area of design. Her knowledge of the possible problems design could address was considerably enlarged and her circle of friends now encompassed scientists and philosophers in addition to artists and editors. This was a world to which she would have had no other access. Pineles and Golden had been part of a small media world attached to certain business sectors. With Burtin she had entrée to wide, international academic and scientific circles and other business sectors. Any relationship is a source for individual expansion, but the worlds of Pineles and Golden had almost overlapped. With Burtin, most of the territory was wholly new.

In an interesting echo of her private sphere, Pineles would also enlarge her professional one from practicing design to teaching design. During the years of her magazine career, Cipe Pineles had participated in many conferences, symposia, workshops, and public discussions about publications. During the academic year 1950–51, while in transition between *Seventeen* and *Charm*, she had been a visiting critic at Parsons School of Design. She had not, however, been involved with design teaching in any formal or regular way. This changed in 1962, when she had been away from the magazine routine for two years and was just establishing an independent practice out of Burtin's office. Parsons offered Pineles a faculty appointment that would continue, without a pause, for twenty-five years of annual contracts. Now fifty-four years old, Pineles embarked on a second career.

Cipe Pineles exuded an
almost mystical grace.
She was a woman with a
powerful magnetism . . .
with a seductive person-
ality that totally enrap-
tured me. . . . When
Cipe spoke, [I] listened.
But her requests (or
rather demands) were
always that we do things
for *others*, and most of
all, for her incredibly
fortunate students.

(George Lois in funeral remarks)

She was at heart a
teacher; if you [were]
willing to learn, she
[was] willing to teach.

(Baron Stewart interview)

[Second Career]

[P]arsons School of Design, at the time Pineles began her academic career, was an independent art and design school with fewer than 500 students in lower-midtown Manhattan. As is common with urban schools of this kind, it had a commuter student body who often worked part-time, if not full-time. The faculty comprised creative professionals working in the metropolitan area who could afford a break in their daily routines to teach a three-hour course once a week. For the students this structure provided intense classes of focused critiques by practicing designers who were often well known and well connected. At the same time, however, there were no opportunities for the valuable discussions that occur during the process of design, only limited time for supervised construction of projects and long hours of necessarily independent work.

For the first eight years of her involvement with Parsons, Pineles taught one three-hour, weekly course each semester in the Fashion Illustration department. For this she initially was paid $1,000; at the end of her eighth year, her salary was $1,216.[1] In the preliminary negotiations, she was leery of the quality of the students, suggesting that Cooper Union students were superior. The department chairman persuaded her: "You will enjoy the full freedom at Parsons to be what you are, and to teach what you believe. This, in fact, is what you would be hired for." She would teach the third-year class; her students would already have basic drawing skills and would be ready for conceptual problems. Pineles was reassured that while the salary was low, it was comparable to that paid to others.[2] Later, with another chairman, she would ask to be the highest paid teacher; he paid her one dollar more than he paid Henry Wolf and she was satisfied.[3]

In 1970 her class Graphics for Illustrators was described as the "application of fashion illustration skills to the field of general illustration."[4] In the beginning, she said, "I didn't like teaching. . . . Nobody in class was interested. They were in art school, it looked to me, because it was easier than going to college."[5] Pineles herself had been an enthusiastic student; now she had to motivate her classes. "I didn't know how to get twenty captive people interested in what I wanted to say. Marvin Israel was teaching a class next door, and when there was a small recess, I told him, 'It's all too much.' He tried to calm me down and said, 'Look, stay with it a little longer, and I'll tell you what to do. Teach them what interests *you*.'"[6] This worked and she was hooked. She could talk about her own illustration assignments or the challenges she gave to her magazine artists; she could recall her days with Agha or how she overcame boredom with given materials at *Glamour*. Later, she reflected, "Recently and only by chance, I discovered that what impressed one very talented student most in my publication design course was that I made him and everyone else in the class hang up their coats and put away their paraphernalia before we went to work. He said I created a special ambiance in my class. What a droll way to come to the realization that graphic design, communicating, has a lot to do with making order out of chaos."[7]

left: Editorial Design class at Parsons c.1971, Pineles and David Levy standing right of center while student presents to visiting critic, a senior editor at *Life*.
below: Early mark for Parsons School of Design by Cipe Pineles.

Good teaching in a school setting is more than presenting the problem, helping the students through the process to solution, and critiquing the final product. A contract is developed between the teacher and the students; the act of teaching, especially design teaching, which uses a studio or laboratory methodology that demands close interaction, requires trust. It is also necessary to "catch" the students' attention and interest. Pineles's personality was well matched to the task. The students with whom she connected found her an engaging presence: beautifully turned out, she always had style—in the 1970s this meant Marimekko dresses, multiple necklaces and a favorite starburst pin, earrings, and hair coiled up in a bun and decorated with a scarf. She had her Austrian-accented voice, her sparkly charm; she was funny and full of life. She was up on the latest trends even if she did not like them, and she was full of practical information and cultural depth. She had energy to spare and she was there, with them, to work.

In 1970, her teaching schedule increased, most likely because the regular Lincoln Center work had ceased. For about six years, Pineles taught two or three classes each semester, first dividing her time between the Fashion Illustration department and the Graphic Design department, where she taught Editorial Design and Publication Design. In the end all her classes would be in Graphic Design, or Communication Design as it later became. Finally, in her second design career, Pineles could put all her talents to work and teach from the fullness of her knowledge and experience.

Pineles established a sequence of courses, Editorial Design in the fall and Publication Design in the spring, that allowed interested and advanced students to move from the hypothetical and ideal to the practical and real. The catalog described the courses: "C218: concept and design of a magazine or other publication subject. Comprehensive layout due at end of the semester. Emphasis on editorial concept as well as format and other design considerations" and "C318: a continuation of C218 at an advanced level with concentration upon the production and implementation of an actual publication."[8] This combination later

would be the basis for Pineles's reconception of the college yearbook, when she and her students created several publications that were so intriguing and inventive they escaped the confines of the school and their expected and captive student audience.

For the first course, Pineles marshaled her considerable experience and contacts in the publishing world. Her teaching approach, as she summed it up, was "encouraging my students to do enough work in school so they will have the confidence to solve the problems that a graphic designer must cope with in the professional world."[9] The semester's work included the following: a concept, shown in a logo, for a new magazine based on the student's interests; four magazine covers; a masthead and contents page; two sample spreads; a complete sequence mapped out for one issue; and an advertisement for the magazine that would run in the *New York Times*. The class brainstormed ideas for subjects, describing appropriate audiences and defending the marketability of their concepts. Pineles always argued for connection with the real world and enthusiasm for the subject. She wanted each student to decide on a personal "turn on" and figure out how to communicate it. She once said in class, "You are not here to do a product, this [magazine] is who you are as a person."[10]

Pineles was an inveterate newspaper clipper and turned this into a teaching method. As one student from the 1970s described, "Every morning she would start class by having students go through the *New York Times* with scissors—she had a favorite pair with gold handles. She taught you to go through and cut out what you liked and put it in a file folder, so you were constantly bringing into life the latest ads, articles, ephemera of the time. She was a classy collector of anything that caught the eye: nice type, nice ad, something fun like gardening— things that connected to the world." Because of time constraints, the class only lasted two or three hours per week; in most cases the students were picking up and reusing images from a variety of sources, though some would do their own photography for covers. The class "was not heavy into art director philosophy. It was more about design; how do you make up a page, balance a page, how does an image work."[11] Pineles's teaching philosophy followed her magazine experience closely; she had trusted her illustrators and photographers to do their best, and she would collect and compose their work into the whole.

Pineles helped her students figure out what was successful communication. Hierarchy was learned by studying the newspaper and analyzing many different kinds of publications. She taught them to organize and articulate the space and how to structure the material. She introduced them to the grid as a structure for typographic cohesiveness. She taught the value of establishing a visual and typographic hierarchy and choosing a set of related and proportional column widths and a set of sizes and proportions for images and the spaces between them. She showed them how to create sequences of spreads and how to control the visual relationships and rhythms between and among the pages that emerge as a reader turns through a magazine. The students began by working at the scale of thumbnail sketches, just as Pineles had always planned her work. A former student who became an assistant remembered, "She taught me that the first thing you do is read the copy; she stressed designing from the inside out, making the work logical before thinking about it in an esthetic sense."[12] The students were not to create only a pretty magazine; Pineles was adamant that "there was no dressing up by design. The point was to create something structurally and conceptually. . . . The concept has to be communicated above all else. The form was subservient to the concept. This was classic design theology. She was good at transmitting that to the students."[13] A student who became a magazine art director described Pineles's teaching: "She doesn't teach style—she teaches content. She teaches you to start with the contents of the magazine and then work from there, rather than just think about what design is going to look nice on the page. It's a very integrated approach to magazine design. It was hard for students to deal with something that unified."[14]

Pineles was open to any and all suggestions on subject matter. One year (1980) the subjects included "College Commuter," "Street Smart," "Peep" (about vision), "Dreams," "New Wave" (music), "Freetime," "Footwear Fetish," "Leftovers," "Travel Bug," "Silks, Satin & Lace," "Garden Indoor," and "Outpatient." Pineles did not try to influence or censor the students' perspectives. One student, whose subject was sex and relationships, wanted to use a short and vulgar word on the cover. Pineles was not shockable; she only commented on the choice of typeface for such a word. Only if an idea was unsellable was it shot down. "I want them to know what is the important problem they have to solve, to respond to the basic communication need of the problem and not to deviate," she explained. "Students have a very big tendency to be mysterious about a problem. They frequently come in with very complicated concepts, and when I ask them to explain, they say they want to avoid being obvious. This is a very common misconception."[15]

During the semester there were critiques of the students' work. Pineles was the same one-on-one as she was when discussing the work with the group: she was tough, she asked questions to keep the students on track, and she made sure the design decisions were about connecting the subject with the audience. The critiques were constructive: she liked to suggest alternatives and was encouraging rather than disparaging.[16] One former student felt she was telling him, "You are a good designer, you have capabilities, you have to stay with it." Self-confidence is one of the biggest things for a designer to develop, especially for women designers, and the student felt Pineles was teaching this by taking the class into her "salon," introducing them to practicing designers, and saying they were good enough to compete.[17] From a former student two years out of school Pineles received a letter saying: "I now think of you with great admiration. You are a highly respected designer, but most importantly you conquered this so-called 'man's world'—a women's libber before it was the fashion."[18] The class envi-

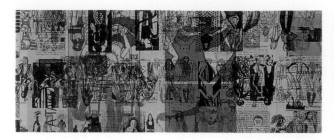

1971 *Yearbook* cover of make-ready sheets and inside gatefold pages of student and faculty self-portraits; 10½ by 8¾ in.

ronment supported real criticism, sometimes not polite. A student remembered that Pineles "was strict but allowed students to work as they liked. She was compassionate with people working hard but ruthless with those who did not come through: she didn't allow much slack. If excited, she would spend extra time after class. She was giving if you were interested."[19] Pineles understood that many students worked at other jobs, with limited time for involved assignments, and often allowed them extra time to complete their projects.

Occasionally, visitors reviewed the work during the semester. At the end of the semester, the students dressed up and presented their work to outside critics invited by their teacher; these were well-known practitioners in publishing who would test the students' work against real-world criteria. Over the years, Pineles invited, among others, Allen Hurlburt, art director of *Look* and writer of design books; Fabio Coen, art director at Pantheon; Lou Dorfsman of CBS; Ivan Chermayeff, designer; Steven Heller, art director and writer on design; Louis Silverstein, art director at the *New York Times*; Walter Allner, former Bauhaus student and corporate art director; and Helen Valentine. In addition to art directors and designers from magazine and book publishers, Pineles invited individuals from sales departments, editors and writers, a writers' agent, a radio commentator on books, and many others known to her through her contact with the design world.

In the spring semester each year, those students from the fall who were particularly interested in the problems of editorial design took Pineles's next course. Here they put into immediate practice what they had learned in the previous class by producing (on a tight schedule) a real book: the Parsons annual yearbook. The yearbook projects were a perfect extension of Pineles's teaching and professional experience. They redefined what a yearbook could be, and some of them "escaped" the school and became popular trade books. The yearbook projects took Pineles back to her days of happy and highly motivated collaboration on magazines; the students were eager and given an unusual opportunity very early in their careers to shape a publication's total content and message. Teachers often bring "real" projects into the classroom for hypothetical solutions; in this case both the creative problem and solution were real. Over time, the yearbooks would provide a forum where the students could explore themes and subjects that interested them: themselves, food, clothes, love, and New York.

While the tradition of yearbooks may be common among schools,

Parsons was an exception. Parson's new dean, David Levy, son of Edgar Levy and Lucille Corcos, initiated the Parsons yearbook in 1970, and by the following spring a new tradition was born. *Yearbook* (1971) was introduced in a preface by Cipe Pineles:

> This is Parson's first yearbook conceived, assigned, designed and executed by a class of third year graphic design students. It was produced as part of normal class room work in the second semester of a course I teach, "Editorial Design."
>
> When Dean Levy asked in December: "How would you like to do a yearbook in the second half of your course and can you get it out by May one?" I answered without thinking: "I'd love to and we will try."
>
> From our first meeting in January with representatives of the Student Council who voted to finance our adventure, it became clear that what everyone wanted in a yearbook was a life-size portrait of Parsons, and no faking, no double images, and no retouching.
>
> We started on January 20th and handed over the mechanicals to the printer April 6th, only two sleepy days and two sleepless nights late.
>
> We invited every student and teacher to add their talents to ours. By the last count we had contributions from 112 first year students, 84 second year students, 72 seniors, 6 writers, 12 photographers, and 43 illustrators. A total of 363 contributors.

The first year, Pineles and seven students put into production a sixty-four-page casebound book, printed in four signatures with two printed black only, one printed black and red, and one printed in process colors, with a tipped-in gatefold section on warm brown paper printed in process colors. The endpapers were portraits of the graduating seniors, printed in black and dark red on the brown paper. Among the acknowledgments in the back of the book is this notice, "Will Burtin—for putting up with two weeks of scrambled eggs for supper, not to mention the layouts for the endpapers which he re-designed, and for which his wife (Cipe Pineles) is taking the credit." The jacket made each book unique: each was cut from make-ready sheets printed on the tan kraft paper; each was a combination of the yearbook's interior drawings, photographs, and type layered in varying combinations of black, red, and green.[20] This small economical step harkened back to Pineles's love for press checks, when she would often carry off the make-ready sheets. In this case, she had taken the students to watch the press run. They were appalled at the waste of paper involved in the setup, and they decided to use the paper for the jackets. It was also a way to bring to the foreground the process and production parts of the book project, which educated the whole student body.

As part of what would become the pattern for the "total yearbook experience," the class started with a solicitation for contributions of ideas and/or artwork for the yearbook. A standard-sized, mimeo-graphed sheet asked for portrait contributions from the faculty, size and media specified—due in two weeks. Pineles contributed a delight-ful sketch of herself in Marimekko, with purse and a Parsons publica-tion in hand. The faculty self-portraits, in addition to the student por-traits on the endpapers and the gatefold, were complemented by departmental group photographs and descriptions, a photo essay, pho-tographs from around the school, some examples of student work, and a reproduction of the Hudson River panoramic mural sketch by Lucille Corcos that dominated Dean Levy's office. A final photograph of the editorial design class managed to incorporate their teacher through a mirror reflection.

Just as Pineles was establishing this course sequence and begin-ning the years of energetic and high-profile teaching and publication for Parsons, her special attention and care was needed by Will Burtin. In May 1971 Burtin received the AIGA Medal, the highest award from the most prominent American professional graphic design organization. Many old friends and professional colleagues attended the dinner and reception at the gallery where an exhibition of his work was mounted. David Levy remembers that Burtin collapsed at the reception, marking the beginning of his declining health.[21] At about the same time, Up-john's corporate organization changed and operations were reduced, re-sulting in the termination of Burtin's consultant relationship. Pineles later saw this professional blow as a contributing factor to his health problems.[22] When Will Burtin died on January 18, 1972, it was of a form of cancer caused by asbestos exposure; in the 1930s he had used an asbestos modeling compound. The funeral service was held in the chapel at the United Nations, where he had been working on a large exhibition for its Human Environment conference. The tributes were many and international. That September, Pineles and Carol went to London to attend a memorial exhibition of Burtin's work at the Ameri-can Embassy, organized by the Society of Typographic Designers.

In her diary for December 12, Pineles wrote: "unfair to suffer so twice; alternative? no happy marriage, no love." Again, she threw her-self into her work; this time she had the enthusiasm of her youthful companions at Parsons to engage her.

The *Bread Book* (1973) started as simply as other yearbooks. Little did anyone realize that the teacher's deep attachment to this most basic food would be matched by a similar level of public interest and appreciation. The students received a valuable lesson in connecting to the zeitgeist. A poster issued the call with an overworked pun to stu-dents and faculty—"We knead your help." They were invited to a bread and cheese party on March 19; they were to bring a recipe and an example of any edible home-baked bread ready to be photographed. Potential participants were reassured that they did not have to be eth-nic for the recipe to be published (a slightly obscure reference to the very popular advertising campaign started in 1965, "You don't have to be Jewish to love Levy's rye bread" [no relation to the dean] and

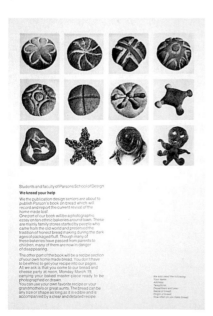

Poster soliciting recipes for *Bread Book* yearbook project.

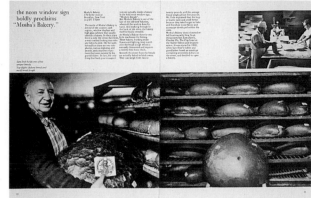

showing a broad cross-section of New York's obviously non-Jewish population).

    Before the poster went up, during the brainstorming session with Pineles, some students were skeptical about her suggestion of bread and baking. To convince them of the potential richness of the subject, she invited them to a party at her house, where she provided wine and cheese to go with all the breads they were to ferret out or to make. The excursion and discoveries of the variety of breads persuaded them.[23] As the yearbook preface put it, eleven students, all Editorial Design seniors, "sifted, kneaded, cut, rolled and shaped" the book under Pineles's direction. The impetus for the subject was the contemporary revival of interest in home bread baking, arising out of the environmental and health food movements. New York City was touted as "a virtual treasure trove of cultures and traditions, . . . [with] more varieties of bread, representing more different nationalities, than can be found anywhere else in the world." Approximately half the book was a photo essay featuring eleven bakeries, many of them family operations, that served Italian, French, Jewish, Egyptian, Scandinavian, and Health/Natural foods. The students did the photography, reporting, and writing. The pages following the photo essay provided recipes and commentary illustrated with photographs of bountiful loaves. Breads and recipes were submitted by many but only twenty nine could be used. These came from students, faculty, family, and friends; among them were Edgar Levy; Dorothy Maas, an illustrator friend of Pineles and Golden; Cleo Fitch, neighbor and wife of James Marston Fitch; and Christine Russo, wife of John Russo, the department chair.

    The book was printed in warm brown and black on flecked and textured wheat-brown paper. There was a loosely used, four-column grid for the type; composition was probably by IBM Selectric. The text was printed in black, as was a recurring bread knife. The breads were all brown and shown as large as possible. While the knife functioned formally as a dark, crisp accent to the soft, brown shapes and as a useful spatial organizer (not unlike a heavy rule), John Russo, Graphic Design department chair and erstwhile bread photographer, said the knife was used because, at one point in the shoot, Pineles thought one

Bread Book, 1973 yearbook, selected spreads showing bakery profiles and recipe pages; 8½ by 11 in. (continued overleaf).

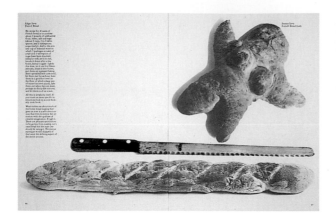

above and opposite: *Bread Book* spreads; note the two printed colors and the bread knife for scale and accent.

large loaf looked like a muffin and added the knife for scale.[24] The cover was a typographic composition, front and back, of the word "Bread" in many sizes and typefaces, printed in black and brown on white. The inside front cover was printed flat brown, and the inside back cover had a surprise: a painting by Pineles of a cut round loaf with a fat bread knife.

Even before the book was delivered by the printer, a writer for the *New York Times* interviewed the class and reprinted one of the recipes.[25] That was only the beginning of the attention paid to this "college yearbook," which drew requests for copies from across the country. The following year Harper and Row picked up the book for a trade edition named *Parsons Bread Book*, published with a new four-color cover, the interior pages printed only in brown, and the visual impact somewhat diminished. While the typographic cover worked for the original design audience, Pineles thought home-baked bread needed to be communicated differently to a mass audience. Her design for the new cover required the collaboration of the Russo family: "Christine had an old family recipe used to make Fastnachts, a holiday fried dough treat. Because I had always been interested in drawing hands, she baked the dough in the shape of hands. We arranged these in a circular pattern for the photo. My brother, Eugene, a professional photographer, took the photo with the bread hands on a wood stained breadboard. Only after we had restained the breadboard numerous times with pine, cherry, walnut, etc., was Cipe satisfied with the color shading contrasting the bread to the background breadboard, and it was accepted."[26] The student group was pictured on the back.

This edition of the book was an extraordinary commercial success, selling out the first printing of 10,000 copies in days; total sales reached 60,000 copies. The book had the odd distinction of having the largest circulation of any college yearbook in the United States.[27] It was reviewed by the radio commentator Stendahl in New York City and in newspapers across the United States, with the only negative note sounded in an Iowa newspaper that (missing the point) did not appreciate the focus on New York bakeries. The book gave Parsons an attractive and respectable face; people from all parts of the country could

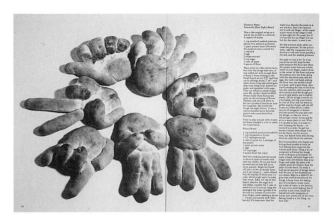
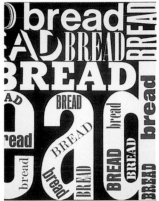
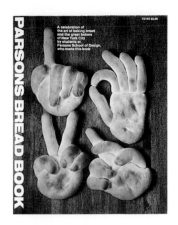

appreciate and relate to the subject matter. Even better, from the viewpoint of Parsons and the students, was the fact that the book was named one of the Fifty Best Books of 1974 by the AIGA and traveled around the world in an exhibition. The students were thrilled, and, of course, their teacher threw a party.

On July 24, 1973, Condé Nast, promoting *Glamour*, ran a full-page advertisement in the *New York Times* with the headline "Think of everything that's happened since they were born and you'll begin to understand the new college generation," followed by a list of forty-seven extraordinary (if not revolutionary) social, cultural, and political changes from the last twenty years. Either Pineles saw this advertisement during her daily reading/clipping or she was shown it by its creator, Estelle Ellis. In any event, it became the inspiration for the next yearbook, *Since We Were Born* (1974), produced by a student group of five. As David Levy said, this publication was more than a yearbook—it was a "generation book," the students' visual response to the events of those twenty years. A partial selection from the book's list of events includes drug culture, women's lib, black power, Lyndon B. Johnson, Vietnam, Berkeley, the Beatles, legal abortion, Cesar Chavez, Ralph Nader, school desegregation, Martin Luther King, Jr., transistors, amnesty, stereo, Pope John, Carnaby Street, coed dorms, the computer, Kent State, Richard M. Nixon, the pill, Chicago '68, Woodstock, Watts, John F. Kennedy, man on the moon, and the eighteen-year-old vote. Parsons students and some faculty illustrated and commented on the issues through typography and lettering, photography, drawing, painting, collage, three-dimensional exhibition, assemblage, printmaking, photocopying, and magazine design. Their work appeared on the pages printed in black and a variety of process colors. The book covers and endpapers consisted of small headshots of the graduating class, printed as duotones with silver type. The old trio was united on this project: Helen Valentine, in her seventies, was a guest critic who blessed them with "You've got a book." (See next page.)

Just as Pineles began teaching two courses at Parsons in 1970, the school acquired a new dean. This was David C. Levy, the eldest son of Pineles's closest friends, Lucille Corcos and Edgar Levy. Pineles had

top center: *Bread Book* typographic cover based on Pineles's painted sketch shown above, approximate size.

top right: Trade edition photographic cover of *Parsons Bread Book*, 1974.

Since We Were Born, 1974 yearbook cover and spread; 11 by 8½ in.

watched Levy grow up; William Golden had encouraged Levy's jazz music interests by giving him a record player and records from CBS. A much younger family friend of many years was now Pineles's boss. She made her teaching contracts with him; she also became involved as designer and art director in the comprehensive promotional and publication programs envisioned and implemented by David Levy as he expanded the school and its programs, of which the reconfigured yearbooks were only a small part.

Within a few years, the complexity of Pineles's relationship with Dean Levy was increased by an additional private and happy tie known to friends and family. Cipe Pineles and Edgar Levy, David's father, were lovers from sometime in 1973 or 1974 until his death in the summer of 1975. Lucille Corcos had died about a year after Will Burtin. Of the three couples who had moved to the country, lived in proximity, shared the childhoods of their children, and occasionally commissioned each others' work, now only Cipe and Edgar were left. Though it may appear odd from the outside, David Levy observed that there was a kind of internal logic for the group, and like the "ten little Indians, there were now fewer and fewer."[28] The children (Carol, Tom, David, and Joel), three of them already parents themselves, were amused by and pleased for their parents, who were now in their mid-sixties. Pineles and Levy both had been seriously affected by their spouses' death and found common ground and companionship. Serendipitously, they also found love and passion.

After Will Burtin's death, Pineles had taken a while to pull herself together. As usual, she did this through work: during that period she produced some of the best of the Parsons yearbooks and enjoyed what were arguably her best years of teaching. Carol Burtin recalls that her mother was in some physical and mental disarray following Burtin's illness and death; she needed people around. "She may have been a feminist in some ways but not in others. She needed a man around."[29] After a time, she and Edgar found each other. The combination was unlikely, given their personalities and contrasting approaches to professional life. When Corcos died, Levy felt threatened by women coming to visit (or so he said). Over the years he had even been discomfited by Pineles. He had been critical of her; his son Joel said, "I remember [him] in his usual intolerant way saying things I felt were not nice at all to her."[30]

However, as survivors, their relationship was more equal; he was rather helpless and she did not like living alone. They complemented each other. Their houses were in close proximity and they shared personal space and activities. Their circles of friends overlapped—they could be both together and separate.

Edgar Levy was an outspoken, paradoxical creative presence. Firm in his ideas about what art should be (his opinions were well informed by his scholarship), he had turned against the work of the Abstract Expressionist artists who were his friends and neighbors. Devoted to art, he painted in isolation for thirty years, refusing to participate in the art scene he saw as only a marketplace. He had been devoted to Lucille, who largely supported the family with the success of her illustrations for major magazines of the day. Levy maintained close friendships with designers and other creative individuals who saw him as a "complex and greatly talented man" and who revered "the breadth of his vision, the vigor of his intellect, the gentleness of his feelings, the impeccable taste of his expressive means."[31]

By the late 40s, Levy became a writer of art criticism and articles in art journals; for a while his exhibition reviews were on radio. His main subjects were art theory and philosophy, and he rejected the work of Abstract Expressionism and other nonobjective art at the point when it was developing and laying the groundwork for the New York School. Levy was stubborn and outspoken; he viewed the success of the new movement as market-driven and as the end of the principles of the modern movement. Levy taught painting and drawing at Pratt Institute during the 1950s and 1960s, and in the 1970s he taught closer to home at Rockland County Community College, where a selection of his work was finally exhibited in 1984.[32]

The relationship between Pineles and Levy was quite different from what each had previously experienced. Levy and his wife had come to terms with his professional choices and their financial and emotional consequences. Pineles, highly successful in design, had shared the design stage, sometimes uneasily, with her two husbands. There was a slight degree of tension and competition, as all were in the same general field, if not in actual competition. Part of Pineles's success was her ability to resolve or live with these conditions. She had adapted to each new situation as she moved forward. She was a different person with each man.[33] Differences in age and maturity during each of these relationships may provide some explanation. She was in her thirties and forties with Golden, in her fifties with Burtin, and in her mid-sixties with Levy. The men themselves had different temperaments and professional outlooks. With Bill she was somewhat adoring and subservient; she cared enormously what he thought of her. Though she expressed her opinions, political and otherwise, Bill was the one who entered the room talking and continued to hold forth. With Will she was more confident and less concerned about his opinion, though it did matter to her that their design methods were different and she learned from him. With Edgar, she was free and easy: "They were like children in a playpen."[34] Work and professional life moved along independently; there was no intersection. She could simply enjoy herself and consider him an adventure. The older Levy son described their divergent personalities: "Cipe was an elegant, sensitive designer with style, not intellectual or analytical in any conventional sense. Edgar was a complicated, intellectual person. It was an odd match."[35] For both it was a liberating experience.[36]

They were together for, at most, two years. All family and friends agreed that their relationship was wonderful while it lasted, and all were saddened by its end. In late June 1975, the couple helped David Levy and his wife fix up their Fire Island house by building a porch. They walked to Ocean Bay Park over the sand and picked up supplies with a wagon. Levy told his son he had had some recent angina attacks but was on medication. They all worked the next day as well. The following holiday weekend they were together again; they attended a party where they ate, drank, and danced late into the night. That night, back home in Stony Point, Levy died in bed. In her diary for that day Pineles copied out this:

> Dearest Cipe: I came upon this paper while doing my mail this morning and I could not resist the impulse to write to you about love—years ago, in San Francisco, when I bought it I knew it was for love letters only. That I love you immensely you know but it sometimes occurs to me that I tell you so most often in bed. I want it on record—our private record perhaps now, but sometime publicly—that I have truly loved two women only and that were beautifully chosen for me (as well, somehow, by me.) And to correct any other impression I must say at once that I do not think it even a little bit amiss that saying "I love you" makes me want you very much, and that having you makes me say "I love you." So having said that loving you one way is equivalent to loving you in all ways, it is the sheerest delight to realize that our very best loving and our very best nights are ahead of us. E February 21, 1975

Pineles had practice with death's aftermath; she increased her activity through freelance design work, teaching, committees of professional organizations, presentations, juries, and travel abroad with friends and to the Aspen Design conferences. Alone again, she carried on, as she always had.

The 1975 yearbook project was engrossing and explored a theme dear to Pineles's heart: food. Class discussion centered around the common student experience of sustenance on a tight budget of money and time. The phrase "cheap eats" seemed to sum it up and the posters went up around school (this time in November—the process was getting better organized). The notice read "I'm Virginia Ham, Fry Me" (another advertising take-off, based on an airline's advertisement quoting a stewardess). Students and faculty were urged to come forward

Poster soliciting recipes for *Cheap Eats* yearbook project.

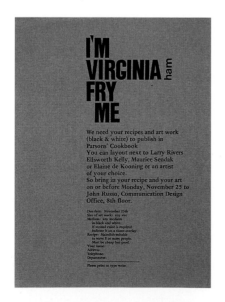

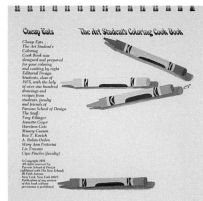

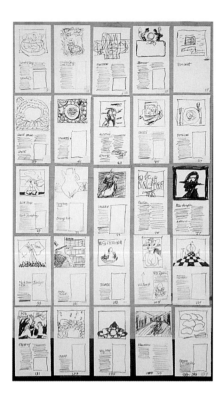

with recipes (main dish, cheap but good) and artwork, to join some
"names" already signed up: Larry Rivers, Ellsworth Kelly, Maurice
Sendak, and Elaine de Kooning. Apparently the response was sluggish;
in late November students in original sandwichboard creations
marched on a red-checked tablecloth in front of the school on Fifth
Avenue to drum up recipes for what would become *Cheap Eats*, *The
Art Student's Coloring Cook Book* (1976).[37]

Eight students worked on this square-format, 144-page book
with double-wire spiral binding at the top and heavy covers designed to
stand up on the kitchen counter. The paper was similar in color to the
Bread Book but more textured, and all art and text (set in Caledonia)
was printed in dark brown. The covers were black and white, combining artwork of a fish head and scales with very trendy contemporary
phototype, the soft and backslanted Watusi.[38] The students described
their philosophy: "For students of art it is the atmosphere, the presentation, the visual temptation of the food that sets it apart from being
'just cheap eats.' . . . The style is in the color, the scale, the original and
unusual use of common items and of art materials. The recipes and
ideas in this cookbook are made with the same ingredients any student
on a budget would buy; but it is the resourcefulness and inventiveness
as well as the artists' love for cooking which make for good design and
especially creative meals. Eating is more than food . . . it is visual impact, contrast, style, scale, mood, fragrance, color." They had been
taught well.

The book opens with illustrations on the top pages and recipes on
the bottom, arranged in a two-column format. The recipes and artwork
were sometimes contributed by the same artist. Recognized artists were
included with others from the art world and Pineles's world: David
Levy's onion soup, illustrated by Edgar Levy; scallops by Robert
Gwathmey (an artist from *Seventeen* and father of architect Charles
Gwathmey); Rudolph de Harak's recipe and fish in one typographic
concrete poem; bulgur salad from Joe and Evelyn Kaufman, with a detail from Joe's work for William Golden at CBS; paella and drawing by
Polly Binder (a friend from London, she had lectured at Parsons for
Pineles); choucroute garni with a drawing by Bernarda Shahn; kasha

top left: *Cheap Eats*, 1976 yearbook cover; 8⅛ in.
square.
center: Title page embellished with crayons painted
by Pineles in personal copy.
above: Layouts for *Cheap Eats* painted by Pineles.

Selected spreads from *Cheap Eats*, illustrated by, left to right, Edgar Levy, Joe Kaufman, and Cipe Pineles (from her family recipe book).

from Pineles, with a painting from her family cookbook; rice and peas from Roslyn Rose, her Jamaican housekeeper; hot liverwurst and a photograph by Robert Motherwell; lentils from Dorothy Dehner, artist and widow of sculptor David Smith; and finally a recipe for fasting from Dutch artist Willem Sandberg and a drawing by Karel Appel, with cautionary note from a doctor (who happened to be Pineles's brother-in-law).

The book was enthusiastically reviewed in the *New York Times* by food critic Mimi Sheraton and promoted in the school newsletter. Given the commercial success of the *Bread Book* and rising production costs, the school decided use the book as a fundraiser and to sell it through the school's bookstore for $5.00 (the trade edition *Bread Book* had sold for $2.95).

For the next year, ten members of the Editorial Design class researched New York City and collected interesting facts about their city. Posters for the school were designed listing these facts and asking for photographs and illustrations of a chosen fact. John Russo said that, as was the case with earlier yearbooks, "There were so many pieces submitted that it was a difficult job to select the ones that were used and explain the rejected ones. This illustrates the interest that this type of project generated in the school."[39] David Levy wrote in the preface that *NYC People Directory & 1977 Desk Diary* (1976) is "an optimistic and loving look at beleaguered New York City, by a group of young people

who find this town to be the source of their vitality as well as the most exciting place to live and work in the world."

The book, again double-wire spiral-bound with heavy boards, was laid out with a double-page spread for each week, days on one side of ruled page, image facing, with the "fact" running vertically along the image. The facts viewed New York through the eyes of different types of people, presented alphabetically from "actors and actresses," "babies," and "motorcyclists," through "pickpockets," "school kids," "tourists," "trees," and "yentas." The artwork ranged from photographs and drawings to posters. One by Pineles illustrated the page on "U.N. people." The front cover, designed by student Mies Hora, was a numerical composition, using days of the years '76–'78 arranged into three skyscrapers, printed in reverse to look like building lights. The back cover photograph gathered the editorial group and advisor on Parsons' roof.

The next year, for *T-Shirt* (1977), which became the second year-book to go mainstream as *Parsons Iron-On Art* published by Pantheon, the class began as described in a letter from a student:

The first semester [fall, while working on their own magazines], the class members were assigned to think of an idea for the publication that would have a wide student appeal; five ideas were produced. Some of these ideas were: a Hands and Feet Book, an Illustrated and Word Book of Current Expressions, a Craft Book on How to Make Unusual Presents, an Owners and Operators Manual for College Students, and a T-shirt Book.

At first, the body manual, which was a guide to maintaining physical fitness proved to be most popular. Unfortunately, this idea was soon discarded, because the class felt that there would be a poor response from the student body to the specific illustration assignments which this book required.

After the ideas were viewed by a wide number of distinguished faculty members, a publisher was asked to voice his opinion. For this occasion, the students were required to present a dummy of each separate idea, with a poster for a call to students requesting illustrators, contributors. The publisher [Fabio Coen, art director at Pantheon] was very impressed with all the ideas. Particularly the T-shirt book, upon which he made the suggestion that the T-shirt book would be even more exciting as an iron-on book. After this suggestion, the class decided upon the T-shirt book.

top: Selected spreads and cover from *New York City People Directory & 1977 Desk Diary* yearbook; 8⅛ by 9⅛ in.; the "people" shown are sanitation workers (photograph by Mies Hora) and telephone callers (illustration by John Russo).
above: Poster requesting submissions for yearbook project, designed by Pineles.

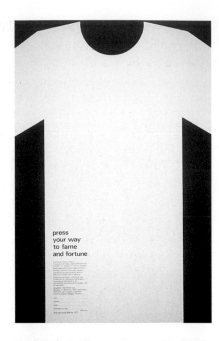

top: Poster requesting designs for T-shirts, to be drawn directly on the poster.

above: Cover of *Parsons Iron-On Art*, 1978 yearbook and trade edition.

The second semester of the publication design class, the poster for the call for the T-shirt book was distributed to the Parsons student body, by the class members, who also took it upon themselves to talk personally to the students in each class.

Because the nature of the design of the poster for the call supplied the students with an ample work space for their art work, the response was extremely successful. About 160 entries were submitted, which were properly seen by the judging committee, composed of the faculty chairman of each department of the school.[40]

The poster, "Press your way to fame and fortune," provided a real-size T-shirt in silhouette, allowing for direct application of the design to be submitted. It also claimed that "Body decoration is the oldest art form, and the t-shirt is its modern version." Artwork had to be black and white, line, or halftone. The forty-six designs selected ranged from word and typographic play to body humor (printed brassiere) to black humor (tire track across chest) to a maze and a San Blas mola design. Pineles submitted a rather chipper Uncle Sam. When the trade edition came out in 1978 the *New York Times* gave it a brief plug.[41]

For the 1978 yearbook, the students proposed the theme of courtship and marriage. The poster asking for contributions listed some famous couples, from Adam and Eve to Jackie and Ari, including Henry VIII and six wives. Again they asked for any kind of artwork on this subject that "has intrigued poets, writers, philosophers and artists since the beginning of time." When the students started to develop the theme, Pineles invited a researcher friend to the class and they discussed the custom of marriage through history and in different cultures, as well as the variety of perspectives by which this theme could be viewed. The class decided on Courtship and Marriage; they researched its position in literature, theology, law, tribal customs, economics, government, ceremonial customs, mythology and ancient history, and the women's movement. Having brainstormed images, symbols, and associations (hearts, rings, rice, veils, flowers, garters, etc.), the students did picture research with help from the art history teachers and used the visual resources of the New York Public Library.

The students' research turned up a vast array of material. The quotations they found were divided into the following categories: self-love, passion, illusion, a good marriage, women's beauty, equality, women's rights, wife, law. Pineles provided a clippings, mostly from the *New York Times*, of articles on the latest research on marriage, sex, careers, relationships, and kissing. Images from art history, cultural history, and anthropology were assembled. The texts were edited down to 333 quotations and combined into a dummy for the planned book, to be 8½ by 10 inches and 96 pages, half text and half image. The images comprised fifteen pages of student artwork, fifteen pages from history, ten pages of documents, and four pages by Parsons faculty. The general design was based on a three-column grid, a column of text (set in Caledonia) at the outside of the left-hand page, facing large-scale artwork on the right. The class proceeded through the usual stages; an outside critic reviewed the dummy. Several cover design ideas were prepared for presentation (one with typography imitating Herb Lubalin's reversed or back-to-back capital Rs from 1965).

No one ever saw this yearbook; it was not published. Years later, in response to an interview question about "the most difficult design job you ever worked on," Pineles said "We tried to do a book on marriage, but when we started researching it, we found very few quotes on marriage that weren't cynical. And to this day, I have this uncompleted project that's been staring at me."[42] No further explanation has been found.

The yearbooks were obviously a valuable and unique apprentice-like experience for the students. With their entertaining subject matter and unusual design, the yearbooks that became trade books went a long way toward raising public awareness of Parsons and its programs. They were a part of Parson's ambitious plan for growth, which would also produce promotional materials reinvented by Pineles.

As is true for all teachers, Pineles had her passionate followers and her detractors. Some students never understood what she wanted; many would only understand what she had taught them much later in their careers. Those who connected with her ideas, her openness and enthusiasm, and her teaching style were richly rewarded. "She enjoyed being with young people; she felt younger. She liked the give and take; she liked being challenged by them," Carol Burtin reported. "She criticized some of their sloppier things, but she thought it was politically correct to stand up for students even if doing a rotten job. I don't think my father would have made allowances for his students. . . . In Cipe's case, she was much more understanding of what these kids were going through at the time. She was aware of the movements going on, the philosophies."[43]

Through her knowledge of and contacts in the design field, Pineles opened doors and made suggestions for graduating students. Even those who had not fully appreciated what she taught and who had resisted her "spell" were always warmly greeted later at professional meetings and were helped if possible. David Levy, who, as dean, was privy to many students' tales, reported in 1985, "She has a very loyal following of students who really feel that she changed their lives, despite the fact that they objected to it while it was happening. Students come back to me all the time and tell me that she was the most influential force in their whole education."[44] Another student, who became art director of *Town and Country*, said, "[I] felt I never got it, then I ended up in it." She continued, "[Six years later] when I started teaching I modeled my class on hers. After doing [magazines] it all made more sense. . . . The connections really came when I started teaching."[45]

In April 1976, a short article in *Art Direction* magazine featured Pineles and her work and noted her most recent professional accomplishment: membership in the Art Directors Club Hall of Fame. Just as

Poster for submissions to *Marriage*, the 1978 yearbook that died of negativity.

she had been the first woman member of the ADC, Pineles now was the first woman admitted to its Hall of Fame. This was probably the high point of her career in terms of public and professional attention, and it was high acclaim and true acknowledgment of her work. Established in 1971, the Hall of Fame, then in its fifth year, had only nineteen members. Now, according to all the established standards and rules, Pineles was allowed into the inner sanctum. She was declared as good as those who were already members: M. F. Agha, Lester Beall, Alexey Brodovitch, Will Burtin, A. M. Cassandre, René Clarke, Charles Coiner, Robert Gage, William Golden, Leo Lionni, Paul Rand, Paul Smith, and Jack Tinker. She was also equal to those joining with her: Gordon Aymar, Herbert Bayer, Heyworth Campbell, Laszlo Moholy-Nagy, and Alexander Liberman (who, for unknown reasons, did not attend the celebration). Implicitly acknowledging the difficulties over her basic club membership in 1948, when Golden pointed out the club's sexist hypocrisy, Pineles's profile in the ADC annual of 1975 stated: "It is appropriate that C.P. breaks new ground. The first woman member of The ADC gives us the privilege of welcoming her as the first woman elected to our Hall of Fame."[46] It was also sweet in that while both her husbands had been given membership posthumously, Pineles was alive to relish hers; with three family members, they made a unique case in American design.

The reception and dinner commemorating the induction of new members was held on November 19, 1975 at the United Nations Delegates Dining Room. Pineles gathered her extended family and friends around her and fully enjoyed herself. Joe Kaufman remembered a detail revealing her politics: longtime friends Isabel Johnson and her companion, Alger Hiss, joined Pineles at the head table.[47] Dr. Frank Stanton, old friend and client of Pineles and former boss and protector of William Golden, was the official presenter for Pineles. Any uncharitable thoughts or feelings she may have had about her peers' tardiness in recognizing her were never expressed. As Estelle Ellis remembered it, "Cipe stood up with grace but never gratitude; [she] accepted nicely. She neither gloated or genuflected, never with bitterness or resentment."[48] Tom Golden recalled that she loved the ceremony: "She liked the limelight and had great things to say, quickly. She never expressed an 'it's about time' attitude; she was established [even without it]."[49] Her attitude here was consistent: Pineles was stoic about slights, real or perceived. She never dwelled in the past and was always outwardly positive. At the same time, she did not say things she did not mean. David Levy summed up her attitude and put it in perspective: "She did not come from a generation that would have understood [the idea that the recognition was late]; a sad fact, Cipe was pleased with the recognition and never said [it] should have been earlier. She was very proud of being the first woman in the ADC Hall of Fame."[50] As Frank Stanton said, "It was the . . . time when women were still not given recognition, even in design."[51] Sadly, she could not share her triumph with Bill, Will, or Edgar.

Portrait of Cipe Pineles, taken at time of her election to the Art Directors Club Hall of Fame.

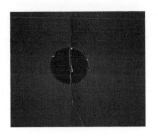
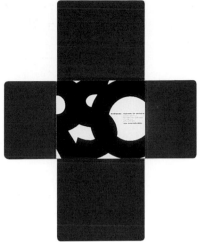

When Parsons became affiliated with The New School for Social Research in 1970, the professional design curriculum was augmented by a liberal arts program. While the school had maintained a modest publications schedule of the usual admissions poster, graduating class placement poster, summer session announcements, precollege poster, school catalog, and materials for the annual fashion show, Dean Levy proposed an expanded publications program to Pineles and asked her to be in charge of it. Her title would be director of publications, and the first year she would receive a retainer of $6,000. For this she would design all school publications, forms, and stationery. She would also help select and supervise any student work used. Some illustration would be done by faculty, such as John Russo, who would also handle mechanical preparation.[52] Records show that this arrangement continued for ten years, later excluding the catalog from the fee, which would rise to $10,000 by 1980.

Pineles began with an overhaul of Parson's stationery, which changed the school's overall visual identity. The basic letterhead used two weights of Helvetica in all capitals: regular weight and bold condensed for emphasis. In the early 1970s, the choice of Helvetica provided the clean, neutral look that was extremely popular (it visually defines the era) and had been adopted by many institutions and corporations. This association was not incidental. Parsons had become a serious business: the design school had recently merged with a respected educational institution and thereby increased its credibility, and its dean intended to expand the student population, which went from 550 in 1970 to 12,000 in 1990.

The first catalog Pineles produced for 1970–71 was like a layered surprise package: a flat medium-gray box with side flaps that folded back to reveal red surfaces and a small booklet with huge letters bleeding off the edges. The school name was formed by overlapping capitals of Futura Bold, covering the front and back covers and fold-out flap, printed black on white. The stacked name and address from the letterhead sat in the counter (or center space) of the *O*.

above: Parsons catalog for 1970–71: box, emerging from box, cover folding out, and selected spread; 8 by 10 in.
below right: Parsons letterhead by Pineles in 1971.

Parsons catalog for 1971–72, cover, inside cover and selected spreads; 9 by 8 in.

Pineles enjoyed the typographic variations she could play with Helvetica: the catalog's interior typography was light and small and contained within grids, which contrasted with the cover. After the shock of exterior scale, the interior was orderly and quiet, printed in black on tan paper. This publication was produced over the course of two weeks at Pineles's house: in the living room she laid out the pages; in the kitchen, at the butcher block counter, David Levy did the typesetting on an IBM Composer; John Russo sat on the floor, pasting up the mechanicals.[53] The overlapping letterform idea would later be used for the fashion show invitation, but it would be drawn out over the space of several pages, producing a dramatic and cinematic effect. The early Parsons materials were established typographically as part of a family of materials; however, with Pineles in charge, the family was subject to all sorts of genetic permutations.

By the next year, Levy was clear in his concept: "In thinking over school catalogs, it did occur to me that while it is very nice to see pictures of studios, etc., studios and hallways are pretty much the same . . . and what is really important about a school like Parsons is what its students do."[54] He proposed a "portfolio and catalog" with the first sixteen-page signature printed four-color on glossy stock, showing the best student work from each department; he warned Pineles and Russo of another "paste-up orgy" and promised them more careful typesetting this time. Levy says this approach was innovative in the marketing of art schools at the time. In fact, Parsons had a five-year lead on the other art schools. The portfolio-catalogs "put Parsons on the map; the audience was art teachers not guidance counselors. The teachers are the main source for advice and information, so we had to reach the teachers and show student work."[55] The work was carefully selected and reproduced on a large scale to create a presence. For the first five years, the catalogs shared the same format. They were eight by nine inches, had Helvetica and variations of Helvetica typography, occasionally used a serif face for text, and used a three- or five-column grid. The interior printing was constrained to black plus a flat color, often on tan paper. The budget was spent on the covers and first signature; the covers were bold and bright and used photographs of student activities, student work, or urban objects.

As the publication program grew and the dean and department chairman were no longer willing to spend their spare time at her house cutting and pasting, Pineles acquired the help of students for the more routine and mechanical tasks. In 1977 she hired Mies Hora, a former student and recent graduate, as a formal assistant. Hora was also the son of a designer neighbor in Stony Point, and Pineles had encouraged him to attend Parsons. He worked with her for three years and considered it an extraordinary apprenticeship, especially in typography. "She undertook to train me from the bottom up; it was her finesse with type that influenced me." She taught him the way she did it: drawing lines on tracing paper for each line of type, carefully drawing each letter to resemble the chosen typeface and to find the correct fit. She would set down one or two paragraphs of text to see how it felt and looked before ordering composition. She worked with typesetters she had known for years and who knew her particular requirements. She knew the best foundry cuts of her favorite faces, Bodoni, Didot, Clarendon, and Helvetica. Pineles shared credit with her assistants and collaborators, even going as far as insisting that Hora come up on stage with her to receive the ADC Silver Award for Parson's first apples and oranges catalog. "She didn't have to do that; it was a moment in the sun for me and very exciting."[56]

After they had done several jobs together, Pineles invited Hora to visit during the weekends.

> [It was] about nine or ten o'clock after dinner; Cipe was on the couch knitting or crocheting and reading the letters of James Joyce from a thick book. "Why don't you read a little bit for me?" So I opened book up, started reading passages of a letter from Joyce to his wife who was traveling in Europe—extremely ribald passages. Right-wingers would say pornography, scatology. I was sitting there in this quaint living room with this little old lady with a bun knitting, and I was shocked I was reading this out loud. She said, "Go ahead, keep going," contentedly listening to me, turning red, reading all these things. That was Cipe all the way, enjoying my embarrassment, challenging me as an old lady again. Breaking down ideas of what was acceptable and what not. She had a broad intellect, it was fine. That's an old person, a great old person to me; she kept broadening."[57]

The catalogs that truly gained attention from their intended audience (and from the design community) were the series built from a single idea in response to a new problem: in 1979 Parsons merged (organizationally, not physically) with The Otis Institute of Los Angeles County, establishing what was commonly called "Otis/Parsons." The problem of how to promote two schools, a continent apart, in one publication was a difficult one to tackle. During a discussion with David Levy, Pineles said she was working on an idea using a cat. Levy disagreed with the idea and suggested using an apple and an orange (conflating two expressions—the comparison of two things and New York's nickname); he imagined a photograph of the fruits with labels for the cities like brand names. Pineles's response was "Who ever heard of apples and oranges?"—the common expression triggered nothing for her and she liked the cat idea. According to Levy, she was "extraordinarily

above: Parsons catalog for 1973–74, cover and inside cover; 9 by 8 in.
below: Parsons catalog for 1974–75, cover and inside cover; 9 by 8 in.

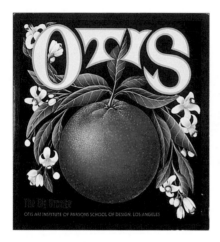

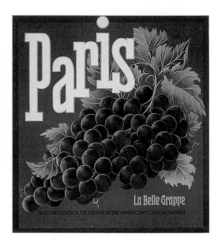

top row: Parsons 1979–80 catalog covers with The Big Apple and The Big Orange; 9⅛ by 10 in.; illustrations by Janet Amendola.

center row: Parsons 1980–81 catalog covers with fruit crate labels theme and addition of Otis/Parsons; illustrations by Janet Amendola (assistant designer, Mies Hora).

bottom row: Parsons 1981–82 catalog covers with The Big Apple Sunrise and The Big Orange Sunset; illustrations by Janet Amendola.

stubborn, but once there was an idea that could work, then all the barriers were down. She could fight one day, go home and think, show up two days later with lots of sketches for the idea resisted; now the idea was hers and it was fine." Levy waited. Directly following the discussion, Pineles left for a visit to California. She called Levy from the airport, told him to go downstairs to the student exhibition, and explained that there was a girl there who did wonderful drawings of plants and

OTIS/PARSONS, LOS ANGELES

PARSONS, NEW YORK

top row: Parsons 1982–83 catalog; surrealist covers by Richard Hess.
center row: Parsons 1985–86 catalog covers; photographs by George Ancona.
bottom row: Parsons 1986–87 catalog covers; illustrations by Janet Amendola.

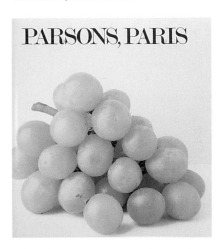

frogs and that this was the person to do the apples and oranges. By the time Pineles returned, Levy had two sketches from Janet Amendola. He proposed adding the text "The Big Apple" and "The Big Orange" in Helvetica, like other school typography. Instead, Pineles used a script similar to that on the old botanical prints she had collected for years, and she immediately produced "a smash." [58] The catalog's novel structure addressed the two-school problem as well; it could be opened

properly from each side (front and "back"), so the schools were presented equally.

For the next eight years Pineles and Levy played with variations on this theme for catalog covers, posters, and smaller brochures. Amendola was the illustrator of the majority of the materials, but other artists contributed work as well. Richard Hess played surrealist by paying homage to Magritte for one cover; Richard Kulicke painted another apple and orange pair. Photographers Arthur Beck and George Ancona (a neighbor of Pineles) were also used. When Parsons expanded its program in Paris, grapes were added to the theme. Ingenuity did not extend to a catalog with three covers, so Paris became an interior page. Together, Pineles and Levy thought up different concepts using varieties of the basic apple, orange, and grapes themes. They changed the number and varieties of fruits, and they provided various interpretations by using different artists' styles. The geographical distance between the two schools was depicted through sunrise and sunset. The fruit photographs showed a certain "perfection" in contrast to the illusion of the illustrations. In addition to the art historical allusions to surrealism, they made reference to vernacular visual styles through use of the fruit-crate-label style.

According to Levy, he proposed "orange crate art" to his art director for the second year (1980–81) of the fruit theme. Apparently not knowing what it was, Pineles thought it ridiculous and stormed out of the office. He sent her books from the library and she returned with her idea of orange crate art, "better than the originals" and exquisite at thumbnail size. Janet Amendola rendered her versions under Pineles's direction.[59] Amendola had not been a student of Pineles. When she first met her as art director, the young artist found Pineles "grandmotherly" and easy to work for; her positive attitude was welcome after years of criticism from teachers.[60]

The theme using the city/school association with apples and oranges was obvious (once done) and might have paled in interest, but Pineles and David Levy continued to present it in new, amusing, and

beautiful ways. Once a theme is stated and variations on it are played out, anticipation builds in the publication's audience. Though the apples and oranges theme was communicated most frequently through the catalog covers, the identifying images were probably seen by more people (including potential students) when the school's posters were distributed. A school program sent the posters to schools across the country and also placed them in the New York subways. They ranged from general information posters to more targeted ones for summer sessions, international programs, lecture series, student exhibitions, competitions, scholarships, and evening classes.

Pineles's magazines had been consistent in their general approach to the combination of text and image, and the interior design of the Parsons publications clearly followed a slowly evolving format based on a confident handling of the International style in typography and design. By contrast, it was with the posters and smaller promotional items that Pineles allowed her imagination to expand and her good eye for quality to roam. She found talented students and incorporated their work into these items. As David Levy recalled, she "used existing materials; anything that was good that she saw. Though egocentric . . . [she] was never threatened by other good people . . . she incorporated others' talent into her work" in the tradition of magazine art direction.[61] One time, Pineles played art director to Rembrandt, using his drawing with her headline "ART was Rembrandt's major (*what's yours?*)." She often recycled historical work, and she also used work from her own past practice: an old botanical print used in the 1940s for Green Mansions reappears on an invitation for the student exhibition and a cover for the Evening Division.

Sometimes a drawing would inspire the piece; sometimes the concept came first. John Russo remembers drawing while he attended Levy's school meetings. Levy would be talking about a new promo-

left: Poster for Parsons Design for the Environment competition, 1971; illustration by Lawrence Peters.
center: Poster for Parsons recruitment, printed on vellum.
right: Poster for Parsons summer programs, 1972; illustration by Rembrandt van Rijn.

above: Subway poster for Parsons; small figures illustration by John Russo.
below: top, Invitation to Parsons 1975 Student Exhibition, interchangeable 6-inch squares; bottom, Invitation to Parsons 1983 Student Exhibition, folded; 4-inch square.

tional piece, would glance at John's sketches, and would promptly interrupt himself, declaring "no need for further discussion, we have it here." Russo drew constantly; Pineles would see a drawing and say, "Oh, John, can I have that?" Russo says he was "used" like many others, but Pineles was charming, and, though he was not paid, he did not mind being used in this way.[62] They also collaborated on a clever poster that the New York subway system did not appreciate and refused to hang. Based on a story about Dorothy Parker, who sent a telegram saying "We knew you had it in you" to a friend after a long pregnancy, Pineles came up with the headline "Have you got it in you?" to go with her outline of a silhouetted pregnant figure filled with little figures by Russo.[63] Pineles was only worried about getting the correct bosom shape, but the real problem lay elsewhere: a solid black figure carrying a portfolio among the other outline figures defined the pubic area of Pineles's pregnant silhouette.[64]

Always interested in materials and processes, Pineles experimented with several kinds of paper for her posters, brochures, and invitations, and exploited their inherent qualities of color, texture, weight, and transparency. Different printing techniques were used as well. For years the catalogs had been printed with the first signature on glossy stock for the student work and the following signatures on colored stocks. The yearbooks had used a variety of binding methods. Posters for scholarship programs and for student exhibitions were printed on translucent vellum (arriving folded, these were layered mysteries to unfold) and were hung in windows, where the colors would glow and the white type (on white paper) would then be legible. She also enjoyed the manipulation of papers with diecut shapes and folding. Frequently, larger materials would be folded for handling and mailing, and the folded shape would be a square. The square became another "sign" of Parsons; the catalogs were almost-square and many invitations were exactly square.

As art director and designer, Pineles used a wide range of images (as she had for magazines). Just as the sources were varied (students, faculty, famous artists, etc.), so, too, were their media and styles. Parsons produced artists and designers with a variety of styles and approaches; to attract them as students, the school chose to communicate its openness to variety by showing examples of student work in all media and representational modes. The annual Student Exhibition (an effective way to introduce the newest crop of creative people to possible employers) was the stimulus for whimsical invitations. Pineles could indulge her love of bright colors, historical typography, and paper folding here, too. One invitation arrived in the square envelope as four bright squares, color on one side, large type on the reverse, ready to be assembled into a larger square for reading. Another started as a square of abstract bold letter forms and unfolded on the diagonal to produce a legible strip of typography and text.

An important annual event, the Parsons Fashion Show was an occasion for the school and its students in this field to shine in front of

some of the best fashion designers (and alumni) in the business, at home in New York. Elaborate invitations were sent out and elegant program booklets with photographs and sketches were part of the event itself. Early in the 1970s, one program had overlapping bold capital letters for "Parsons" starting on the outside cover, with "Fashion" continuing on the inside cover and flap. Other pieces would reflect Pineles's addition of Bodoni to the typographic tool kit for Parsons. Another program picked up on the fashion illustrators' use of brush lettering for the designers' names inside and on the cover, printed red on red. All the lettering was by Pineles, who also tested several combinations of reds, along with the more usual white and gold, in a series of little painted sketches.

A huge volume of printed pieces for the publication office was produced (in 1985, Levy estimated forty books a year, plus posters, invitations, etc.).[65] Pineles was also responsible for the covers of the inexpensively produced course listing for the division of Continuing Education (earlier the Evening Division). First as 5½ by 9 inch rectangles, then as 9⅛ by 10 almost-squares, the covers were another place to play. Three times a year for several years, she went back to her historical sources, finding old engravings to illustrate proverbs or using Edward Lear's *Nonsense Botany* of 1871. She used Russo's drawings, a student-designed maze from the *T-Shirt Book*, and some historical mazes. She did a riff on communication with a series of alternative alphabets: Hebrew, the manual alphabet, and semaphores. Nature appeared in a botanical print of grasses and in a tree for fall, with leaf/letters on the ground. A collection of sun faces came from a book by Mies Hora and his father. Even with something relatively unimportant, as this catalog was, Pineles used all her resources and amused herself.

Pineles's projects to promote Parsons had collected awards from the beginning: she received a 1973–74 Certificate of Excellence from the AIGA and reached a high point in 1974, when the *Bread Book* was one of the Fifty Best Books of the year. In 1980 the ADC gave three awards for a Parsons catalog, a mini-catalog, and a poster series; in 1981 there were two awards for a catalog and a poster. The Type Directors Club also awarded three certificates for the Parsons materials.

Parson's design and identity system—its "look"—was established, loose as it was. By 1980, assistants increasingly took over the design details and production of the promotional materials, allowing

above: Parsons Fashion Show brochure, cover unfolded.
below: Parsons Evening Division catalog covers, 1975–1982; using Edward Lear illustration, mazes, sign language, and suns.

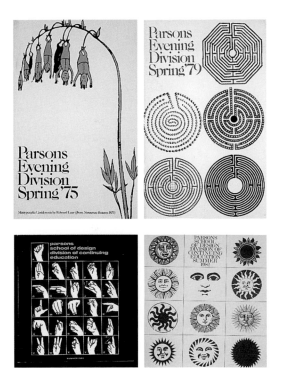

Pineles, who was now in her early seventies, to concentrate on teaching and practice more distanced art direction. Over the years, when she had traveled with Burtin or to professional meetings, Pineles had asked other teachers who were friends and former students to take her classes for her. During the mid-80s, her age and waning mental energy began to show. David Levy encouraged the class visits from many of these same teachers, as well as outside designers and critics to help keep the classes focused and pertinent. Though Pineles had mellowed in her critique style, her assignments were the same and the usual numbers of students were enthusiastic or uninterested. Her reputation at this time was as positive as always, but it was of the "legendary" kind and no longer tied to design work that the students knew or could appreciate.

Fortunately, Pineles's reputation was not dependent on the short attention span of students or on their limited knowledge of recent design history. Appreciation for her work came from unexpected sources. Through Will Burtin, who was the American president of the Alliance Graphique Internationale (AGI) for several years, Pineles was well acquainted with the organization and its many members worldwide. Since its founding in 1951, AGI has been an elite graphic design organization limited to invited membership. In the mid-70s, after Burtin's death, Cipe Pineles was recommended by the then-American president, Rudy de Harak, and invited to join; he said, "I was appalled at so few [women members]."[66] While Pineles was well known to the members through her association with Burtin and her years in the American design circuit, her admission to this elite group was based on her professional work on magazines, at Parsons, and for Lincoln Center, as well as on her illustration.[67] Not the first woman member, she was certainly among the earliest and well aware of it.[68] In a 1981 draft letter to a British design magazine contemplating including her work in an article about AGI members, Pineles added this note: "It's just that AGI has had some problems in the past—problems about recognizing that there are women in commercial graphic design as well as men and has only recently included me into their exclusive organization."[69] AGI members congregate annually, often taking a trip together. Newly widowed, Pineles attended the AGI conference in Amsterdam in 1972; she traveled to Poland in 1974 and Greece in 1975 with Bernarda Shahn and Gertrude Snyder. She joined AGI members in Venice in 1977 and in 1980 returned to Vienna, her birthplace. Pineles went to the 1985 meeting on a ranch in California with Ray Eames (a member with husband Charles Eames since 1978).[70] An observer was amused by the physical similarities of the two women designers: they both had short, stocky figures and were dressed in their own idiosyncratic styles.

International peer notice notwithstanding, Cipe Pineles could still be forgotten at home. Even with her example and those of many other successful women designers, as a group they were often overlooked on their own turf. This exasperated Pineles, and on one occasion she expressed her frustrations to designer Paula Scher. Commenting on current magazine design, Scher had written a short piece for the *AIGA*

Journal called "The Mystery of Conde Nasty."[71] The 1984 article had apparently delighted Pineles, who had used the term herself, and she invited the much younger Scher to visit, never having met her. At this meeting, Pineles was quite exercised about a poster for an ADC lecture series and was waving it around. "Have you seen this?" she asked Scher. The title for the series was *An Evening with One of the Best* and there were to be a dozen or so talks by male designers (some of whom were good friends of Pineles). The photograph showed a group of prominent art directors and designers—but there was a problem. "'Not one (even lousy) token woman!' She was furious. She suggested another event: *An Evening with One with Breasts*. The poster and the event were the last of their kind."[72] It was unusual for Pineles to express so vehemently her professional frustrations, even to a sympathetic female colleague (whom she did not know well). This event may signal a change in her "gracious" attitude and a willingness often found in older women to risk being "outrageous."

After Levy's death, Pineles's life beyond Parsons was lonely. She had lost the three men in her life, her son was living on the West Coast, and her daughter and grandchildren were in Toronto. She stayed at the big house in Stony Point during long weekends and had a small apartment on 10th Street for her business and teaching days in the city. She used both for socializing—weekends in the country and parties in the city. She had learned to make things happen, not to wait for others to act. She regularly invited people for dinner at the apartment. Among her friends were the "great" designers, former students, young people she met, and anyone visiting. About every two weeks she walked to Balducci's market for a roasted chicken; other meals she prepared herself. She had always preferred home cooking and entertaining to restaurants.[73]

For years Pineles had been generous with her space and hospitality: friends and their children from around the world had stayed with her during visits. She had frequently taken in young people getting started in the city; this was especially true for young women, to whom she also gave contacts, professional recommendations, and advice ("First be yourself, then be a couple"[74]). During the late 1970s, when she was traveling often and wanted someone at the house for "cats and lights," she took in a boarder for the summer. This turned into a twelve-year arrangement with Baron Stewart, a young Jamaican math teacher at the Rockland Country Day School who later worked for IBM. It also became a significant friendship. As he describes it, she took under her wing an unsophisticated, young black man, taught him about New York City, and introduced him to the world. "She was Henry Higgins to my Pygmalion; she even gave me a reading list."[75] Dressed as if for the office, she often worked at home all day at her glass-topped table overlooking the Hudson River. She would stop at the end of the day for drinks when Stewart arrived home, talk about the news (she loved the Op Ed page of the *New York Times*), and make dinner. Stewart accompanied Pineles to many events, both professional

Cipe Pineles in Paris, 1979; research for a French "bread book," project abandoned (photograph by Mies Hora).

and for personal entertainment.[76] He took her dancing in the city and introduced her (and some of her friends) to reggae music. He accompanied her shopping, to galleries, and to the theater. He was part of her parties at home and met prominent people from her many worlds; she liked to put provocative, opinionated people together to see what would happen. At Pineles's urging, Stewart began taking annual summer trips to Europe; he visited some of her friends, too. Often they went to the same place during the year, and, when they returned, they would compare notes and discover totally different experiences. Stewart called Pineles "at heart a teacher; if you are willing to learn, she is willing to teach." He was only one of many to whom she offered lessons, formally and informally, throughout her life.

Pineles began to receive the kind of awards that reflect on many years of practice and dedication. In 1983, Parsons established the Cipe Pineles Scholarship in Communication Design. Two hundred and fifty of her friends and colleagues came to mark the occasion at a luncheon; many were from far back in her career. Instead of giving a speech, Pineles chose to read a petition that students had circulated and signed in the mid-70s. The petition began "I've had it with Cipe Pineles," went on to list some grievances, including her use of their work in her role as "Publication Czar," and closed with the remark that since everyone knew she was related to Dean David Levy, it was unlikely she would be fired. Pineles was not upset but rather interested and challenged by the fact that some students did not understand her. She said at the luncheon, "I try very hard to find a way to get different kinds of talents, different capabilities, different initiatives to respond to an assignment with equal enthusiasm and interest," and she went on, "I find it very inspiring to be in contact with a whole new wave of young future designers."[77] Pineles told the petition story again the next year when she received the Herb Lubalin Award from the Society of Publication Designers. Interestingly, the award was presented by the President of the Society that year, Melissa Tardiff, a former student and a signer of the petition. "Cipe thought it was all very funny, all part of the process of teaching. She never held a grudge and was always cordial whenever we met over the years."[78] Following closely on the two awards that honored her for teaching and professional achievement, in 1985 her alma mater, Pratt Institute, gave her an Alumni Achievement Award and her work was exhibited at the school.

Right up to her retirement in 1987, Pineles continued to participate in her profession through AIGA conferences, jury work for the Society of Illustrators, and by speaking at schools like Cooper Union. For the AIGA, Pineles was chair of the Medalist committee that selected Romana Javitz, the creator of the picture reference library at the New York Public Library. In 1985, she served on the jury for the *Communication Graphics* show. In that same year she made the case for a posthumous medal for William Golden; Golden received it in 1988. A good professional "citizen," Pineles befriended the next design generation through her participation in organizations. Though the younger

Pineles and fall 1984 Editorial Design class at Parsons (photograph by Margaret Gregor).

designers were barely involved in design when Pineles was in her prime, this is how they got to know her, and they related to her more in her "maternal" role.

In 1982, James Craig asked her to contribute to his chapter "How I got my first job" in his book *Graphic Design Career Guide*. In her contribution, Pineles reiterated many of her stories about bull pens, Contempora, meeting Mr. Nast, and working for Dr. Agha. Her advice to students warned them against being concerned about pay scale, title, office decor, and repetitive, lowly tasks. What they should care about was "to choose your first job as though you were choosing a postgraduate course in graphic design at some university that's very costly. . . . Apply for a first job by showing your portfolio to every top designer whose work you especially admire." When this short list was exhausted, the student was to go on to the next three hundred designers, "who, though not well known or as much publicized . . . are nevertheless designers you can learn a lot from."[79]

The AIGA sponsored a symposium on magazine design in 1985; she was one of the participants (in the company of Henry Wolf, Leo Lionni, Sam Antupit, Milton Glaser, Will Hopkins, Walter Bernard, Ronn Campisi, and Paul Davis). The panel discussion was an opportunity for Pineles to reflect on the changes in magazine design in the twenty-five years since she had left *Mademoiselle* and to comment on what she saw currently in practice. In answer to the question "How have magazines changed in the Eighties?" she replied, "Magazines today are so timid. They have no self-confidence. There aren't many magazines that are so certain of their mission that they don't put the whole ball of wax on the cover. The entire contents are given away. The decline of the magazine rests on the need to outdo the competition on the newsstand." She further explained that when she started "this business was a free-for-all for inventive layouts and ideas. The editors frequently turned with great eagerness to the art department to solve their problems—ideas were needed and wanted. More important, it was a time when advertising looked to editorial for inspiration, not the other way around." She connected this surrender to advertising to changes in spatial planning, where more than four spreads in a sequence had become rare. "Now the *well* has been relinquished to the advertisers, which underscores the problem because the *well* defines the magazine. It's how the magazine fulfills its promise to the reader." Later in the discussion, she commented on current design, calling it "middle-of-the-road kind of work without any real peaks of brilliance." She said exciting graphics were no longer found in new magazines but rather in coffee-table books. In answer to a question about talent, Pineles commented that she perceived a current lack of talent, in contrast to her days at *Vogue* when "there was a studio where photographers were given space in which to experiment. There was a great deal of interest in finding new talent on the part of the editors."[80]

When graphic design history in the United States started to be organized as a field of study and published in the early 1980s,[81] Pineles

Original painting by Pineles for cover of 1985 *Print* containing retrospective article on her work.

received some attention and was featured or included in several articles and exhibits. A long retrospective article about her and her work was published in *Print* magazine in 1985; she was interviewed by the author and submitted a large number of slides of her work from all periods; seventy were used. She also painted the magazine's cover illustration, a characteristic gouache of some of her favorite things: antique cups with lettering, letter blocks, natural objects, and food. She rendered the magazine's name with the letter blocks and was slightly annoyed when the editors decided to overprint with the standard logo.[82] In general, however, she felt satisfied with the article and her cover.[83] A few years later, in 1988, women designers in Chicago organized a small exhibition of work by women designers and published a catalog; Pineles was included and interviewed.[84] The first major exhibition of American graphic design was organized by the Walker Art Gallery in Minneapolis, and an associated book was published in 1989. Pineles was one of fifteen designers Steven Heller interviewed for the book; she discussed her early work in magazine design.[85]

More often, however, Pineles was used as a valuable resource who could provide information about her husbands and other prominent figures in the design world. In 1985 she was interviewed about William Golden and Will Burtin in conjunction with research for *Nine Pioneers in American Graphic Design*, a book that profiled significant designers.[86] In all interviews—those about her contributions as well as those about her husbands—Pineles was quite helpful and forthcoming about facts, professional relationships, and the early years of modern magazine publishing and corporate design. Though she answered factual questions about her relations with husbands and colleagues, she never revealed her emotions. Some of the stories (about Dr. Agha, how she got started, and Golden's CBS eye mark) she had told many times, but occasionally the interviewer would ask a question that revealed a new fact or connection.[87] When queried about why she had not written about her husbands (she had only edited the Golden book), Pineles replied that a wife writing about her husbands would be "sensational" somehow, that she would be "exploiting" herself and the marriages.[88] To those who did not know her well, Pineles appeared to be a sharp older woman in full command of her memory and power of judgment. This was not completely true. She willingly did the interviews; if she felt afterwards she had been unclear or mistaken, she would call back with the correct facts or the more accurate memory.[89]

Many friends have described Cipe Pineles, even late in life, as a woman with innate and striking style in her person as well as her surroundings. Her way of dressing was perfectly suited to her work and her short body. She found simple shapes—suits in her early days, shifts later—and always used fine fabrics and wonderful colors (she was said to dye her hose to match her dress before such choices were available in stores). When she found a "perfect" coat, for example, she continued to wear it, made up successively in different fabric and colors. Pineles assiduously developed her image over the years and controlled it carefully. She prepared herself daily for her professional role, wherever it might be.

When Pineles worked at home, she had several places to settle. In the winter, it might be downstairs in front of the fireplace or at the round table in the light-filled bay of windows in the dining room. Upstairs she had created a pleasant nook—at the end of the central hall was an alcove with a large window looking out on the garden and the Hudson River. Here she kept a neat desk with notes and friends' postcards under its glass top. The walls were dark green and lined with shelves. Photographs and a set of four miniature books in a slipcase created by William Golden were displayed. The title *LIFE WITH CIPE* could be read correctly when the books were placed side by side: arranged on the spines, the words were stacked top to bottom and read horizontally, with each letter of each word placed on a separate spine. The books were filled with 35mm contact-sheet-sized photographs Golden took of their life together. Pineles always surrounded herself with the ephemera of family and friendship.

Pineles had been going strong professionally for close to sixty years. Privately, she had weathered the deaths of three beloved men, among the other stresses of family life. Not unexpectedly, she was beginning to slow down and her daily activities had to change. For most of her adult life she had struggled with the common problems of smoking (which she gave up in the early 1960s after witnessing its effect on William Golden) and weight gain. In 1981, after an operation for a benign tumor in her back, she felt "marvelous" but frequently walked with a cane. Around 1985, she began to have serious kidney problems.

She had always had household help. When Tom was young there was Roslyn Rose, a Jamaican woman who had first worked for the Levys, and she continued to help Pineles until she retired in the early 1970s. Beginning in about 1977, Utah Mascoll, a Trinidadian, came on weekends and holidays. In addition to doing household chores and entertaining, Mascoll became Pineles's friend and went with her to parties, galleries, and lectures. Mascoll, too, got to know many of the friends and people in the design world. The two women connected on a personal and emotional level, developing this relationship to the point that Mascoll was in daily contact and finally living at Stony Point in 1988, when Pineles was first hospitalized for chronic problems that would end her life.

Another change occurred in the household around the mid-80s. Tom Golden had been pursuing a musical career in California but decided to return east and wanted to live at home. He had maintained a physical and emotional distance from his family for years. Even as an adult, Tom's relationship with his mother was complicated by his perception of his childhood spent with inattentive and accomplished parents and the burden of their expectations. The early loss of his father added to this troubled picture. In one of her truly rare unguarded interview moments, Pineles, about age seventy-eight, talked about her career and child. When asked about when Tom was born, Pineles said she

Cipe Pineles, about 1985.

had to choose between staying home for his first three or four years or to continuing work. Commenting that she "had worked too long to be able to make such a big switch," Pineles explained that she and Golden had tried to remain open-minded about the decision. They wanted to "see how it work[ed] out; if it didn't, I would give up the job. I thought it worked out, but you never know."[90] She was counseled against sharing her home with her son at that stage in their lives; Pineles, finding it almost impossible to deny her son anything, did not hear.

Her teaching at Parsons continued, though Pineles's health intruded on it. In the academic year 1986–1987, difficult decisions had to be made at Parsons. Pineles, now seventy-eight years old, was still teaching at a time when most colleges and universities had a mandatory retirement age of sixty-five for their full-time faculty. Albert Greenberg, the department chairman, had always shared student evaluations with faculty members, and Pineles had been reading hers for years, even the recent ones that were sometimes devastating. Student evaluations of Pineles's classes were mixed. Some students were still able to learn from and appreciate her, while others wrote that they felt "ripped off by a living legend" and believed what Pineles was teaching was no longer relevant to the field.[91] The visiting critics she invited could not salvage the situation. This student letter seems to sum up the situation:

> I found her unable to teach effectively. . . . Many assignments were given with one set of instructions, but critiqued on another. . . . I did not learn any skills or techniques of editorial design. . . . I found Ms. Pineles's erratic teaching style very frustrating and quite a waste of time. I pity her future students who sign up for her course because her name is (or was) highly regarded in graphic design.[92]

In addition, many noticed a most telling (and poignant) loosening of her grip on her stylish image. Greenberg initiated a discussion with Dean Levy about Pineles, her teaching, and the student complaints. He felt that Levy, as dean and old family friend, should "take the bull by the horns and have her do something else." He suggested she come in once or twice a semester, saying that "the two daily classes seemed to be too much for her."[93] At the semester's end, Greenberg reported to Levy that there was no enrollment for Pineles's four classes in the next term. David Levy described what happened as a "bad, sad story." Aware of Pineles's powerful ego, he proposed to Greenberg that she be employed by the department as an outside critic for weekly visits, since "her critical faculties were still sharp [and] she still can be put in front of artwork and . . . tell you what she thinks." Greenberg was not enthusiastic about the idea but agreed.

It was July by this time, when Parsons faculty traditionally had their contracts in hand. Levy took Pineles out to dinner and told her he was concerned about the pressure of classes requiring her to drive into the city so frequently. He proposed, with no reduction in salary, that she create her own schedule as department critic. She turned it down cold, saying she did not like the idea and wanted to teach. He did not have the heart to tell her she had no students for the next term.

Levy called Greenberg the next day and discovered he was on vacation until early August, when Levy would be away. The dean wrote the chairman a lengthy memo about the problem, outlined a strategy, and left Greenberg to handle the situation. When Levy returned, Greenberg reported what had happened. By mid-August Pineles had realized she had no contract for the coming year, and she called Greenberg. Put on the spot, Greenberg told her the truth: that she was not hired back. Not in favor of the visiting critic plan, he apparently did not reiterate the offer. Essentially, Pineles was fired—over the phone—after twenty-five years of teaching.[94]

As might be expected, Pineles's reaction was one of extreme anger and depression, and the decline in her health accelerated. After being a family friend, his mother's best friend, his father's lover, his employee, collaborator, and surrogate mother, Pineles refused to speak with David Levy. She would, in fact, see him only once more before she died. Levy called it "the greatest tragedy of [my] life and terribly sad because we had been so close."

After the shock of the Parsons firing, Pineles had little energy for creative work. She painted a cup, a group of green tomatoes, a wildflower.[95] She participated in interviews, made a few trips to exhibits, and arranged to give some materials to the archives at Rochester Institute of Technology. Gradually, she took to her bed. Some of her friends (the "tough old women" as one younger described them) and former students visited. Cipe Pineles slowly declined and died in the hospital of a heart attack as a complication of chronic kidney failure on Thursday, January 3, 1991.

We cannot know how Cipe Pineles saw her future when it seemed to be an Eastern European one, but from the moment she stepped off the boat in New York and took the "sub-train" to Brooklyn, she seemed to join in the optimism and share the strength of character and self-assurance that have marked so many immigrants and pioneers to America. Her creative talents were recognized early by family and teachers, and she understood that her gender was only a societal obstacle to be overcome and not an impediment to her ambitions. She took advantage of the lucky breaks, such as meeting Condé Nast, that are only useful for the individual prepared to move forward. Dr. Agha was an engaging, difficult and valuable mentor; as Pineles seems to be the only woman designer he trained and promoted, the chemistry between them (perhaps aided by shared European roots) was a significant ingredient. From the beginning of her career in publication design, Cipe Pineles took her talents as an illustrator and designer and went on a merry and satisfying ride in the world of American design.

An energetic and expressive creative individual, Cipe Pineles found outlets for her interests and talents in a myriad of places. When the magazines she art directed did not provide the opportunities for illustration she seemed to need, she found freelance assignments and invented projects for her family and friends. The picture book of her days in Paris with Golden and the many illustrated letters she wrote him were major expressions of her pleasure and love for him. Painted and lettered recipes handed down from her mother became family cards and then treasures for friends. The book describing her adventures in Russia with Rose Warren was created for another friend. Birthdays and holidays provided impetus for Pineles's creations, as did her son's hair dispute. Her strange gifts were another way she expressed her wide-ranging reaction to the visual richness that surrounded her. And her home, entrancing to children and adults alike, was an ongoing environmental experiment reflecting her joy in the colors, forms, and textures of the physical world. That many of these objects and places also found their way onto her magazine pages was only one example of the ways in which the line between private and public was blurred in Pineles's practice.

Many of Pineles's projects profited from her ability to work with groups of people, combining their talents and skills with her own to enhance the project at hand, whether it was a magazine, yearbook, or party. Possibly her experience in Poland as a member of a close family that moved often influenced her lifelong preference for working and playing in groups. Her ability to organize and lead these efforts certainly strengthened her work at magazines, and collaborations were fed by her personal relationships with the editors, artists, illustrators, and printers. In the same way, her students at Parsons joined her to pursue each year's publication by dint of assigned tasks, group criticism, and schedules. In all these cases, Pineles was part of the whole and shared the accolades that followed. When it was time for vacation, Pineles traveled with groups of friends and family, whether to Fire Island with children or to the Greek Islands with designers. Weekends and parties were for sharing the house and garden, wonderful food, the latest treasures, and political ideas.

Her ability to work with people required her to find connections and comfort with different kinds of individuals. Pineles seemed to care little for society's distinctions by title, class, wealth, or race. She worked with, made friends with, and shared her life with men and women very different from herself and her experience. She created an extended and variegated family, perhaps to compensate for the size of her biological family due to war and immigration. Her ability to relate across vast cultural differences was part of successful publishing and teaching. She did not condescend to her audiences; she presented them with the best of art and design. She could connect with all kinds of students and enjoy their cultures though she was not part of them; she exposed them to the best examples and critics, and many were invited to enter her life.

Pineles's integration of her own life with those of others was most apparent in relation to her two husbands. She was forthright in her appreciation for what she learned from them, especially about typography, and she studied their design methodologies. As they all worked as art directors and team leaders, there were experiences to share and from which they all could learn. On the other side of the equation, the ways in which Pineles directly benefited her husbands were considerable if less tangible. The small world of New York art and design promoted working friendships, and Pineles built on this. Given both men's personalities and ways of working, without her as catalyst, the nature and frequency of their interactions with many of the talented people they knew would have been limited. Pineles was William Golden's connection to Dr. Agha; she was a regular supplier of talented assistants. Pineles probably better connected Burtin, who was less amenable to change, with designers outside the corporate realm; she certainly kept him connected to the world beyond science and technology.

Cipe Pineles was committed very early to her creative life and her design career. Her "self" was intimately connected to creation and this impulse drove her and her decisions. Armed with talent and training, she followed luck and help from friends. The choices she made often eased her "double shift." When family life was a goal, she modified her working life slightly and her son Tom was incorporated into the larger fold of her identity as a working mother. During her second marriage, when she had the opportunity to travel more frequently, she chose the more flexible working arrangement that teaching provided. Creative work was Cipe Pineles's identity and salvation; in the end, she gave it up unwillingly and under protest. The example she leaves us is of a woman dedicated to a creative life and the fostering of that in herself and countless others: artists, photographers, friends, husbands, and students.

All those colleagues, friends, students and family would not allow her work, generosity, wisdom, and spirit leave so quickly and without due notice and humorous remembrance.

[A] few weeks after Cipe Pineles's death, on January 23, a "celebratory service of remembrance" was held at the ADC. Friends and colleagues attended and spoke: Henry Wolf, Joe Kaufman, George Lois, Estelle Ellis, James Marston Fitch, and others. Lou Dorfsman assembled a slide show of Pineles's work. George Lois told a story, which many of the attendees had heard before, about getting William Golden's attention by dropping a dictionary; this time he added a coda: Cipe sent him a large dictionary wrapped in Wiener Werkstätte paper several days later with a note: "Keep up the good work. Love, Cipe Pineles." Though Lois had never met her, he knew well who she was and felt appreciated by the Goldens and cared for by Cipe. He went on to mention other strong mentors and called Pineles the "mother of them all, a *den* mother with every *bit* of talent as any one of us, but with a persona, presence and compassion that conquered and consumed all who knew and loved her."[96]

Joe Kaufman recalled William Golden's estimation of his wife's talent by relating an exchange he and Golden once had. Golden was using several illustrators for a series and asked for Kaufman's suggestions. "'How about Cipe?' I asked. 'Of course,' said Bill, 'she would do the best one of all, but there would go our vacation!'" Kaufman spoke of Pineles's "rare capacity for enjoying life," and ended: "Cipe had a special gift for friendship. She always managed to find time to do all the small, meaningful things that keep friendships alive and make people feel good: dashing off an amusing note (often liberally illustrated with her incomparable sketches), sending a clipping, making a telephone call to cheer someone up. On top of that, she was a fabulous cook, a renowned party giver, and a devoted mother. Her talent encompassed her entire life. Everything she did had that unique Cipe touch. She really 'had it all.'"[97]

Estelle Ellis, the last of the troika from *Seventeen* and *Charm*, recalled the Parsons luncheon for the scholarship in Pineles's honor, when she read the petition from students to have her fired. Ellis spoke of the way Pineles had defined herself from her start in 1930 as an art director and of the barriers she had vaulted in her six-decade career. She spoke of Pineles's perception that the "new generation was ready for and would be responsive to fine art and good design" and that images should therefore be created by the best artists of the day, and she commented that this perception had significantly shaped her own values. She spoke of Pineles as teacher and mentor to several generations, starting with herself: "After I left her and Helen to strike out on my own, she called me every day for three months. She'd prod me to meet her for lunch . . . to go to a gallery opening . . . or to walk with her through MOMA and the Met. All the while reminding me that I was enough. She'd say 'You don't need to be someone from a magazine to be *someone*.'" Ellis went on to describe Pineles's enjoyment of things: "Cipe loved misprints—she taught me to see the beauty in *imperfect* fabrics and papers, explaining that mistakes proved a human being was there and produced something truly unique. . . . Cipe was an original. She was, in fact, very much like that one-of-a-kind discovery she made you appreciate. . . . An excursion with Cipe was always an adventure. Nothing beat going with her to a printer and standing with her in the press room and listening to her talk to the men who she asked, ever so gently, to go back again and again to get the colors right. 'Get to know the foreman in the printing plant,' she told me. 'Don't wait for them to send you the proofs, go down to the printer and stay with the job until they get it right.' Who will ever forget those make-ready press sheets that she'd bring back and hang on the wall like a work of art? Cipe made the ordinary extraordinary."

Estelle Ellis reminded Pineles's closest friends of an event a few years previous when they had gathered and shown Cipe's ephemera: the letters, notes, cards, envelopes, gift wraps, labels, and birthday and anniversary collages they had all received over the years. "We discovered that no one could ever bear to throw away any form of communication we received from Cipe. It was a wondrous collection of things bearing Cipe's inimitable handwriting and artwork." And finally, "She made a difference to everyone she ever met, touched, taught, worked or lived with. How many women do you know who could have 'made it' with (and been a equal partner of) men like Bill Golden and Will Burtin? And in later years with Edgar Levy?"[98]

Cipe Pineles's qualities as a catalyst among diverse people and her ability to link individuals from many different realms were nowhere more evident than at her memorial service. An observer said that without her they would never be in the same place and never connect again. Artists, designers, writers, editors, art directors, typographers, and printers; doctors, professors, and scientists; a Trinidadian housekeeper, a Jamaican mathematician, and a former lord chancellor—these people made up her extended family.[99]

After a private funeral, Cipe Pineles Golden Burtin was buried in a Nyack cemetery with her husbands and Burtin's first wife. After Burtin's death, Pineles had ordered the gravestone from the John Stevens Shop, fine stone carvers in Providence, Rhode Island. She worked out an unusual inscription to fit the grouping of people, complete with her own chosen birth year: "In memory of Hilde Munk Burtin [dates] wife of Will Burtin [dates] who married Cipe Pineles ["revised" dates] widow of William Golden [dates]."

When recently interviewed, some former colleagues were critical of Pineles. Looking back on her example and career, they were less impressed than many others have been. Lillian Bassman, the fashion photographer and earlier collaborator with Alexey Brodovitch at *Harper's Bazaar* and *Junior Bazaar*, had attended the Parsons Scholarship lunch and recalled that she was amazed that so many prominent, creative people seemed to think so well of Pineles. She commented that she never thought Pineles was "top notch; there were other younger designers who were better. Pineles's work was beautiful but not innovative; she was living on her husbands' names."[100] Naomi Rosenblum, a good friend of Pineles and historian of women photographers, thought that Pineles had compromised her relationship with her son by her dedication to her work and her need "to control every aspect of her life."[101] This is echoed by a member of a younger generation, who, watching her and working with her, had learned some hard lessons: "She was a control freak. She demanded strength or else . . . [she] pushed me to a high level of expertise. . . . It [was] hell but you learn from the master/slave role. . . . She was a total career women and she paid the price."[102] These comments reflect a common problem for women who have been successful publicly. Doubt about their accomplishments exists if they have been connected with husbands or male collaborators; there is the implication that anything less than perfection in combining public and private responsibilities is unacceptable.

Others assessed Pineles's work and example positively. Rosenblum commented on her work: "It was intelligent; you could read it. It was designed with the idea of communication. The designs were always very stylish . . . the graphic design did not have [an] 'I did this' look. She paid attention to the purpose of design, without the ego. I think this is important; it may be the difference between male and female designers. . . . Cipe did not have the idea when she designed that it had to be known as her thing."[103] Sara Giovanitti remembered Cipe as a "thinking art director, like an editor in charge of art, not a decorator. She designed based on subject matter. Art direction was packaging. She was a seminal pioneer, she was different."[104] These comments point out Pineles's lack of individual ego in her work (even as she was driven to be at the top of the game); she was a happy collaborator and committed to visual journalism.

Ivan Chermayeff (who was too young to know her magazines) said he knew Pineles by her position in the design community but not as a designer: "Cipe represented the older generation [that was] respected. [She was] always involved. That was why she was a good teacher—she was active." He speculated that she greatly influenced the way both William Golden and Will Burtin behaved toward the profession and their level of professional involvement.[105] By position or personality or both, each of these designers could have been more aloof; it was partly by virtue of Pineles's involvement with people and her attention to organizations that her husbands connected to the community and provided leadership.

Finally, picture this: Awarding her its 1996 Medal, the AIGA called Pineles "[one of] those individuals who have set standards of excellence over a lifetime of work or have made individual contributions to innovation within the practice of design." They mentioned her pioneering role as autonomous art director and member of professional organizations, as well as her many years of teaching and her position as a role model.

The legacy of Cipe Pineles to American graphic design comprises these words: *Seventeen, Charm,* Parsons, role model. In two separate and lengthy careers she was able to influence American culture and American design education. She continued on the path set for her by

Dr. M. F. Agha to be a responsible, effective, inventive visual journalist. *Seventeen* and *Charm* were unique publications because of their audiences and editorial visions, and Pineles was responsible for the visual interpretation of those visions. *Seventeen* has been joined by other magazines eager to address the audience it identified and captured. *Charm* disappeared after having made room on the publication spectrum for working women. Through mentoring publishing assistants, the nature of her teaching methods and projects, and her continuing interest in young designers, especially women designers, Pineles was able to further the interests of several generations of beginning designers. From the start of her own career she was a role model for women when there were no others; her value only increased with each of her achievements and the gathering of professional recognitions. Her particular combination of talent, accomplishment, professionalism, assertiveness, charm, teamwork, lively engagement, and generosity make her a valuable model for all involved in design and a significant figure in American graphic design history.

Dedicated, inspirational, dependable, imaginative, persuasive, perceptive, enthusiastic, intuitive, pertinacious, indefatigable, 99% infallible, durable, and wonderful, wonderful Cipe.

(John Russo letter)

[Notes]

Preface (pages 9–12)

[1] See Scotford, "Is There a Canon of Graphic Design?" in Steve Heller and Marie Finamore, eds., *Design Culture: An Anthology of Articles from The AIGA Journal of Graphic Design* (New York: Allworth Press, 1997) and "Messy History vs. Neat History: Toward an Expanded View of Women in Graphic Design," *Visible Language*, v. 28, n. 4, part 2 (1994).
[2] Ann deForest, "Women in Graphic Design: Building a Velvet Ghetto?" *AIGA Journal*, v.6 n.3, 1988.
[3] See Scotford, "The Tenth Pioneer," *Eye* 18 (Autumn 1995).

Chapter 1 - To America (pages 18–29)

[1] Cipe Pineles essay of 25 October 1923, "My first impression of New-York" (Cipe Pineles Archives, RIT). Original grammar intact, spelling corrected.
[2] This birth year may be surprising, as all previously published documents have given it as 1910. However, she appears to have been more honest on her marriage license in 1942 than she was later in her career. The license also gives Austria as her birth place. In 1926, when Pineles graduated from high school, a newspaper article about her writing prize identifies her as Polish and discusses her experiences in Gliniany; the vividness of her stories of Poland may have colored or confused others' perceptions of her real origins.
[3] Cipe Pineles essay of 26 November 1923, "The life of the peasants in the Polish country." (RIT).
[4] Family background from Dr. George Forster, stepson of Cipe's oldest sister, Regine; interview by the author, tape recording, Tenafly, NJ, 16 October 1994. His natural mother, Lucia, came from the same town as the Pineles family and is shown in several childhood photographs with Cipe and Debora. The family name Pineles was a regional Austrian name and was not changed when the family immigrated.
[5] Cipe Pineles essay of 11 November 1923, "The wood" (RIT).
[6] Cipe Pineles essay of 26 November 1923, "An excursion in the mountains" (RIT).
[7] Cipe Pineles, "Bolsheviki," from *The Maroon & White*, Bay Ridge High School monthly publication, June 1926 (RIT).
[8] Carol Stevens, "A Companion of Design," *Print* (January/February 1985).
[9] Cipe Pineles essay of 1 November 1923, "How I spent my vacation" (RIT).
[10] There is some discrepancy in family stories. Irving Schor, Debora's husband, says Bertha Pineles and two (or three) daughters began the trip around 1921 but were stopped in France when U.S. quotas were changed and they were without the correct visas. According to Schor, they lived near Cherbourg for about two years and were supported by Sam and Jack. They eventually received the correct visas and proceeded. No one else has mentioned this French sojourn; Cipe Pineles had no noticeable knowledge of the French language.
[11] Rose Warren, interviewed by author, tape recording, New York City, 19 October 1994.
[12] Nancy Cacioppo, "She's been a designing woman all her life," *Rockland Journal-News* (NY), 11 September 1985 (RIT).
[13] Stevens, *Print*, 1985.
[14] Cipe Pineles interview in exhibition catalog *Ten Years: Women in Design*, Chicago, 1988.
[15] Dixie Maura, "Polish Girl, 18, Here 3 years, Declared Best HS. Writer," *Brooklyn Daily Times*, 4 July 1926 (RIT).
[16] "Types of Recent Work Done by Art Illustration Class," *The Evening World* (Brooklyn, NY), 30 March 1926 (RIT).
[17] Stevens, *Print*, 1985.
[18] Exhibition catalog, Chicago.
[19] Promotional materials, "Everfast-Contempora," about 1931 (RIT).
[20] Gertrude Snyder, "Pro.File: Cipe Pineles," (RIT). From published and unpublished text.
[21] Ibid.

[22] Unsigned newspaper article, "A Coast-to-Coast Display of Linen Costumes," no name, no date, (RIT). Includes photograph of window display model, presumably by Cipe Pineles.

Chapter 2 - Getting Started in Design (pages 30–51)

[1] Caroline Seebohm, *The Man Who was Vogue: The Life and Times of Condé Nast* (New York: The Viking Press, 1982). General background on Condé Nast, the man and the empire.
[2] Ibid., theories and examples, 10, 38, 76, 77.
[3] Ibid., 164.
[4] Ibid., 226–228.
[5] Agha liked to be called "doctor." Remington and Hodik ascribe this to his desire for the traditional Germanic respect given to all scholars; Seebohm claims he had a doctorate in political science.
[6] Nast, Condé. "Dr. Agha in Berlin." *PM*, v.5 n.2 (August/September, 1939).
[7] R. Roger Remington and Barbara Hodik, *Nine Pioneers of American Graphic Design* (Cambridge, MA: MIT Press, 1989). General background.
[8] William Golden, "The Man Who Knew Too Much," *PM*, v.5 n.2 (August/September, 1939).
[9] Seebohm, 233.
[10] William Owen, *Modern Magazine Design* (Dubuque, Iowa: William C. Brown Publishers, 1992), 48–49. General discussion of Agha's work.
[11] Seebohm, 229–231.
[12] Ibid., 229.
[13] Gertrude Snyder, "Pro.File: Cipe Pineles." *U&lc* (Fall 1978). From published and unpublished text.
[14] Seebohm, 220.
[15] Remington and Hodik, 14.
[16] Cipe Pineles interview by R. Roger Remington, tape recording, RIT, 12 February 1986.
[17] Joyce Morrow interview, Remington and Hodik, 13.
[18] Cipe Pineles interview, Remington.
[19] Owen, 48.
[20] Stevens, Print, 1985, 50.
[21] Snyder, "Pro.File: Cipe Pineles."
[22] Ibid.

[23] As these are mostly uncredited, I have depended on Pineles's portfolios and collections of tearsheets to sort out what is to her credit. It is not always clear whether she kept pieces because she was the designer or the art director or both. Some works have been previously published in articles about her and on which she collaborated; these I consider solidly hers.
[24] Cipe Pineles, interviewed by Phil Meggs, tape recording, 15 October 1987.
[25] Rose Warren interview, 1994.
[26] From research by Benno Schmidt, Washington, D.C.
[27] Gertrude Snyder, "Pro.File: Bill Golden," *U&lc*, v.2 n.1 (1975).
[28] This was during *House & Garden*'s "recovery" period. Challenged by Hearst's *House Beautiful*, launched in 1933, Agha thought *House & Garden* an ugly magazine, harmed by "idea" editing like *Life* rather than "visual" editing; by the late 1930s it was competing again. Seebohm, 329–330.
[29] Remington and Hodik, 71.
[30] Snyder, "Pro.File: Bill Golden"; and government employment records (William Golden Archives, RIT).
[31] The date here is a year earlier than published accounts; with the special issue published in April 1937 and the summer trip, she must have returned that same year.
[32] Seebohm, 331–335.
[33] Jeanie Esajian, "Pineles Sisters: High Achievers in Their Fields," *Times-Delta* (Visalia, CA), 15 January 1976.
[34] Stevens, *Print*, 1985.
[35] Joel Levy, interviewed by author, tape recording, New York City, 18 May 1995. The earliest example found was in December 1939 *Glamour*.
[36] "C.P.," *Print* (September/October 1955).
[37] Rose Warren maintains that William Golden got his job through her husband, Norman, who worked briefly at CBS in advertising.
[38] Cipe Pineles letter to William Golden, "Tuesday night, Dearest Willie!," probably early 1943 (William Golden Archives).
[39] Cipe Pineles letter to William

Golden, dated approx. February 1943 (William Golden Archives).
[40] Cipe Pineles letter to William Golden, dated approx. May 1943 (William Golden Archives).
[41] Cipe Pineles letter to William Golden, dated approx. 1943 (William Golden Archives).
[42] Cipe Pineles, letter to William Golden, dated approx. May 1943 (William Golden Archives).
[43] Cipe Pineles, letter to William Golden, "Sunday night," probably March/April 1943; also, Frank Stanton, letter to William Golden, "Saturday Night, Dear Bill," probably May 1943 (William Golden Archives). He writes: "Note: Cipe did a beautiful job on the questionnaire. Now if the CBS boys don't sabotage it in production we will have our first good job since you left."
[44] *Overseas Women*, April 1945, v.1 n.1, p. 1. The first five issues were forty pages with self covers, measuring 6¾ by 9 inches, printed in black and occasionally second colors.
[45] Historical speculation can be amusing: How might Pineles's professional life have been different if Alexander Liberman had not come to America? If his wife, Tatiana, who was earlier in love with Russian Revolutionary poet Vladimir Mayakovsky, had gone back to the Soviet Union with him, she would not have married Liberman and urged him to emigrate from France during the war. Liberman worked in a controlling way, especially compared to Agha. Following Pineles, Priscilla Peck, a talented and influential woman, assisted Liberman for many years. He gave her some autonomy in page layouts but he never allowed her individual credit in awards. Liberman was not alone in maintaining this degree of control: Alexey Brodovitch never gave Lillian Bassman independent credit for her *Junior Bazaar* work.
[46] Isabelle Johnson, phone interview by the author, October 1995.
[47] Cipe Pineles letter to William Golden, "Dear Fresser," probably early 1943.
[48] Carol Burtin Fripp, interview by

the author, tape recording, Toronto, Canada, 29 July 1995. Fripp is the daughter of Will Burtin and became the adopted daughter of Cipe Pineles after his death.
49 Snyder, "Pro.File: Cipe Pineles," published and unpublished.

Chapter 3 - At *Seventeen* (pages 52–75)

1 Bradbury Thompson, phone interview by the author, 7 February 1995.
2 Kurt Weihs, interview by the author, tape recording, New York, NY, 19 May 1995.
3 Sara Giovanitti, phone interview by the author, 2 February 1995.
4 Eleanor Perenyi, phone interview by the author, 13 February 1996.
5 Stevens, *Print*, 1985.
6 Snyder, "Pro.File: Cipe Pineles," unpublished.
7 Stevens, *Print*, 1985.
8 Quentin Reynolds, *The Fiction Factory* (New York: Street and Smith, 1955), 231.
9 (No author) "*Seventeen*: A Unique Case Study," *Tide*, 15 April 1945, 19. *Tide* was an advertising trade magazine; all facts for the first eight months are from this cover article.
10 Most of the background on Helen Valentine and the beginning of *Seventeen* is from Reynolds, *The Fiction Factory*.
11 Both of these studies were directed by David Hertz, Helen Valentine's son-in-law. There were other familial connections as well: Valentine's daughter Barbara V. Hertz wrote a monthly science column for *Seventeen*.
12 Jean Campbell, "Why Snub 8 million Customers?" *Cosmetics and Toiletries*, August 1949. The author was health and beauty editor for *Seventeen*.
13 Stevens, *Print*, 1985.
14 At the time of writing, Ellis is in her late seventies and a recent book author.
15 Estelle Ellis, interview by the author, tape recording, New York, NY, 18 October 1994.
16 Ibid.
17 Barbara V. Hertz, phone interview

by the author, 31 January 1995.
18 Estelle Ellis interview, 1994.
19 Stevens, *Print*, 1985.
20 Cipe Pineles, interview by Steven Heller, *Graphic Design in America* (New York: Abrams, 1989), 175–177.
21 Hermon More, Director, Whitney Museum of American Art, letter to Cipe Pineles, 29 November 1948 (RIT).
22 D. S. Defenbacher, Director, Walker Art Center, letter to Cipe Pineles, 27 November 1948 (RIT).
23 Frederick A. Sweet, Associate Curator of Painting and Sculpture, The Art Institute of Chicago, letter to Cipe Pineles, 3 December 1948.
24 Those who received mention by three or more museums are of interest: Louis Bouche, John Carroll, Stuart Davis, Julio DeDiego, Philip Evergood, Lyonel Feininger, Philip Guston, Robert Gwathmey, Joseph Hirsch, John Heliker, Julian Levi, Jack Levine, Pepino Mangravito, Henry Poor, Ben Shahn, Franklin Watkins, Max Weber, Karl Zerbe.
25 Snyder, "Pro.File: Cipe Pineles," unpublished.
26 Cipe Pineles, talk delivered at the AIGA, 13 November 1948, on occasion of Ben Shahn's medal presentation (RIT).
27 Ibid.
28 Ibid.
29 *Print*, 1955.
30 Comments recorded at "The Art of Teaching Art: a study institute," March 1951, Mass Media panel. Digest of 9th Annual Conference (RIT). Another time she named Jon Whitcombe, Al Parker, and Bradshaw Crandall as examples of magazine illustrators who were ubiquitous and cliched (AIGA talk).
31 Stevens, *Print*, 1985. Work done for commercial commissions by many of these artists is collected as readily as other work, privately and by institutions.
32 Joe and Evelyn Kaufman, interview by the author, New York, NY, tape recording, 17 October 1994.
33 *Seventeen*, September 1948, pp. 108–109.
34 Cipe Pineles letter to Allen F. Hurl-

burt, chairman, AIGA Magazine Show, 17 November 1964. Handwritten draft (RIT).
35 Cipe Pineles talk to AIGA, 1958.
36 Valentine Kass, phone interview by author, 27 July 1996.
37 Cipe Pineles letter to Hurlburt.
38 Quoted in catalog, Art Directors Club, *Annual National Exhibition of Advertising and Editorial Art*, 1948, 153.
39 Stevens, *Print*, 1985.
40 Ibid.
41 Tom Golden, now owner of the bronze ruler; interview by the author, tape recording, Stony Point, NY, 16 October 1994.
42 Snyder, "Pro.File: Cipe Pineles," published and unpublished.
43 Bradbury Thompson interview, 1995.
44 Estelle Ellis interview, 1994.

Chapter 4 - *Charm* and Family Life (pages 76–101)

1 Helen Valentine, "Memo: To all whom *Charm* concerns," 17 April 1950 (RIT).
2 Figures from *Charm*, July 1951.
3 Esajian, "Pineles Sisters."
4 Elaine Louie, "Cipe Pineles," *Art Direction*, April 1976.
5 Ellis speaking; Stevens, *Print*, 1985.
6 Stevens, *Print*, 1985.
7 Barbara V. Hertz interview, 1995.
8 Valentine's speech appeared as an "extension of remarks" of Senator Henry M. Jackson of Washington, printed in the Congressional Record—Appendix 28 April 1954. Could this be the first time "feminist" appeared in this publication?
9 Muriel Batherman Sheldon, phone interview by the author, early February 1995.
10 Carol Burtin Fripp interview, 1995.
11 Snyder, "Pro.File: Cipe Pineles."
12 Janet Levy, interview by the author, tape recording, New York, NY, 16 October 1995.
13 David Halberstam, *The Fifties* (New York: Villard Books, 1993), 588–598.
14 Carol Burtin Fripp interview, 1995. In 1962 Tom and Carol would be-

come step-siblings.

15 Snyder, "Pro.File: Cipe Pineles," unpublished.

16 Estelle Ellis interview, 1994.

17 Jack Cowden, "A Tribute to William Golden," *The Visual Craft of William Golden* (New York: Braziller, 1962), 142.

18 Roger Schoening, letter to the author, 13 November 1996.

19 Cacioppo, "She's Been a Designing Woman all her Life."

20 James Marston Fitch, interview with wife Cleo by the author, tape recording, New York, NY, 19 January 1995.

21 Most information from John Driscoll and Janet Marqusee "Lucille Corcos 1908–1973," catalog for her exhibition at Babcock Galleries, New York, 1992. Other information from Gene Davis "Corcos," *Art Direction*, December/January 1940/1941; and interviews with sons David and Joel Levy.

22 Joel Levy interview, 1995.

23 Carol Burtin Fripp interview, 1995.

24 Lou Dorfsman, phone interview by the author, 16 August 1994.

25 Frank Stanton, interview by the author, tape recording, New York, NY, 18 October 1994.

26 Jay Rae Offen, "A Home That's a Work of Folk Art," *The Record* (Rockland Co., NY), 9 January 1968.

27 James Marston Fitch interview, 1995.

28 Snyder, "Pro.File: William Golden."

29 Kurt Weihs interview, 1995. Many have remarked on Golden's handsomeness. As a younger man in California, he had been asked to take a screen test but refused. Instead, the family story goes, Hollywood found Gregory Peck.

30 Estelle Ellis interview, 1994.

31 Carol Burtin Fripp interview, 1995.

32 Snyder, "Pro.file: William Golden."

33 Kurt Weihs interview, 1995.

34 Tom Golden interview, 1994.

35 Muriel Batherman Sheldon interview, 1995.

36 All was not always so perfect in the office. Another assistant, Roger

Schoening, wrote "Cipe was a formidable but kind boss. She was not universally liked at the magazine. Many thought her arbitrary and domineering and many feared her"; letter to the author.

37 Schoening letter.

38 Tom Courtos, phone interview by the author, 19 July 1996.

39 Schoening letter.

40 Lillian Bassman, interview by the author, tape recording, New York, NY, 17 May 1995.

41 *Print*, 1955.

42 Tom Courtos interview, 1996.

43 William Helburn, phone interview by the author, 1 April 1997.

44 Tom Courtos interview, 1996.

45 William Helburn interview, 1997.

46 *Print*, 1955.

47 Ibid.

48 Joe and Evelyn Kaufman interview, 1994.

49 Schoening letter.

50 Eleanor Perenyi interview, 1996.

51 Esajian, "Pineles Sisters."

52 Cowden, "A Tribute to William Golden," 146.

53 Kurt Weihs knows the genealogy of the "eye"; Golden was inspired by a Pennsylvania Dutch birth certificate he saw in an issue of Brodovitch's "Portfolio."

54 Cipe Pineles interview at RIT 1986.

55 Bernarda Bryson Shahn, interview by the author, tape recording, Roosevelt, NJ, 13 October 1996.

56 Frank Stanton interview, 1994.

57 Fred Friendly, *Due to Circumstances Beyond our Control*, (New York: Random House, 1967), 34.

58 George Lois, "George, Be Careful" (New York: Saturday Review Press, 1972), 31.

59 Friendly, 97–98.

60 Cipe Pineles letter to Fred Friendly, 14 December 1966 (RIT).

61 Friendly, 98.

62 Kurt Weihs interview, 1995.

63 Joan Perlstein, interview by the author, tape recording, New York, NY, 16 May 1995.

Chapter 5 - New Lives (pages 102–125)

1 Snyder, "Pro.File: Cipe Pineles," published.

2 Schoening letter.

3 Stevens, *Print*, 1985.

4 Schoening letter. Years later, after working closely with Liberman, he went to a party for Pineles and met Liberman, who asked how they knew each other. Schoening said she was his first boss, to which Liberman replied, "She was my first boss too."

5 Carol Burtin Fripp interview, 1995.

6 Ibid.

7 Kurt Weihs interview, 1995.

8 Gertrude Snyder, "Pro.File: Will Burtin," *U&lc*, v.7 n.1, March 1980.

9 Pineles archives, RIT.

10 Snyder "Pro.File: Cipe Pineles."

11 Interview, *AIGA Journal* #18, 1971. This may be Burtin's last interview; he fell ill in May and died in January 1972. For a concise and illustrated review of Will Burtin's career, see Remington and Hodik, *Nine Pioneers*. Burtin's use of "non-Ayran" is unusual; it can only be explained if as the husband of a Jew he was "tainted" in Nazi eyes, and this assumes they knew about his wife.

12 Carol Burtin Fripp letter to the author, 28 November 1995.

13 Snyder, "Pro.File: Will Burtin."

14 Ezra Stoller, photographer, in letter to Chris Mullen, 5 October 1984 (from Carol Burtin Fripp).

15 Interview, *AIGA Journal*.

16 Carol Burtin Fripp interview, 1995.

17 Tom Golden interview, 1994.

18 Cipe Pineles letter to Fabio Coen, art director at Pantheon, 9 January 1968 (RIT).

19 Snyder, "Pro.File: Cipe Pineles," published and unpublished.

20 Ibid.

21 Cipe Pineles Burtin, Kurt Weihs, Robert Strunsky, editors, *The Visual Craft of William Golden* (New York: George Braziller, Inc., 1962).

22 Ibid.

23 Estelle Ellis interview, 1994.

24 Snyder, "Pro.File: Cipe Pineles," published and unpublished.

25 Stevens, *Print*, 1985; in fact Burtin approved of his daughter's residence

in Toronto, in part because the airport signage used Helvetica.

26 Carol Burtin Fripp interview, 1995.

27 Ken Garland letter to the author, 28 November 1995.

28 Background on Lincoln Center from Edgar Young, *Lincoln Center: the Building of an Institution* (New York: New York University Press, 1980); from various publications of Lincoln Center, Inc.; and from phone interviews by the author with John O'Keefe (9 August 1996), John Mazzola (9 August 1996) and Edgar Young (6 June 1996).

29 John Lahr, *Print*, May/June 1967, 15–23.

30 Lincoln Center press release, 21 February 1967 (RIT).

31 Contract terms and conditions between Cipe Pineles and Jack deSimone, Vice President for Public Information, letter 1 July 1966 (RIT).

32 Cipe Pineles letter to deSimone, 16 December 1966 (RIT).

33 Lahr, *Print*, 1967.

34 Ibid.

35 Cipe Pineles letter to Larry Creshkoff, 3 August 1966 [some punctuation added] (RIT).

36 Ibid.

37 Some evidence of the importance of, and maybe some stress related to, these presentations: Pineles kept a short note written by Will Burtin on his yellow pad wishing her well.

38 Cipe Pineles notecards, 1 June 1967 and 13 July 1966 [her mistake: it would have to be 1967.] (RIT).

39 John O'Keefe interview, 1996; he was Vice President for Publicity in 1968 after consulting for a year.

40 Bernard Taper letter to Cipe Pineles, 3 April 1967 (RIT).

41 John O'Keefe, John Mazzola, Edgar Young interviews, 1996.

42 Lahr, *Print*, 1967.

43 Cipe Pineles letter to Jack deSimone and Henry Bessire, 15 August 1968 (RIT).

44 Cipe Pineles letter to John O'Keefe, 23 May 1969 (RIT).

45 Edgar Young letter to Cipe Pineles, 28 May 1970 (RIT).

46 Edgar Young interview, 1996.

47 John Mazzola interview, 1996; he was made President and CEO of Lincoln Center in 1968.

48 Cipe Pineles letter to William de-Majo, 12 April 1966 (RIT).

49 Interview, *AIGA Journal*.

50 "The Design of The Cell," *Industrial Design*, August 1958, 56–61.

51 Will Burtin, "The Brain," *Industrial Design*, August 1960, 66–69.

52 "Walk-in Portrait of a Gene at Work," [*Life?*], c. 1966.

53 Remington and Hodik, *Nine Pioneers*.

Chapter 6 - Second Career (pages 126–169)

1 Cipe Pineles Burtin with Parsons, contract letters, dated 1962–1970 (RIT).

2 Alan Gussow, chairman, Fashion Illustration Department, Parsons, letter to Cipe Pineles, 24 May 1962 (RIT).

3 Albert Greenberg, interview by the author, tape recording, New York, NY, 17 February 1994.

4 Notes in Pineles's hand, 14 July 1970 (RIT).

5 Snyder, "Pro.File: Cipe Pineles," unpublished.

6 Louie, "Cipe Pineles."

7 Snyder, "Pro.File: Cipe Pineles," unpublished.

8 Parsons School of Design catalog, 1973–1974.

9 Exhibition catalog, Chicago.

10 Mies Hora, interview by author, tape recording, New York, NY, 17 May 1995.

11 Ibid. Pineles practiced what she preached; to show the comprehensiveness of her interests, one file folder found among her materials and marked "Keep Class" contained the following thirty-eight items: letter from art director of Americana thanking Cipe Pineles for talk to Society of Publication Designers, dated 2/9/81; letter from Society of Illustrators thanking Cipe Pineles for help with exhibition of America's Great Women Illustrators 1850–1950, dated 1/14/85; promotional brochure from Museum of American Folk Art; letter from librarian at Cooper Hewitt Museum giving hours and rules for use of museum, dated 1/31/85; brochure from The Pierpont Morgan Library; postcard from Burden Gallery about Japanese photographs; three sections of Dover reprints catalog, about nature, paper dolls, ornament; *NYT* newspaper article dated 5/24/84 about Cooper Union commencement and first honorary degree recipients (Frank Stanton was one of five); *NYT* newspaper article dated 12/15/69 about Edward Lear manuscript coming to dealer; *Village Voice* newspaper article dated 12/15/84 about two photograph shows reviewed by Lucy Lippard; *NYT* article dated 11/8/70 about body suit designs, two photographs; *NYT* article dated 11/21/67 about children's art the same the world over, examples; *Home Furnishings Daily* article dated 2/16/68 about Bonnie Cashin and apartment; *NYT* full page from 3/17/65 with Macy's fashion drawings and note "Tony Zocchi"; *NYT* full page from 12/4/66 with Henri Bendel's fashion drawings; *NYT* full page from 11/3/69 with lots of buttons, urging people to vote, paid for by A&S department store; *NYT* page from 6/21/70 with article about French medals and decorations; advertisement for chairs, photograph; *NYT* page dated 12/19/70 with article about designer Charles James; brochure from American Heritage Society Tours 1971; *NYT* page dated 10/27/69 with shipyard advertisement, lots of ship silhouettes; *NYT* advertisement dated 12/30/68 for Pappagallo shoes, with many old shoe drawings; *NYT* advertisement dated 12/30/85 for Leger exhibit at Janis, uses Leger signature; *NYT* advertisement dated 8/13/69 for Lucidity, drawings of clear objects; *NYT* advertisement, no date, for Cartier with photograph of pearls in goblet; *NYT* editorial dated 10/27/69 about endangered species, leopards and alligators (copy); four pages of brochure from Victoria and Albert Museum about 19th century women's fashions, with drawings; brochure from Bethnal Green Museum; Cut out Fashion Doll from V & A; *NYT* full page dated 2/25/70 with Macy's ad-

vertisement, drawings of shawls; page, copied, of twenty hockey goalie masks in grid; *NYT* Op-Ed page dated 6/4/1975 with piece by Lillian Hellman on truth, justice, and American way, copy; page of typewriter patterns; reading list for Editorial Design, Communication Des, Parsons, Spring 1982, Cipe Burtin listing: Hurlburt, *The Grid*; Müller-Brockmann, *Gestaltungsprobleme*; Vignelli, *Grids: their meaning and use for federal designers*, to be put on reserve; grouped items: brochure from Metropolitan Museum on African sculpture with photographs, and timeline, *NYT* page dated 12/2/84 with article about states and education policy, with statistical chart, page from *Time* dated 12/5/83 with article about football with visual chart, statistics, *NYT* page dated 4/19/84 with article about wages and benefits, arranged in huge chart; *NYT* article dated 11/9/84 about design of *NYT* and awards; magenta sheet with small poster soliciting submissions from students for cookbook project "I'm Virginia ham, fry me"; *NYT* article dated 4/14/78 about Saul Steinberg art.

[12] Linda Levy (no relation to family) quoted in Stevens, *Print*, 1985.

[13] Mies Hora interview, 1995.

[14] Melissa Tardiff quoted in Stevens, *Print*, 1985.

[15] Stevens, *Print*, 1985.

[16] Melissa Tardiff, phone interview by the author, 5 April 1996.

[17] Mies Hora interview, 1995.

[18] Francine Rappaport letter to Cipe Pineles, 15 March 1975 (RIT).

[19] Mies Hora interview, 1995.

[20] Make-ready sheets are created during the printing process as printers are testing their presses for correct color and ink coverage before the actual printing job begins. Using the same sheets for several different jobs, the layers of images and colors build up into a complex and random composition that many in the business find magical and beautiful.

[21] David Levy, interview by author, tape recording, Washington, D.C., 15 December 1994.

[22] Carol Burtin Fripp letter to Cipe

Pineles, 28 January 1973; sadly, much the same would happen to Pineles (RIT).

[23] Angela Taylor, "The problem: to do a yearbook that's actually something else," *New York Times*, 17 May 1973; this article was picked up in newspapers across the country.

[24] John Russo, phone interview by the author, 29 May 1996.

[25] Taylor, *New York Times*.

[26] John Russo letter to the author, 3 June 1996.

[27] Parsons School of Design Newsletter, December 1974.

[28] David Levy interview, 1994.

[29] First her stepmother, Pineles asked to become Carol's adopted mother shortly after Burtin's death; as Pineles explained it, she had always thought of Carol as her daughter, never had another, and wanted to make the relationship legal. Carol Burtin Fripp interview, 1995.

[30] Joel Levy interview, 1995.

[31] James Marston Fitch, introduction to memorial publication of work by Lucille Corcos Levy and Edgar Levy, family publication, 1975.

[32] Most biographical information from Emily Harvey, *Edgar Levy, Selected Themes*, Rockland Community College, Cultural Arts Center, January 8–February 15, 1984. The remainder from interviews with the two sons.

[33] Joel Levy interview, 1995; Estelle Ellis interview, 1994.

[34] Estelle Ellis interview, 1994.

[35] David Levy interview, 1994.

[36] Janet Levy interview, 1995.

[37] Director of Public Relations at Parsons letter to ABC-TV producer urging coverage, 20 November 1975.

[38] "Watusi" according to Pineles's notes; author's type book calls it "Smoke."

[39] John Russo letter.

[40] Carmen Salazar, student in the class, written for Dean Levy, 12 April 1977 (RIT).

[41] Enid Nemy, "Discoveries: New Life for Old Shirts," *New York Times*, 19 July 1978.

[42] Exhibition catalog, Chicago.

[43] Carol Burtin Fripp interview, 1995.

[44] Stevens, *Print*, 1985.

[45] Melissa Tardiff interview, 1996.

[46] *Art Directors Club Annual of Advertising and Editorial Art and Design*, 1975.

[47] Joe and Evelyn Kaufman interview, 1994.

[48] Estelle Ellis interview, 1994.

[49] Tom Golden interview, 1994.

[50] David Levy interview, 1994.

[51] Frank Stanton interview, 1994.

[52] David Levy contract letter to Cipe Pineles, 4 June 1970 (RIT).

[53] David Levy interview, 1994.

[54] David Levy letter to Cipe Pineles, 26 May 1971 (RIT).

[55] David Levy interview, 1994.

[56] Mies Hora interview, 1995.

[57] Ibid.

[58] David Levy interview, 1994.

[59] Ibid.

[60] Janet Amendola, phone interview by author, 11 March 1997.

[61] David Levy interview, 1994.

[62] John Russo interview, 1996.

[63] Stevens, *Print*, 1985.

[64] John Russo letter to author; he thinks the poster was hung for a few days and removed due to public complaints.

[65] Stevens, *Print*, 1985.

[66] Rudolph de Harak, phone interview by the author, 25 March 1997; he puts the date at 1973; she did not submit any portfolio, "did not start that nonsense until the '80s." Lou Dorfsman says she joined in 1977.

[67] Lou Dorfsman, phone interview by the author, 7 January 1997.

[68] As of summer 1997 there are ten American women members and approximately ten other women designers from around the world.

[69] Cipe Pineles letter to Jane Lott, *Design* magazine, London, 9 July 1981; there are two handwritten letters to Lott; it is not clear if these were drafts to be typed, nor which version (with and without this sharp comment) was sent (RIT).

[70] Helen Federico, phone interview by the author, 4 March 1997.

[71] *AIGA Journal*, vol. 2, no. 2, 1984.

[72] Paula Scher, phone interview by the author, 24 September 1996.

[73] Mies Hora interview, 1995.

[74] Baron Stewart, phone interview by author, 8 October 1996.

75 Baron Stewart interview, 1996.

76 Stewart and Robert Schor (Debora's son) were with her at the ADC Awards dinner where Pineles and Mies Hora won an award for a Parsons catalog. Someone came up and asked who the men accompanying her were; she delighted in answering, "Baron lives with me, Mies works for me, and Robert is my nephew."

77 Stevens, *Print*, 1985; to address the rumor of a family relationship between Pineles and the dean: At the time of the petition she was involved with David Levy's father, Edgar; this may have been known by the students. Moreover, the close ties between the two families since the 1930s were undoubtedly known, leading to student imprecision and rumor.

78 Melissa Tardiff interview, 1996.

79 Craig, James. *Graphic Design Career Guide*. (New York: Watson-Guptill, 1983), p. 107.

80 Steven Heller, ed., "Symposium: Magazine Design, The Rationalist's Dream." *AIGA Journal of Graphic Design*, v. 3, n. 3, 1985.

81 Two graphic design history conferences were held at RIT; Philip Meggs, *A History of Graphic Design*. (New York: Van Nostrand Reinhold, first edition 1983).

82 Jan Uretsky, interview by the author, tape recording, New York, NY, 16 May 1995.

83 Utah Mascoll, phone interview by author, 12 September 1995.

84 Exhibition catalog, Chicago.

85 Cipe Pineles interview with Steven Heller.

86 Remington and Hodik, *Nine Pioneers*, 1989.

87 Tapes of interviews by Remington and Hodik (1985, 1986), Philip Meggs (1987) as well as video clips made at RIT in conjunction with an exhibit there of Golden's and Burtin's work in 1986.

88 Cipe Pineles, interview by Remington and Hodik, January 1985.

89 Utah Mascoll interview, 1995.

90 Cipe Pineles interview by Roger Remington and Beth Jelsma, no date (around 1986).

91 Editorial Design class, student evaluations, fall 1986 and spring 1987.

92 Bridget M., Parsons student, letter of 3 August 1987.

93 Albert Greenberg interview, 1994.

94 David Levy interview, 1994.

95 Utah Mascoll interview, 1995.

96 George Lois, notes from memorial, faxed to author 11 May 1995.

97 Joe Kaufman, notes from memorial, given to author 17 October 1994.

98 Estelle Ellis, notes from memorial (RIT).

99 Baron Stewart interview, 1996.

100 Lillian Bassman interview, 1995.

101 Naomi Rosenblum, interview by author, tape recording, 16 October 1995.

102 Mies Hora interview, 1995.

103 Naomi Rosenblum interview, 1995.

104 Sara Giovanitti interview, 1995.

105 Ivan Chermayeff, phone interview by the author, 14 February 1996.

[Appendix]

Bolsheviki
Awarded First Prize in the Atlantic Monthly Essay Contest for High Schools

"I wonder how they look!" "and what they wear!" "and how they act!" These were the questions asked over and over again while we awaited our guests—the Bolsheviki. We by no means desired their coming, but their visit was inevitable.

It was the summer of the year 1920 that the Bolsheviki, after a hard struggle in Russia, invaded the Ukraine and part of Poland. They came down in masses, overcrowding towns and villages, roads, and forests, spreading horror and fear among the people.

At this particular time my family and I lived in a little town very near the capital of Poland. Much interest and excitement centered in Gliniany, for such an invasion meant the invasion of the capital and consequently all Poland. Different reports, mysterious stories, new announcements, were heard every day. Rumor had it that the Bolsheviki were in the habit of killing men, women, and children—of destroying whole towns and villages. Others reported that the Bolsheviki were concerned with rich people only, that they confiscated their property and gave it to the poor. We heard also that the Bolsheviki came down to reform the world and the people; and, on the other hand, that they were against all humanity. Of course, with these stories came reports of the dreadful murders of mothers and children, accompanied with descriptions of terrible tortures of men, of bloodshed, of fire, and disease.

So we lived, week after week, in suspense, excitement, and uncertainty. Just such a thrilling life as is sometimes depicted in the movies.

Naturally, preparations had to be made for the coming guests. Here I must stop and describe somewhat fully the hiding places that were invented and discovered for the hour of need.

We occupied a convenient house of eight large rooms. Of these, at this time, the two kitchens played the most important part. One of them, the larger, had entrances to two cellars. One of these cellars was continually used, but the other was a long-forgotten and deserted affair. It was not liked because of its inconvenience. Entrance could be made only through removing a few boards from the floor. The black opening which was thus revealed led to some underground passages, unknown and unexplored. We often wondered at the idleness of it, until one day my brother discovered it would make a splendid hiding place. Hither, then, went all our precious things: carpets, draperies, linens, clothes, furs, china and silverware, even pieces of furniture. The treasures of our town church, including heavy silks and velvets, magnificent gold and silver precious jewels, were hidden there too, thus making the old, forgotten cellar a veritable glory-hole.

The other hiding place was less mysterious. It was simply a storage room adjoining the kitchen. The door leading to it was so small that it was entirely hidden by a large trunk placed in front of it. This room was to be used as a place of refuge.

Within a few days our rooms, usually so pleasantly and conveniently furnished, were bared of their ornament and beauty. All things except absolute necessities of life were hidden, and the house took on an air of poverty and desertion.

At last the day, the hour, the moment arrived. Our forces could hold out no longer, but had been forced to retreat to guard the capital. We were left unprotected before the coming wolf. At the last moment twenty loaves of bread were baked. This course of action, we were told, would mitigate the wrath of the invaders, for their ferocity had been largely caused by the lack of food in Russia.

The night came when no on slept. Everyone awaited the approach. Some heard them coming; others saw them coming, but were they? Dawn crept over the watchful town, but none appeared. Morning—no one came. Eight o'clock—half past eight—nine—half past nine—and still there was no sign. Would they ever come?

I was standing at the window in one of the rooms facing the street. Everything around and over me was silent. Suddenly innumerable violent pistol shots—three horsemen galloping through the street—a cloud of dust. With the breathless shout, "They are here! They are here!" I ran to inform the rest of the household. In a few moments the news spread that the three Bolsheviki, who had just invaded the town, were the patrol. They announced that a large army was coming right behind them, and begged the people not to be afraid, saying that they were "comrades" to everyone and would do no harm.

We were amazed. Here we had expected a wild tribe ready to kill and destroy, but instead were to come plain and harmless soldiers. In the afternoon of that same day the large expected army came. As the soldiers approached form the distance under the hot August sun, they looked horrible and splendid. The red of their flags and coats and caps seemed redder; the shining buttons and trumpets sparkled and shone. The thrilling communist song was growing stronger, louder, as they came nearer and nearer. That was all I saw that day. The experience had been so thrilling; the sensation, so new; the picture, so astonishing; and the surroundings, so strange, that I felt weak and in need of repose. Not until the second day did I begin to notice the defects of the unwelcome guests. First of all, no two soldiers wore the same uniform. This was brought about not so much for variety's sake as for the lack of uniforms and money. French, Servian, German, and Russian uniforms were to be seen. Second, the soldiers were very poorly and shabbily dressed; every kind of footwear could be found. In case of shortage, women's garments were used also: coats, jackets, blouses, nightgowns, and hats. Above all, there was no distinction between soldier and officer. They were all comrades—all equal.

I shall never forget the entertainment that the would-be officers held in our house the third or fourth day. Supper consisted of soup, bread, tea, and songs. My mother was assigned the task of tea-making—no easy one. After innumerable kettles of tea had been served, our supply became exhausted. When the news reached the officers that the tea had given out, one soldier produced a large package of coffee and bade my mother "make tea out of it, quick." Such a tasteless, brown, boiling drink that was served! But the Bolsheviki seemed not to note the difference and consumed it with the same splendid appetite. Both the officer of the highest rank and the soldier of the lowest degree enjoyed the same feast and ate from a common dish. As for cleanliness, it was not known among them.

One night a party of about fifty Bolsheviki broke into our house. We had accustomed ourselves to sleep in our clothes, and were used to being waked at night by shooting, noises, and soldiers. We were surprised, then, only by the numbers. New forces had arrived suddenly and the soldiers must be quartered. All night long it had rained, and the soldiers were wet from head to foot, their boots clogged with mud. In this attire they made themselves comfortable in our house. I don't want to mention how the white bedding and the clean floor looked the next morning.

And yet, whatever may be said of the Bolsheviki, one thing was sure— they were honest. I remember one night at twelve o'clock some one violently knocking at the door and ringing the bell. Trembling all over, my mother went to the door and to her great surprise, was asked by a soldier "to please lend him a spoon." After two hours the same knocking and ringing was repeated. This time the soldier returned the spoon, thanking her most politely.

There were all sorts of people among the Bolsheviki, from the illiterate Russian peasant to the most educated of men. Two officers who had lived in our house spoke, besides Russian, German and French and came from one of the wealthiest and most aristocratic families of Russia. It appeared that when the revolution broke out, they had turned away from their father and joined the Bolsheviki Army. Later, they had confiscated their father's property, and given it all to Russia. The story was told with great pride and satisfaction.

Our town was as far as the Bolsheviki ever reached. They could advance no farther, for the capital was well guarded by disciplined Polish forces, which continued to move forward. After a two weeks' stay with us, they retreated one August afternoon almost at the same hour and almost in the same fashion as they had come. Suddenly and quickly. Bright horsemen on swift horses—a shot or two—a tumult, and a cloud of dust.

(from *Maroon & White*, Bay Ridge High School yearbook, 1926)

Talk delivered by Cipe Pineles at the AIGA on November 13, 1958, Ben Shahn award medal presentation.

I have a funny feeling that this whole thing is a mistake. I don't mean that Ben Shahn shouldn't be given a medal. He deserves lots of medals. He has lots of medals. But he doesn't even keep them polished. If he would only learn to take care of his things I'd give him a medal myself.

On one side it would be inscribed for schmoosing, story telling or just plain talking. The other side would be inscribed for loafing. Everyone from Dulles to Admiral Rickover is telling us that we must hurry like mad to stay alive. But Shahn not only consciously wants to loaf, but he wants everyone to loaf. He tortures his busy friends who have guilty consciences, by dropping into their offices and saying "come on, let's go for a walk down Canal Street."

More often than not, they're too embarrassed to admit that they aren't free. So they go to Canal Street. And after Ben has ruined their workday, they sneak back to the office and work all night.

I think there is another reason for his loafing. As you might suspect, there is a line of people and museums, from here to Rome, waiting for their turn to buy a Shahn picture. He could afford a swimming pool in no time at all. He is at the point where his signature on a stained tablecloth after lunch at Del Pezzo would bring a respectable price.

Well, this great demand for his work is a burden in disguise.

If Shahn ever gets suspicious that he is working for any other reason that he wants to work—he just quits and begins to loaf.

But to get back to why this presentation might be a mistake. The fact is that Ben Shahn is subversive . . . right now he is undermining the American Institute of Graphic Arts.

A few years ago he agreed to be on the jury of an AIGA Printing for Commerce Show. After a couple of hours of examining the entries he became very depressed and refused to continue as a juror. He didn't quit because the pieces were so bad! He was depressed because they were so good. All this talent and resourcefulness was being used to extol the great contribution to mankind of, let's say . . . a laxative.

But what upset him more deeply, however, was his conviction that the people who made these graphic impressions obviously had enough talent to quit whatever they were doing and just draw. He wants everyone to draw. It is his solution for whatever ails you. All of you in the American Institute of Graphic Arts are now in danger of having your entire careers changed. If you have achieved some sense of satisfaction from being a publisher, a typographer, a printer or any of the crafts that go into printing for commerce, you are now doomed.

By this very act of awarding the Institute Medal, you have demonstrated that Shahn has conquered you. You have included his work in many of your exhibitions. You have circulated an entire exhibition of his printed works and from this day on you will have to listen to him.

I know one case where Ben persuaded someone to quit going to an analyst and follow the prescription of Dr. Shahn, which was to make a drawing every day with a 6H pencil.

It probably doesn't matter what this man's profession was or if he can still pay his rent. For Ben, he has become a useful member of our society. He draws. And so will you if you listen to him for very long. Maybe there is too much printing in America anyhow. Maybe we could do with a few less magazines, newspapers, and books. I can imagine the day when Ben will rush to a phone book to look up a number, only to find that no new phone books have been printed since 1958, the year he captured the AIGA and all the printers stopped printing and began painting. It will serve him right.

I imagine that most of you are sort of in love with type. You have a number of convictions about its uses. You are fond of explaining its refinements and its subtleties. Well that too is doomed.

One of your great purists, Joe Blumenthal, who is drawn like a helpless moth to the brilliance of Shahn, nevertheless for years has been protecting the printed page from the menace of Shahn. He will print any book that Ben makes. He will print his drawings, that is. But he won't print Shahn lettering. Oh he won't, won't he? Since Joe first refused to print the text pages Ben had lettered, almost every major theatrical advertisement in the Sunday Times and I don't know how many book jackets in every part of the world, have had their titles drawn in Ben Shahn Grotesque. How long do you think that Joe can hold out?

I said at the beginning that I had the feeling that this whole thing is a mistake. I have read in a number of trade papers which announced tonight's event, a very inadequate description of Ben Shahn's work, which concludes with this statement: "His work is a fresh note in American Graphic Art, and in recent years he has produced more and more (quote) commercial (unquote) art." If this is what we are honoring him for, then we have missed the whole point of what he has done.

Ben has never produced commercial art since he left the lithographer's shop some 35 years ago. The distinction between the so-called "fine" artist and the commercial artist is clear enough.

They are two different people. As far as I know, Ben is concerned only with being an artist.

To label art that is printed as "commercial" has done and is doing an enormous amount of damage to artists and to everyone in the Graphic Arts.

This label has kept some great talent away from us. It has been terribly confusing to the artist himself. Most American painters have worried about this horrible label to the point where they look on an assignment for publication in a mass medium as a fall from grace. Something to be done furtively, if at all. They don't want it to be confused with their "real work" and as I have learned from my own experience, their "commercial" work is usually rejected because it is awful. And it's awful because they tried to make it commercially acceptable.

I suppose I was asked to speak tonight because some years ago I tried an experiment. I wasn't the first American art director to introduce the work of painters into mass publications, but I did have an opportunity to do it on an important and consistent scale. I was the art director of a new magazine called *Seventeen*. It was then a stimulating publication edited by Helen Valentine, who had discovered a new world of young people. People who didn't yet know all magazine illustrations had to be made by Jon Whitcombe, Al Parker and Bradshaw Crandall, and who hadn't enough experience to know what an acceptable illustration should be.

These young people seemed to represent as nearly an uncorrupted and unprejudiced audience as one could find.

I thought there was an opportunity to give them a new experience in seeing, that was spoiled for an older generation. It seemed to me, that if the magazine fiction pages were illustrated by painters and that no fuss was made about it or special attention was called to that fact, the readers would either accept or reject them without being challenged to judge them as Art. And maybe some young people would be moved by these paintings.

At that time, all fiction to be illustrated in *Seventeen* was commissioned to illustrators in the following way: the fiction editor would type out the specific passage to be illustrated. This passage was arrived at through conferences, and represented the best editorial opinion on just which morsel in the story was the most likely to lure the reader into reading the piece.

My idea was to allow the artist to read as well as to illustrate the story and even to choose the part he wished to make a picture of. This was an unthinkable proposal, but since I was new on that job, and insisted that the artist be allowed to make his own contribution, on the wild theory that he might have a more valid instinct about pictures than a fiction editor could have.

It might surprise you to know that most painters are frightened by a publishing assignment. They usually want to be told just exactly what it is that you want them to do. Then, when they're told, they protest that you've taken away their freedom. At this point they will either run away to the safety of their studios or do a job they would be ashamed to put their signature on.

I wasn't going to let them off that easy.

The plan was to give the artist a story, let him decide what to paint, and insist that we would publish the picture only if he liked it well enough to exhibit in his own gallery.

It would have to stand on its own as a painting—even when it was divorced from the magazine pages it would appear in.

Obviously, the only way a program like this could work was by example. I needed a fellow conspirator. A painter of stature, integrity and courage.

So I asked Ben to help.

I remember the first story he did. It concerned a 14-year-old boy, a keen tennis player, who is ashamed of his mother because she is very pregnant, and he is determined to keep this fact from his friends. To do this he keeps them from using the family tennis court, which up to the time of the pregnancy had been the center of social activity. I gave Ben a two week deadline. He could do anything he pleased, in any shape and any number of colors.

There was only one restriction. The hero and his friends must be clearly recognizable as youngsters in their teens.

Three days later the finished job came in and it was plenty clear. There was no hero. There were no friends to be seen. Instead, stretching across two pages in a long, thin picture, was the most deserted, clearest, biggest tennis court in a brilliant color, marked with the sharpest, neatest, traditional white lines. It was a breathtaking beautiful shock of a painting to go with what story. It was also a wonderful painting if you had never heard of the story.

With paintings like this for a beginning, the success of the project was assured. Ben has opened the way for many more painters to work in the magazine, made it easier for other publishers to open their pages to the work of non-commercial artists.

Why did Ben do it? I liked to think he did it as a favor to me, but I don't think that's the reason.

I imagine it is because he thinks it's unhealthy for an artist to steal away to a world of his own. I imagine he did this and many other things for publication because he knows that an artist can be an artist all the time. That he needn't be a different kind of man of different days in different circumstances.

I know that he has never done a job (or anything else for that matter) that he didn't want to do. Everything he has done for print, has later been bought by a museum or an individual. I know that several projects that began as a result of a commission, were later made into important paintings.

A drawing of empty chairs in an empty radio studio is as stunning on the walls of the Downtown Gallery as it is in an advertisement for CBS.

He makes a series of drawings of the Centralia Mine disaster for *Harper's Magazine*, and later a group of paintings based on this experience appears.

Where is the line of separation?

There is a story that might come close to the answer, and it comes right out of Ben's home town—Roosevelt, New Jersey.

This is a community that was built during the depression for unemployed garment workers who moved there from New York (together with Ben Shahn).

It was the habit of the people of Roosevelt to meet every morning in their post office not only to collect their mail, but also for a little schmoos.

One morning two elderly cloak and suit men came over to Ben and one said: "nu, are you working?" Shahn said "yes." Then the other one asked, "Stock, or orders?"

Unlike most painters Ben's got both.

Ben Shahn's convictions are in his pictures, where everyone can see them. You can see them on the walls of museums, as well as in the millions of impressions on the printed page, and you can come to your own conclusions about them.

My conclusion is that we ought to cut out all this nonsense about honoring Ben Shahn. Let's just admit that he has honored us by making it possible for so many other American artists to bring their talents to the world of print. And that he has enriched the field of the Graphic Arts by the gift of his own enormous body of work.

We need it very badly.

Cipe Pineles Golden, 11-24-58

(from galley found in archives, dated January 6, 1959.)

[Bibliography]

General

Attfield, Judy, and Pat Kirkham, ed. *A View from the Interior: Feminism, Women and Design*. London: The Women's Press, 1989.

Bateson, Mary Catherine. *Composing A Life*. New York: The Atlantic Monthy Press, 1989.

Broude, Norma, and Mary D. Garrard, ed. *Feminism and Art History: Questioning the Litany*. New York: Harper & Row, Publishers, 1982.

Buckley, Cheryl. "Made in Patriarchy: Toward a Feminist Analysis of Women and Design." *Design Issues* , v. 3, n. 2 (fall 1986): 3–14.

Chadwick, Whitney, and Isabelle de Courtivron, eds. *Significant Others: Creativity and Intimate Partnership*. London and New York: Thames and Hudson, 1993.

Ford, James L.C. *Magazines for the Millions: The Story of Specialized Publications*. Carbondale, Illinois: Southern Illinois Press, 1969.

Forty, Adrian. *Objects of Desire*. New York: Pantheon Books, 1986.

Halberstam, David. *The Fifties*. New York: Villard Books, 1993.

Heilbrun, Carolyn G. *Writing a Woman's Life*. New York: Ballantine Books, 1988.

Lupton, Ellen. *Mixing Messages, Graphic Design in Contemporary Culture*. New York: Cooper-Hewitt National Design Museum, Smithsonian Institute, and Princeton Architectural Press, 1996.

McCracken, Ellen. *Decoding Women's Magazines: From Mademoiselle to Ms*. New York: St. Martin's Press, 1993.

Peterson, Theodore. *Magazines in the Twentieth Century*. Urbana: University of Illinois Press, 1964.

Pollock, Griselda. *Vision and Difference: Femininity, Feminism and the Histories of Art*. London: Routledge, 1988.

Rosenblum, Naomi. *A History of Women Photographers*. New York: Abbeville Press, 1994.

Scotford, Martha. "Is There a Canon of Graphic Design?" in Heller, Steve, and Marie Finamore, eds. *Design Culture: An Anthology of Articles from The AIGA Journal of Graphic Design*. New York: Allworth Press, 1997.

Meggs, Philip B. *A History of Graphic Design*. (2nd Revised edition). New York: Van Nostrand Reinhold, 1992.

Scotford, Martha. "Messy History vs. Neat History: Toward an Expanded View of Women in Graphic Design." *Visible Language* , v. 28, n. 4, part 2 (1994): 368–388.

Cipe Pineles

(anon.) "A Coast-to-Coast Display of Linen Costumes." no publication, no date. (RIT).

(anon.) "Cipe Pineles Burtin." *Ten Years: Women in Design*. Chicago: Women in Design, 1988.

(anon.) "C. P." *Print* (September–October 1955): 18–29.

(anon.) Digest of 9th Annual Conference. "The Art of Teaching Art: a study institute." New York: Museum of Modern Art (March 1951).

(anon) "Types of Recent Work Done by Art Illustration Class." Brooklyn, NY: *The Evening World* (March 30, 1926).

(anon.) Interview with Will Burtin. *AIGA Journal 18.* (1971).

(anon.) "*Seventeen*: A Unique Case Study." *Tide* (April 15, 1945): 19.

(anon.) "*Seventeen*'s Fine Art Diet Clicks with Teenagers." *Studio News*, v. 1, n. XI (March 1950): cover, 12–13.

(anon.) "The Cell." *Industrial Design* (August 1958): 56–61.

(anon.) "Walk-in Portrait of a Gene." *Life* [?] (about 1966).

(anon.) "Will Burtin, 63, Exhibit Designer." *New York Times* (January 20, 1972).

The Art Directors Club. *Annual of Advertising and Editorial Art and Design.* New York: The Art Directors Club, 1921–present.

Burtin, Cipe Pineles, Kurt Weihs, and Robert Strunsky. *The Visual Craft of William Golden*. New York: Braziller, 1962.

Burtin, Will. "The Brain." *Industrial Design* (August 1960): 66–69.

Cacioppo, Nancy. "She's been a designing woman all her life." Rockland, NY: *Journal-News* (September 11, 1985).

Campbell, Jean. "Why Snub 8 million Customers?" *Cosmetics and Toiletries* (August 1949).

Chase, Edna Woolman, and Ilka Chase. *Always in Vogue*. New York: Doubleday & Company, 1954.

Cowden, Jack. "A Tribute to William Golden." *The Visual Craft of William Golden*. New York: Braziller, 1962.

Craig, James. "Cipe Pineles Burtin."*Graphic Design Career Guide*. New York: Watson-Guptill, 1983.

Davis, Gene. "Corcos." *AD* (December/January 1940/1941).

Driscoll, John, and Janet Marqusee. *Lucille Corcos*. New York: Babcock Galleries, 1992.

Dougherty, Philip H. "Woman Enters the Hall of Fame." *New York Times* (November 28, 1975).

Eichenberg, Fritz. "The Golden Touch." *AIGA Journal*, v. IV, n. 1–2 (1951 or 1952): 22–24.

Esajian, Jeanie. "Pineles Sisters: High Achievers in Their Fields." Visalia, CA: *Times-Delta* (January 15, 1976).

Friendly, Fred. *Due to Circumstance Beyond our Control*. New York: Random House, 1967.

Golden, William. "The Man Who Knew Too Much." *PM*, v. 5, n. 2 (August–September 1939).

Harvey, Emily. *Edgar Levy, Selected Themes*. Rockland, NY: Rockland Community College, Cultural Arts Center (January 8–February 15, 1984).

Heller, Steven. "Cipe Pineles, 1909–1991." *ID* (May–June 1991): 10–11.

Heller, Steven. "Interview with Cipe Pineles." *Graphic Design in America*. New York: Abrams, 1989.

Heller, Steve, ed. "Symposium: Magazine Design, The Rationalist's Dream." *AIGA Journal of Graphic Design*, v. 3, n. 3 (1985).

Henrion, F. H. K. "Will Burtin." *Typographic 1* (1972): 2.

Kazanjian, Dodie, and Calvin Tompkins. *Alex: the Life of Alexander Liberman*. New York: Knopf, 1993.

Lahr, John. "The Blurred Graphic Image of Lincoln Center." *Print* (May–June 1967): 15–23, 46–49.

Lois, George. *George, Be Careful*. New York: Saturday Review Press, 1972.

Louie, Elaine. "Cipe Pineles." *Art Direction* (April 1976): 48–49.

Maura, Dixie. "Polish Girl, 18, Here 3 years, Declared Best H.S. Writer." *Brooklyn Daily Times* (July 4, 1926). (RIT).

Meggs, Philip. "Women in Design: CP (Profile of Cipe Pineles)." *Print* (November–December 1990): 68–69.

Nast, Condé, "Dr. Agha in Berlin." *PM*, v. 5, n. 2 (August/September 1939).

Natoli, Geraldine, and Jeanne Brand. "Fashion Artist." *Maroon & White*. Brooklyn, NY: Bay Ridge High School, 1938.

Nemy, Enid. "Discoveries: New Life for Old Shirts." *New York Times* (July 19, 1978).

Offen, Jay Rae. "A Home That's a Work of Folk Art." *The Record* (January 9, 1968): A–21.

Owen, William. *Modern Magazine Design*. Dubuque, Iowa: William C. Brown Publishers, 1992.

Pineles, Cipe. "An excursion in the mountains." Essay dated November 26, 1923. (RIT).

———— "Bolsheviki." *The Maroon & White*. Brooklyn, New York: Bay Ridge High School. June 1926. (RIT).

———— "How I spent my vacation." Essay dated November 1, 1923. (RIT).

———— "My first impression of New-York." Essay dated October 25, 1923. (RIT).

———— "The Christmas in Poland." Essay dated December 13, 1923. (RIT).

———— "The life of the peasants in the Polish country." Essay dated November 26, 1923. (RIT).

———— "The schools in Poland." Essay dated October 23, 1923. (RIT).

———— "The wood." Essay dated November 11, 1923. (RIT).

Pineles, Cipe. Letters. (RIT).

Pineles, Cipe. Talk to AIGA. 1958. (RIT).

Remington, R. Roger, and Barbara Hodik. *Nine Pioneers of American Graphic Design*. Cambridge, MA: MIT Press, 1989.

Reynolds, Quentin. *The Fiction Factory*. New York: Random House, 1955.

Scotford, Martha. "Cipe Pineles: The Artist as Art Director." The Annual of the American Institute of Graphic Arts. New York, 1998.

———— "The Tenth Pioneer." *Eye* 18 (autumn 1995): 54–63

Scebohm, Caroline. *The Man Who was Vogue: The Life and Times of Condé Nast*. New York: The Viking Press, 1982.

Snyder, Gertrude. "Pro.File: Bill Golden." *U&lc*, v. 2, n. 1 (1975).

———— "Pro.File: Cipe Pineles." *U&lc* (fall 1978), published and unpublished sections of interview. (RIT).

———— "Pro.File: Will Burtin." *U&lc*, v. 7, n. 1 (March 1980).

Stevens, Carol. "A Companion of Design." *Print* (January–February 1985): 47–61, 117–120.

———— "Cipe Pineles Burtin 1910–1991." *Print* (January–February 1991): 150.

Taylor, Angela. "The problem: to do a yearbook that's actually something else." *New York Times* (May 17, 1973).

Young, Edgar. *Lincoln Center: the Building of an Institution*. New York: New York University Press, 1980.

[Index]